Karolina:

Congratulations on winning one of the copies of Broken Promises, which tells the story of the Heppenheimer family. Because of readers like you, their stories will not be forgotten. I would appreciate any feedback you may have, and would be grateful if you could post a review on Amazon and/or Goodreads. You can also contact me at suchmanbonnie@gmail.com.

All the best,

Bonnie Suchman

BROKEN PROMISES

The Story of a Jewish Family in Germany

BONNIE SUCHMAN

Broken Promises

The Story of a Jewish Family in Germany

© 2021, Bonnie Suchman.

Print ISBN: 978-1-09839-2-062
eBook ISBN: 978-1-09839-2-079

To Curtis Heppen and

the Heppenheimer family members

whose stories had been lost.

May their memories be a blessing.

CONTENTS

Acknowledgments

I started this project as a genealogical search of my husband Bruce's family, who lived in Germany before World War II. However, I soon found myself writing a book about the Heppenheimer family, due, in part, to the amount of information I was able to find about the family. Through my research, I found that German records about the family are primarily in the archives of the individual German states and cities, and I was fortunate to find archivists who were patient with an American trying to navigate the different processes for obtaining documents. I am also very appreciative for the information I received about the Heppenheimer family from the various Holocaust museums and memorials around the world. I also found significant amounts of information about both the Heppenheimer family and German Jews in general through the Leo Baeck Institute (both at the Center for Jewish History in New York and on their website) and through the digital collections (particularly the Compact Memory collection) at Germany's Goethe University in Frankfurt.

The information I received from family members (both known and unknown to me before this project) has helped me to paint a richer picture of the family. I am indebted to Steve Harvey for sharing the transcripts from recordings he made of his conversations with his uncle Herb Harvey (Benny Heppenheimer's son) and to Carol Reynolds (Herb Harvey's daughter) for sharing the pictures of her family, as well as information about the family. Jean Horgen's information about Jacob Heppenheimer (Lazarus' son) provided important details that were missing from my research. I am also grateful to

Alex Heppenheimer (Adolph Heppenheimer's great-grandson) and Kelvin Zane (Gustav Heppenheimer's nephew) for information about their relatives.

Virtually all of the documents I received from the various sources are in German. While Google translator was quite useful, it became clear to me early in my research that I needed to take German classes to better understand the documents. Christina Mockel was my first German teacher, and while I want to thank her for introducing me to the language, I am especially appreciative for her help in translating numerous documents that were either written in the old German script or written in cursive German.

I was especially fortunate to find Stefan Jamin, a genealogical researcher based in Southern Germany. Stefan was able to locate the relevant records of the Heppenheimer family ancestors from the Venningen archives and, most importantly, translate those records for me. The book would have been all the poorer without those records documenting the Heppenheimer ancestors' early years in Germany.

As I began to research the history of Jewish scrap metal dealers in Germany (the Heppenheimers were scrap metal dealers), I came upon the agenda for a program that included a paper that was delivered by Chad Denton, Associate Professor of European History at the Underwood International College at Yonsei University in South Korea, on Jewish scrap metal dealers during World War II. Prof. Denton was kind enough to send me the paper, and we began a correspondence during which Prof. Denton forwarded to me other very useful information about Jewish scrap metal dealers, as well as extremely useful feedback on my own research.

I have been researching and writing this book for three years and have received encouragement from my husband's family all along the way. Before each family get-together, they asked me to present an update on what I had found. Our last Thanksgiving took place over Zoom because of the pandemic, but the family still insisted that I make a presentation on what I had discovered since our last get-together. Bruce's parents always referred to me as their daughter and not their daughter-in-law, and Bruce's family has always made me feel welcome, and that extended to this book. I will be forever grateful.

The lawyer in me wants to provide a source for everything, but I am aware of the number of footnotes already in the book and mindful that too many footnotes can distract from the story. I therefore decided not to cite information I obtained on the Ancestry.com website unless necessary. This site had been critical to obtaining genealogical information about the Heppenheimer family, and often served as a jumping off point for exploring other sites. For purposes of this book, the reader should assume that all gene-alogical information provided about the Heppenheimer family was obtained from the Ancestry.com website unless otherwise noted. I also tended to get lost in the various details about each family member or each time period, and am extremely appreciative of my friend Mark Gunther's suggestions to "cut, cut, cut" to improve the flow of the story. I hope I cut enough.

This book would not have happened if not for my husband, and not just because the book is about his family. Bruce has been totally supportive of this effort, even when it raised issues for him (I sometimes forgot that the horrible things I was discovering and sharing with Bruce actually happened to his family). Bruce has read multiple versions of each chapter, and provided helpful criticism and suggestions. He deserves more thanks than is possible. I also thank my children Emily and Jonathan for their continued support throughout this project. My effort to tell the Heppenheimer family story is really for the two of them, as well as all the other Heppenheimer descendants.

Family Trees

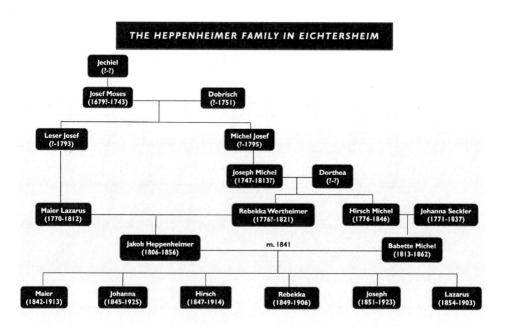

THE HEPPENHEIMER FAMILY IN EICHTERSHEIM

Jechiel
(?-?)

Josef Moses
(1679?-1743)

Dobrisch
(?-1751)

Leser Josef
(?-1793)

Michel Josef
(?-1795)

Joseph Michel
(1747-1813?)

Dorthea
(?-?)

Maier Lazarus
(1770-1812)

Rebekka Wertheimer
(1776?-1821)

Hirsch Michel
(1776-1846)

Johanna Seckler
(1771-1837)

Jakob Heppenheimer
(1806-1856)

m. 1841

Babette Michel
(1813-1862)

Maier
(1842-1913)

Johanna
(1845-1925)

Hirsch
(1847-1914)

Rebekka
(1849-1906)

Joseph
(1851-1923)

Lazarus
(1854-1903)

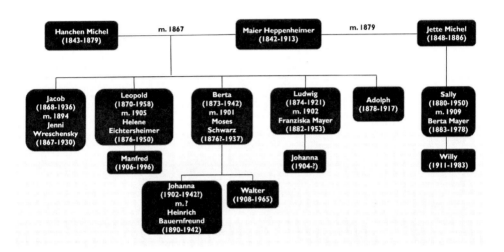

MAIER HEPPENHEIMER'S FAMILY

Hanchen Michel (1843-1879) — m. 1867 — Maier Heppenheimer (1842-1913) — m. 1879 — Jette Michel (1848-1886)

Jacob (1868-1936) m. 1894 Jenni Wreschensky (1867-1930)

Leopold (1870-1958) m. 1905 Helene Eichtersheimer (1876-1950)
— Manfred (1906-1996)

Berta (1873-1942) m. 1901 Moses Schwarz (1876?-1937)
— Johanna (1902-1942?) m. ? Heinrich Bauernfreund (1890-1942)
— Walter (1908-1965)

Ludwig (1874-1921) m. 1902 Franziska Mayer (1882-1953)
— Johanna (1904-?)

Adolph (1878-1917)

Sally (1880-1950) m. 1909 Berta Mayer (1883-1978)
— Willy (1911-1983)

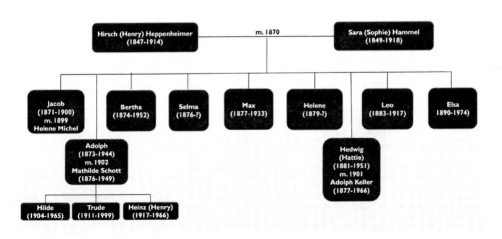

HIRSCH HEPPENHEIMER'S FAMILY

Hirsch (Henry) Heppenheimer (1847-1914) — m. 1870 — Sara (Sophie) Hammel (1849-1918)

Jacob (1871-1900) m. 1899 Helene Michel
— Adolph (1873-1944) m. 1902 Mathilde Schott (1876-1949)
  — Hilde (1904-1965)
  — Trude (1911-1999)
  — Heinz (Henry) (1917-1966)

Bertha (1874-1952)

Selma (1876-?)

Max (1877-1933)

Helene (1879-?)
— Hedwig (Hattie) (1881-1951) m. 1901 Adolph Keller (1877-1966)

Leo (1883-1917)

Elsa (1890-1974)

5

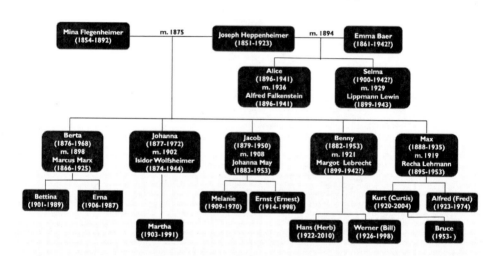

JOSEPH HEPPENHEIMER'S FAMILY

Mina Flegenheimer (1854-1892) — m. 1875 — Joseph Heppenheimer (1851-1923) — m. 1894 — Emma Baer (1861-1942?)

Alice (1896-1941) m. 1936 Alfred Falkenstein (1896-1941)

Selma (1900-1942?) m. 1929 Lippmann Lewin (1899-1943)

Berta (1876-1968) m. 1898 Marcus Marx (1866-1925)

Johanna (1877-1972) m. 1902 Isidor Wolfsheimer (1874-1944)

Jacob (1879-1950) m. 1908 Johanna May (1883-1953)

Benny (1882-1953) m. 1921 Margot Lebrecht (1899-1942?)

Max (1888-1935) m. 1919 Recha Lehmann (1895-1953)

Bettina (1901-1989)

Erna (1906-1987)

Melanie (1909-1970)

Ernst (Ernest) (1914-1998)

Kurt (Curtis) (1920-2004)

Alfred (Fred) (1923-1974)

Martha (1903-1991)

Hans (Herb) (1922-2010)

Werner (Bill) (1926-1998)

Bruce (1953-)

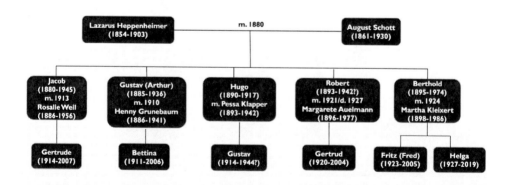

LAZARUS HEPPENHEIMER'S FAMILY

Lazarus Heppenheimer (1854-1903) — m. 1880 — August Schott (1861-1930)

Jacob (1880-1945) m. 1913 Rosalie Weil (1886-1956)

Gustav (Arthur) (1885-1936) m. 1910 Henny Grunebaum (1886-1941)

Hugo (1890-1917) m. Pessa Klapper (1893-1942)

Robert (1893-1942?) m. 1921/d. 1927 Margarete Auelmann (1896-1977)

Berthold (1895-1974) m. 1924 Martha Kleixert (1898-1986)

Gertrude (1914-2007)

Bettina (1911-2006)

Gustav (1914-1944?)

Gertrud (1920-2004)

Fritz (Fred) (1923-2005)

Helga (1927-2019)

Map of
Southern Germany

MAP OF SOUTHERN GERMANY

Germany is my fatherland, my homeland, the
land of all my yearnings, the land in which my
forefathers have been buried, the land of my
battles and my love, and when I return home from
a foreign country I come home...to Germany...

Franz Oppenheimer, renowned German Jewish sociologist
and Zionist. This statement was written before World War I.
Oppenheimer escaped from Nazi Germany in 1938.

Sometimes our own stories are the ones that
we can never tell. But if a story is never told,
it becomes something else...forgotten.

Sarah's Key. Directed by Gilles Paquet-Brenner, Hugo Productions. 2010.

Prologue

It is traditional for Jews to name a child after a deceased relative, and American Jews often give their newborn both an English name and the relative's Hebrew name. When our son was born, we decided to name him after my grandfather, giving him the English name Jonathan and the Hebrew name Nacham. We also decided to give our son the middle name "Max" after my husband Bruce's two grandfathers. While our son would not be given a Hebrew name for his middle name (since the great-grandfathers had different Hebrew names), we still wanted to honor these ancestors. A few days before the bris, when our son would be named, Bruce called his mother to ask her to ask my father-in-law Curtis to speak at the bris about his father.

As our families gathered at our house for the bris, Bruce reminded his mother about his father Curtis' speaking role. My mother-in-law told Bruce that his father would not be speaking because it would be too painful, given how Curtis' father died. Bruce had always assumed that his grandfather had died of heart troubles brought on by "the times" in Nazi Germany. and so he asked his mom why speaking about this would be too painful. She then told him that his grandfather had committed suicide. Shock does not fully convey the reaction Bruce had upon hearing this news. Bruce then asked each of his two siblings if they knew anything about their grandfather's death. Each had also thought the death was the result of natural causes. Curtis shared virtually nothing about growing up in Germany with his children, and his children knew not to ask. Thus, sensing that this, too, was forbidden territory, none of his children asked Curtis about his father's suicide and Curtis volunteered no additional information.

Many years later, and long after my father-in-law's death, Bruce and I visited Yad Vashem, the Holocaust museum in Jerusalem. During our visit, we were encouraged to look up in the museum's database of Holocaust victims Heppenheimer family members, which I did when we came back to the U.S. When multiple Heppenheimers came up, and only one name was familiar to Bruce, I became curious about the connections these other Heppenheimers had to my husband's family. I had an existing Ancestry.com account (from research I had done on my own family) and I began to try to build a family tree of Bruce's family, exploring each name I found on the Yad Vashem website. Unable to make much headway on my existing limited Ancestry.com account, I added the international version and gained greater access to German records. I soon discovered that Curtis' grandmother and two aunts were among the Heppenheimer family member who died in the Holocaust, and that virtually every Heppenheimer listed in the Yad Vashem website was a family member.

Suicide is often an embarrassment for a family, and so one can understand why nothing was said about the circumstances of Curtis's father's death. But why did Curtis never tell his children about the grandmother and two aunts he lost in the Holocaust? And why did Curtis never even mention these losses to his wife?

Wanting to know more about these relatives of my husband (and hoping to understand why they were never mentioned, particularly the grandmother and two aunts), I began looking for more records. I explored the websites of the relevant German states and began ordering tax, reparations and other family records. Knowing almost nothing about German history, I began reading books about the history of the relevant period, particularly Jewish German history. I also reached out to previously unknown relatives I found while doing the family research, discovering things I would not have found in the various archives. Finding much of the relevant material in German (particularly the family records), I started taking German language classes. Through this research, I began to understand the strong connection his family had to Germany, and why it was likely very painful to discuss what had happened. Until this research into the Heppenheimer family history, I did not fully appreciate the extent of this pain, both because they were forced to leave a country they thought had been theirs and because of the loss of those left behind.

When Curtis stepped off the S.S. Pennland in Hoboken, New Jersey on April 13, 1937, he was Kurt Heppenheimer. He was 17 years-old, blonde-haired and blue-eyed, and 5'6" tall, and spoke only German. He had travelled alone from his hometown of Mannheim, Germany, and was met at the boat in Hoboken by a distant and unknown relative, Adolph Keller, who had sponsored his immigration to America. Kurt was given some money by Keller, who had found an apartment for him in New York City. Kurt was on his own in a strange country, and he felt guilty about leaving his family behind. But Kurt would soon be joined by his widowed mother and younger brother.

Because he was Jewish, Kurt had been forced to leave his college preparatory school in 1935, and worked for two years before his emigration as an apprentice at Süpag Süddeutsche Papiermanufaktur, a paper manufacturing plant in Mannheim. During that period of time, Kurt worked to obtain his immigration visa to the United States. But he was subject to constant taunts from fellow workers and at the technical school he was attending for his apprenticeship. Kurt knew he was no longer welcome in the country that had been his home and the home of his ancestors, and feared for his future. Kurt was finally able to leave Mannheim in 1937 for America. As the train approached the Belgium border, an SS officer checked Kurt's passport, causing one last moment of anxiety for the teen. Kurt breathed easier only after the train crossed into Belgium.

Once his mother and brother were able to join him in 1939, Kurt and his family moved to Jackson Heights, a neighborhood in Queens, New York. He had a number of jobs, ranging from kitchen worker to a manager of a hosiery store. He was drafted into the Army in 1943, which shortened the process for becoming a U.S. citizen. Kurt anglicized his name to Curtis Heppen and, after his discharge, attended Pace College in New York on the GI Bill and graduated with a degree in accounting. Curtis embraced his new life and his new country. He married Millie Hertz, also a Jewish refugee from Europe, had three children, and lived the American dream.

But the scars of fleeing Nazi Germany never fully healed. In 1970, Curtis and Millie went on a vacation to Europe. Curtis wanted to visit his father's grave in Mannheim, the first time since he had left Germany in the 1930s. He asked Millie to remain behind at the train station, which was highly unusual, since they did virtually everything together. On his own, Curtis went to the grave, and then took a short walk to visit his old neighborhood. He then went back to the train station and he and Millie immediately left Mannheim. The old feelings of anxiety and fear had returned during Curtis' brief visit to Mannheim, and he breathed easy only after their train crossed the Swiss border. This trip was obviously so painful that he could not even share his time in Mannheim with his wife. Curtis swore that he would never return to Germany, and he never did.

Curtis had some family in and around the New York area—also refugees from Germany—that he and Millie would visit. Because Curtis rarely spoke about his life in Germany to his children, they were often confused about how their Dad was related to these relatives. And they certainly never really understood their family's business interests in Germany. They had heard that Curtis' father was in the scrap metal business and that he had been in the business with his brothers. They understood that, in Germany, the family had been well-off, but hearing about a scrap metal business suggested to them a business like the scrap peddlers in the movies, hawking their wares by horse and buggy. Curtis' children had no idea that the Heppenheimers were quite successful in the scrap metal business and that the scrap business actually helped Germany grow into an industrial power. They were unaware that Jewish families like the Heppenheimers played an important role in the economic development of Germany.

I became part of the Heppen family when I married Curtis' son Bruce. My family origins are very different from the Heppenheimer family origins. My family were Eastern European Jews. Never fully accepted as citizens, my family came from areas that are now part of Belarus and Ukraine, but whose borders and governments were constantly changing. Living in shtetels, or segregated Jewish towns, they only felt connected to their Jewish community and were suspicious, or downright frightened, of the government of the country in which they lived. Subject to one pogrom after another, my ancestors never considered it a possibility that they could become full and accepted citizens of any of the places in which they lived. And so, when the opportunity came to emigrate to America, they all jumped at the chance to become Americans and never looked back.

When I married my husband, I sensed from his family both a great pride in having been German (they boasted that they spoke "Hochdeutch," or German, and not Yiddish) and pain and sadness in having been forced to emigrate. My family had no real emotional connections to the countries they left, but easily spoke about their life in "the old country." Bruce's family had complicated connections that I could sense whenever Bruce or his family spoke of Germany.

Our families' involvement in World War I illustrates the difference between their connections to their respective countries. My grandfather's oldest brother had been drafted into the Russian army at the beginning of World War I. Not wanting his son to fight and die in a war that he did not feel was his, my great-grandfather appeared at his son's army barracks with a suit, told his son to put on the suit, and the two walked out of the barracks, leaving behind the army uniform. My grandfather's brother was then given money and told to leave Russia, which he gladly did. At this same time, multiple members of the Heppenheimer family enthusiastically joined the German army to fight on behalf of the fatherland. Unlike my family, the Heppenheimers felt a strong connection to their country and relished the opportunity to prove their loyalty. None of them ever considered shirking their duty to Germany.

When Curtis came to America, he chose to look forward rather than back. Too many terrible things had happened to him in Mannheim, and he decided not to speak of his past to his wife or with his children. But by not speaking of this past, his family's history was lost to his children and grand-children. And, I believe, the Heppenheimer family history is an important history to tell.

As I researched the family's history, I could have stopped when I found the birth and death records of the various family members. But as I researched the family, and read various histories about Germany's Jewish community, I discovered a much larger and richer story. Moreover, the times we are living in have made me think about the Jewish people's place in the world. Jews have been a minority population, struggling to survive in hostile regions around the world for the last two thousand years. Except in Israel, Jews remain a minority population. In the United States, Jews often forget that anti-Semitism remains a problem. And yet, as was the case in Germany, the situation can change and change quickly. And recent events in the United States suggest that anti-Semitism could become a problem here. The Heppenheimer family story serves as a cautionary tale of what can happen to a minority population—any minority population—even after a country provided full acceptance. And how easy it is for people to fail to see (or ignore) the signs that the country in which they had lived and prospered is no longer safe, until it is too late.

I would occasionally ask my father-in-law questions about his life in Germany. Any time I would ask him questions that had never been asked by any of his children, my husband would get nervous, expecting Curtis to shut down the conversation. But Curtis would always answer my questions, and now I regret not asking him more. Curtis was a doting and caring grandfather and always relished the time he spent with his seven grandchildren. He was especially proud of his grandchildren's Jewish accomplishments, particularly their bar and bat mitzvahs. But when he came to our oldest child's bat mitzvah, something was not quite right with Curtis. He was having trouble following driving directions and smiled a little more than normal. Bruce and I were both a little nervous sending him and Millie home, which was a three-hour drive from our house. A few weeks later, things took a turn for the worse, and 6 months later, Curtis was put into a nursing facility. Only later did we discover that he had Lewy Body Dementia. In a cruel twist of fate, my father-in-law would suffer at the end of his life from a disease that would rob him of his past.

Every year, during the Jewish holiday of Passover, we tell the story of the Jewish exodus from Egypt. We tell that story so that we do not forget that, at one time, we were slaves in Egypt and were oppressed by the Pharaohs. Often, during the Seder, our family also talks about the Holocaust and the importance of remembering the events that led to the Holocaust. We say "Never again" to remind ourselves that we must work to make sure a Holocaust never again happens to the Jewish people, or to any people. I know that my father-in-law would have bristled at the idea of revisiting his past, at least initially. But Curtis was a man who was curious about ideas and history, particularly the history of the Jewish people and the ideas in the Torah, and understood the importance of remembering our past. Elie Wiesel said that "for the dead and the living, we must bear witness." I believe that my father-in-law would ultimately have liked the idea of telling the story of his relatives, particularly those whose stories would have been lost but for this telling. And my father-in-law would have understood the importance in telling the story of the

Heppenheimer family, especially at a time when anti-Semitism is on the rise and the rhetoric of the Nazi era has present day echoes.

While this book tells the story of the Heppenheimer family, this book also tells the story of German Jewry, since Curtis' ancestors experienced first-hand the key moments in the history of Germany's Jews: immigration from Poland following the Thirty Years War in the seventeenth century; the restrictions on economic and civil liberties during the eighteenth and nineteenth centuries; emigration to America in the nineteenth century; Jewish emancipation in the 1870s, followed by migration to the urban centers in Germany; the emergence of a Jewish middle-class; continued anti-Semitism, followed by periods of relief; the emigration of Jews following the rise of the Nazis; and the death of those that remained. This book recounts the critical role Jews like the Heppenheimers—who owned thriving scrap metal businesses—played in the development of Germany as an industrial power and its integration into the world economy, until their businesses and property were stolen and they were either forced to leave or were exterminated.

1.

The Family's Origins in Germany

"Heppenheimer" appeared for the first time as the family's surname in 1809 when Maier Lazarus Heppenheimer (my husband's three-times great-grandfather) was required to adopt a surname. Before 1809, Maier Lazarus Heppenheimer used the names Mayer Leser or Maier Lazarus, using his first name and variations of his father Leser's name as a second name. While the Heppenheimer surname does not appear in the German records until 1809, the family's ancestors can be traced back to around the time Jews first returned to the German lands.

The Heppenheimer Ancestors' Early Years in Germany

The Heppenheimer family ancestors likely emigrated from Poland to Eichtersheim ,[1] a small town in Southern Germany,[2] after the Thirty Years War,[3] when Jews were invited to settle in the German lands. The Jews in the Electoral Palatinate, where Eichtersheim was located, had been expelled in the fourteenth century after having been blamed for the plague epidemics.[4] But the Thirty Years War, which ended in 1648, left large parts of the German lands ravaged and depopulated,[5] so that by the middle of the seventeenth century, the rulers decided that it was in their economic interests to permit

Jews to resettle in their lands.[6] The more prosperous Jews (known as "Court Jews") were encouraged to settle, being seen as reliable sources of income for the ruling entities, but even the poorest of Polish Jews crossed the border into the German lands, drawn to the new opportunities available to Jews.[7]

Eichtersheim was a fief of the Electoral Palatinate and was controlled, along with neighboring towns, by the Lords of Venningen.[8] While the Lords of Venningen permitted Jewish settlement in Eichtersheim, the number of Jews that could live in Eichtersheim was limited and the Jews living in the town were limited in their professions -- Jews could only be money lenders, peddlers (peddling foods, or textiles), or cattle and grain traders.[9] In order for a Jew to live in Eichtersheim, he first needed to apply to the Lords of Venningen for a schutzbrief ("Letter of Protection"), which he could receive only if he was able to demonstrate that he had sufficient resources and that his presence was advantageous to the town.[10] The schutzbrief authorized the holder to engage in a trade, granted residency rights, and was also a necessary precondition for marrying.[11] The rights of the schutzjuden ("Protected Jew," the holder of the schutzbrief) extended to his household.[12]

It is likely that Jews were not permitted to live in Eichtersheim until around 1705, the first year that records were kept on Jewish residents by the Lords of Venningen.[13] In that year, seven Jews in Eichtersheim were listed as having schutzbriefs.[14] The 1705 tax register contains the name "Josef," and this person was likely Josef Moses, Maier Lazarus Heppenheimer's grandfather.[15] The 1710 Beetbuch (the property tax book) identified four Jews who were also homeowners, out of a total of thirty-eight homeowners in Eichtersheim,[16] and one of those who owned property, Michal, may have been Josef Moses' father.[17] Thus, Josef Moses (and perhaps his father) were likely among the first Jewish residents of Eichtersheim, and they either immigrated to Eichtersheim directly from Poland or came after wandering from town to town in the German lands as peddlers until they earned enough for schutzbriefs.

By 1723, Josef Moses was a widower with four sons: Leser Joseph (my husband's four-times great-grandfather), Benedict, Seligmann, and Michel Joseph (my husband's five-times great-grandfather, which will be explained below).[18] It would be nearly a century before German Jews adopted surnames, and Josef Moses' sons Leser Joseph and Michel Joseph used their father's first name as a second name, to distinguish themselves from others in Eichtersheim with the same first name.[19] At the time of his death in 1743, Josef Moses' sons Leser Joseph and Benedict had schutzbriefs—Leser Joseph (likely the eldest of the sons) appeared for the first time in the tax register in 1737 and Benedict appeared in the tax register as "the son of Joseph" in 1740. Josef Moses' third son Seligmann was added to the tax register in 1748, and Michel Joseph was added to the tax register in 1749.

Leser Josef was likely married twice, although we only know the names of two sons. Leser Josef's older son was Michel Leser, and was likely born in the late 1730s. Leser Josef's son Maier Lazarus (my husband's three-times great-grandfather) was born in 1770,[20] so it is likely that Maier Lazarus was from a second marriage. Leser Josef would likely have been around 60 years old at the time of Maier Lazarus' birth.[21]

Since Jews that received schutzbriefs could not easily leave their towns,[22] the Venningens were able to control the size of the Jewish community in Eichtersheim by controlling the number of schutzjuden. Between 1705 and 1710, the number of Jews on the tax register grew from seven to nine. In the 1723 Jewish census, nine families were living in Eichtersheim.[23] For the remainder of the century, the number of Jews on the tax register ranged between 8 and 11, falling because of the deaths of existing schutzbrief holders or rising from the addition of sons of schutzbrief holders. The Lords of Venningen also limited the time in which non-residents (even family members) could remain in Eichtersheim without special permission in order to keep the Jewish population in check. For example, in 1795, Michel Joseph was fined for allowing his two daughters and their husbands (who lived in another town) to remain in Eichtersheim for six weeks without permission.

In addition to the size of the Jewish community, the Lords of Venningen also controlled the behavior of the Jews living in Eichtersheim. An example of such control occurred in 1760, and the Heppenheimer family ancestors played a central role in the event. On a Saturday morning in September 1760, the Jews in Eichtersheim were attending Sabbath services. During services, Leser Joseph, Michel Joseph, and Leser's son Michel Leser approached Moyses Benjamin and accused Moyses Benjamin and his wife of spreading malicious gossip and besmirching the good names of the Jews in the town. Moyses Benjamin had been living in Eichtersheim only a few years, having immigrated from Poland. The men began to argue, and the argument may have become physical. Moyses Benjamin then lodged a complaint with the Lords of Venningen against Leser Joseph, Michel Joseph, and Michel Leser. Leser Joseph was charged with scolding and Michel Joseph and Michel Leser were charged with improper behavior. The Lords of Venningen assessed a fine against Leser Joseph, Michel Joseph, and Michel Leser, and then assessed a smaller fine on all of the town's Jewish men who were at services that morning (including the rabbi) for failing to stop the incident and for failing to report it.

After Leser Joseph and Michel Joseph explained the reasons for the confrontation, the Venningens reduced the fines, but still required that the fines be paid. That the entire Jewish community was punished demonstrates the control the Venningens exerted over the town's Jews. The fines were assessed as a warning against any potential unrest in the community. The fact that Moyses Benjamin may have been the cause of the altercation seemed to be of little interest to the Venningens, who were more interested in maintaining order in the town.[24]

The Heppenheimer family ancestors were among the more successful Jews in Eichtersheim, at least by the late eighteenth century. There are no records in the Venningen archives regarding Leser Joseph's business, but we can guess that he was in the grain business based on the activities of other family members. When Leser Joseph's son Maier Lazarus first requested a schutzbrief (as discussed below), he supported his request based on significant grain contracts. Moreover, Michel Joseph's family was also in the grain business. For example, Michel Joseph's son Joseph Michel entered into a contract in 1781 that provided him with the responsibility for selling oats from the granaries in Eichtersheim and two neighboring towns. He also entered into a contract for the purchase of grain in 1787. And there is a record of a 1793 contract with Joseph Michel for the sale of grain and Mühlfrucht, which is a combination of rye and barley.[25]

The success of the Heppenheimer family ancestors can also be seen by the fact that, as of 1790, three of the four properties owned by Jews in Eichtersheim were owned by Leser Joseph, Leser Joseph's son Michel Leser, and Michel Joseph.[26] The following map shows the location of the properties owned by Leser Joseph, his son and his brother:

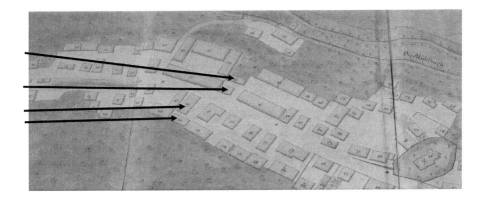

The top two arrows point to the property owned by Michel Joseph. A large property, it was comprised of two houses (represented by the two arrows), a barn, and a garden. The property was adjacent to a very large property owned by a noble family. The bottom two arrows are the houses that were owned by Leser Joseph and his son Michel Leser. Leser Joseph's house (the top of the two arrows) also included the town's Jewish school.[27]

Michel Joseph was an important man in the Eichtersheim Jewish community. By 1784, Michel Joseph was a Judenvorsteher, or a Chief of the Jews, and was responsible for the collection of taxes for the Lords of Venningen from the other schutzjuden in Eichtersheim.[28] Michel Joseph remained the Judenvorsteher until his death in 1795, at which point Michel Joseph's son Joseph Michel became the Judenvorsteher of Eichtersheim.[29]

Leser Joseph died in 1793, and Maier Lazarus inherited a half interest in his father's house. In submissions made in 1795 and 1796 to the Lords of Venningen, Maier Lazarus requested a schutzbrief and permission to marry. In support of his request, Maier Lazarus stated that he owned half a house valued at 750 florin (fl.)[30] and had 1500 fl. in cash, and his future wife was to bring to the marriage a dowry valued at 700 fl. In addition, Maier Lazarus maintained that he had been flawless in his grain trading practices and had a trading route that extended into Mannheim, Bruschal, Phillipsburg, and Heidelberg. Moreover, he was owed monies for deliveries made to the imperial troops for the war effort, which added to his value.[31]

Maier Lazarus received his schutzbrief and permission to marry a "local" woman on January 25, 1796. The local woman Maier Lazarus married was likely his first cousin Rebecka,[32] daughter of his uncle, Michel Joseph.[33] Both Leser Joseph and Michel Joseph were among the few Jewish property owners in Eichtersheim, but Michel Joseph was likely the wealthier of the two brothers (based on the size of his property), and so Maier Lazarus married well when he married his cousin. And this marriage may also have cemented business relationships among the family, since Maier Lazarus entered into grain trading arrangements with his first cousin (and Rebecka's brother) Joseph Michel just after his marriage.

Maier Lazarus' first wife Rebecka likely died in childbirth in 1803.[34] Maier Lazarus then married his cousin Joseph Michel's daughter Rebekka (his first wife's niece), who was born in 1775 or 1776.[35] Joseph Michel was the eldest son of Michel Joseph.[36] With an infant to care for, it is likely that Maier Lazarus remarried soon after his first wife died. Maier and his second wife Rebekka had two children that lived to adulthood, Jakob, who was born in 1806, and Zerle, who was born in 1810.[37] Jakob was my husband's two-times great-grandfather (which is how Leser Joseph is my husband's four-times great-grandfather and his brother Michel Joseph is my husband's five-times great-grandfather).

Around the time of Leser Joseph's death, Eichtersheim began to experience a growth in Jewish schutzbrief holders. In 1793, there had been 11 families on the tax register. In 1794, two additional families were added. In the 1795 register, there were fourteen families on the list. Three more families were added to the 1797 tax registry, the year Maier Lazarus was added to the tax register. By 1800, the number of Jews on the tax registry was 19, as can be seen in the following register (with "Mayer Leser" next to the arrow):

The number of families in Eichtersheim continued to grow steadily during this period. By 1809, there were 22 Jews on the tax register. This number translated to 114 Jews living in the town, out of a total population of 656.[38]

Legal Changes for Eichtersheim's Jews

Around the time of Maier Lazarus's marriage to his second wife, a series of events directly impacted the lives of Eichtersheim's Jewish community. French forces under Napoleon Bonaparte invaded and occupied the German lands in 1796.[39] Under Napoleon, Baden, Bavaria and *Württemberg* were united into the Grand Duchy of Baden in 1805, and Baden also took control of Eichtersheim from the Lords of Venningen.[40]

Baden was required to undertake reforms to improve the situation for Jews.[41] In response, Margrave Karl Friedrich of Baden (the ruler of Baden) issued a number of edicts affecting Baden's Jews, beginning in 1807. In the first edict, Jews were granted citizenship and Judaism was recognized as a constitutionally tolerated religion.[42] In 1808, Jews were recognized as "state citizens", although not as "local citizens," so that Jews could still only live in the areas in which Jews had not been previously excluded.[43] Still, the edict eliminated the schutzjuden (and thus the need for a schutzbrief), and established three categories of citizenship: "burger" (citizen), "schutzburger" (protected citizen) and "einwohler" (resident).[44] A burger enjoyed the full advantages and obligations in the town, while the schutzburger enjoyed only certain defined benefits, and the resident had no benefits or obligations.[45] While Jews could not be burgers, any Jew could become a schutzburger.[46] Further, while a schutzburger was still subject to fees, they were no longer the exorbitant fees charged the schutzjuden for the schutzbrief.[47]

The final edict affecting Jewish life during this period was the Edict of 1809 (often referred to as "the Jewish Edict"), which required the male head of every Jewish family to adopt a last name unless that family already had one.[48] The Edict also placed restrictions on "nothandels," who were persons involved in the so called "irregular jobs" like door-to-door peddling, junk-dealing, pawnbroking, and moneylending,[49] since a key goal of the Edict was the elimination of the nothandel and the movement of Jews to more "regular" occupations.[50] Further, the Jews in Baden were also directed to record marriages, births and deaths; this record became the "Standesbuch" in Eichtersheim.[51]

The Jews of Eichtersheim submitted to the Baden Ministry of the Interior two lists in 1809 in compliance with the Jewish Edict: a list of nothandels and a list of Jewish surnames. Maier Lazarus Heppenheimer was recorded in the nothandel list (the name to the right of the arrow):

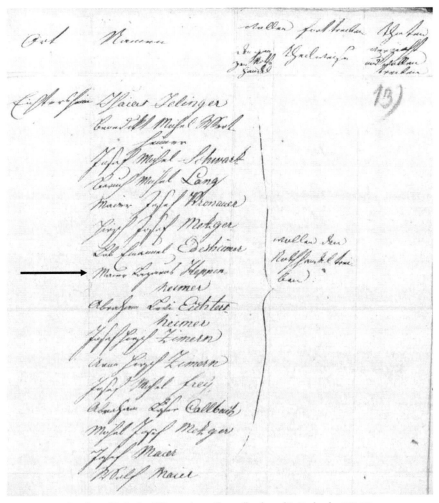

Landesarchiv Baden-Württemberg- Generallandesarchiv Karlsruhe, 185-73.

In terms of the 1809 names list, which is below, the surname "Heppenheimer" does not appear on the list. Instead, there is a Maier Lazarus "Maier," who is at the bottom of the following list next to the arrow:

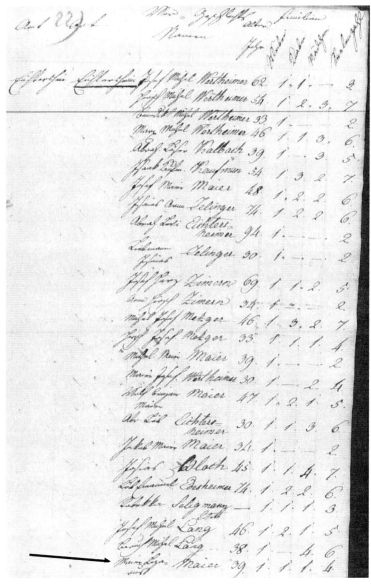

Landesarchiv Baden-Württemberg- Generallandesarchiv Karlsruhe, 185-72.

However, based on an analysis of relevant records, I was able to conclude that this person is very likely Maier Lazarus Heppenheimer.[52]

In trying to understand why Maier Lazarus would have different surnames on the two different documents, Maier Lazarus may have changed his mind about his surname. Both the names list and the nothandels list were submitted to the Baden Interior Ministry, which certified both lists in July 1809, but it is possible that the names list was prepared and submitted first. Thus, it is possible that Maier chose the surname Maier and then changed it when the nothandel list was prepared, perhaps because he discovered that the surname Maier had already been chosen by another and unrelated family in Eichtersheim.[53] It is also possible that a mistake was made when the names list was submitted to the Interior Ministry and that Maier's surname should have been Heppenheimer.

Maier Lazarus was the only Jew in Eichtersheim to adopt the surname Heppenheimer.[54] Maier Lazarus' older brother Michel Leser died in 1808, just before the issuance of the Jewish Edict, but his sons Joseph Michel and Baruch Michel chose the surname Lang, choosing a variation of their father's second name Leser. Michel Leser and Maier Lazarus had different mothers, and Maier may have chosen the surname Heppenheimer because his mother (or her family) came from Heppenheim.[55] The four sons of Maier Lazarus Heppenheimer's uncle Michael Joseph—Joseph, Hirsch, Marx, and Benedict—also chose a different surname; they chose the surname "Wertheimer."[56]

Immediately following the issuance of the Jewish Edict, Maier Lazarus Heppenheimer became a handelsmann and a schutzburger.[57] A "handelsmann" literally means trade man in German and is often translated as a businessman, merchant, or trader.[58] At the time, the Jews in Eichtersheim were mostly trading in cattle or grain.[59] Maier, who was a grain trader, was likely on the nothandel list because the definition of nothandel in the Jewish Edict included "brokers" (those who acted between the buyer and seller, but did not actually purchase the grain), and Maier was likely both a grain dealer and a grain broker.[60] While brokering was no longer permissible under the Jewish Edict, dealing was,[61] so Maier likely became just a grain dealer after 1809.[62]

As Jews began to take advantage of the new opportunities afforded by the Jewish Edict, a supplemental edict was issued in May of 1812 that made it more difficult to obtain "schutzburger" status. Under the new regulation, to become a schutzburger, a Jew needed to demonstrate that he had specific controllable assets or could make a living through a properly learned trade, knew German, and had learned to read, write and do arithmetic.[63] We do not know whether Maier could have satisfied these new conditions, since he died in 1812.[64]

Maier Heppenheimer's death could not have come at a worse time for the family. The farms around Eichtersheim experienced bad harvests in 1809, 1810, and 1812-1815, and a total crop failure in 1816 due to bad weather,[65] and such failures likely had a devastating impact on cattle and grain trade, and thus Eichtersheim's Jewish community. Moreover, Maier's death left his wife with three young children, including 2-year old Zerle. And things did not improve for the family over the coming years—Maier's daughter Rebecka died in 1814 and Maier's wife Rebekka died on May 2, 1821.[66] At this point, Jakob was 15 years old and Zerle was 11 years old.[67] Still, Jakob was old enough to work, and he and Zerle may have been living with some branch of their mother's family, the Wertheimers.

Growth of the Jewish Community in Eichtersheim

After Napoleon was defeated in 1815, Baden became part of the thirty-nine member German Confederation.[68] The issue of Jewish emancipation was returned to the individual states, and the Jews in Baden saw a loss of some of the rights granted under Napoleon.[69] While the schutzbriefs had been abolished, these letters of protection were replaced by a Matrikel, a registration that continued some of the restrictive policies.[70] And while Jews were no longer subject to the schutzbrief taxes, other Jewish taxes remained.[71]

The Jews in Baden experienced increased anti-Semitism following the defeat of Napoleon. The so-called "Hep, Hep" riots (an ant-Semitic rallying cry thought to mean "Jerusalem is lost") in 1819 reminded the Jews of southern Germany that their situation remained precarious.[72] During those riots, Jewish property was destroyed and many Jews were killed.[73] The riots ended only after the rioters achieved their goal, thwarting any additional attempts to improve the Jews' legal situation.[74] Fortunately for the Heppenheimer family, there were no Hep, Hep riots in Eichtersheim.[75]

While the Jews of Eichtersheim may have lost some of the freedoms given under Napoleon, they still enjoyed a certain amount of autonomy over their community as a result of the Jewish Edict. The Jews could enjoy unhindered trade and could officially purchase land,[76] although a few Jews had been able to own property in Eichtersheim for more than a century. Eichtersheim's Jewish community was governed by the "Synagogue Council," a self-governing organization elected by the community that collected taxes and administered the community's day-to-day affairs, including the construction of public buildings and the authorization to marry.[77] But this autonomy only went so far—while the Synagogue Council directly governed the lives of the Jews in Eichtersheim, their decisions were still overseen by the municipal authorities.[78]

Without the earlier restrictions on the number of schutzjuden permitted to reside in the town, Eichtersheim's population grew through the first half of the nineteenth century, and with that growth came the need for improvements. In 1830, due to the poor state of the existing synagogue and the steady growth of the Jewish population, the community decided to tear down the old synagogue and build a new one, which was inaugurated a year later.[79] The following plaque is currently located at the site where the synagogue was built:

Source: https://www.jlk-ev.de/page24/page4/files/Expo_S.PDF.[80]

The plaque reads *"Synagoge Eichtersheim 1790-1938."*

The Synagogue Council also made a decision in 1833 to build a new school for the town's Jewish children. The Jewish Edict had required Jews to educate their children, and to send them to a Christian school if the community did not have a Jewish school.[81] Earlier in the century Jewish lessons had been given in the old synagogue, and by 1832, 16 Jewish children were being taught by a private teacher paid by the community.[82] When a directive was issued in 1833 that the Jewish children were to attend a Protestant school, the Synagogue Council decided to build its own school.[83] While the majority of the Jewish community opposed the building of a new school, the Synagogue Council and the town's mayor made the decision to build the school,[84] again demonstrating the power the Synagogue Council held over the community. The schoolhouse was completed in 1838 and had space for 40 students, a meeting room for the synagogue, a teacher's apartment and a mikvah.[85]

The Synagogue Council was responsible for the operation of the synagogue, and this extended to the drafting of a directive on ways to control order in the synagogue. This directive, which required, for example, that services be conducted on time and that there be no talking during services, is another indication of the control that the Synagogue Council, and ultimately the municipal authorities, exercised over the Jewish community.[86]

As the Jewish community in Eichtersheim continued to grow, the community became more German. The Supreme Council of Jews in Baden was working to eliminate the use of Yiddish both in the synagogue and in the classroom throughout Baden, believing it was holding Jews back from advancement.[87] Moreover, virtually every German Jew born in the second and third quarters of the nineteenth century had an elementary German education and could read and write German, and the use of Yiddish was becoming less prevalent.[88] While Maier and Rebekka were likely Yiddish speakers, Maier's son Jakob and his wife were native German speakers.[89] The average Jewish family in this period also tended to be healthier than the typical Christian family; Jews outlived Christians and their infant mortality rates were lower.[90]

Jakob Heppenheimer's Life in Eichtersheim

Maier and Rebekka's son Jakob married his first cousin Babette Michel on March 3, 1841.[91] By the time he wed, both of Jakob's parents were long dead, and Jakob was 35 years old. At the time of his marriage, Jakob was both a schutzburger and a handelsmann.[92] One can assume that Jakob waited this long to marry in order to have the resources necessary to receive the approval of the Synagogue Council. He and Babette had six children who lived to adulthood: Maier (born May 23, 1842), Johanna (born May 17, 1845), Hirsch (born May 25, 1847), Rebecka (born December 21,1849), Joseph (or Josef) (born August 14, 1851), and Lazarus (born May 16, 1854).[93]

As was the case for Jakob and his father Maier, most Jews in Eichtersheim were traders, trading primarily in cattle and grain, and they played an important role in the Baden economy.[94] The peasant farmers often lacked cash, so the Jewish dealer would loan the farmer money.[95] The Jewish trader would take the coming grain harvest or cattle as security, and would then sell the grain or cattle if the loan was not paid.[96] Jews also acted as middlemen in the grains business, purchasing grain from the growers and selling the grain to the millers in need of grain.[97] Whether they were cattle dealers or grain dealers, Jews paid cash for all livestock or grains they bought, but extended partial or total credit for everything they sold.[98] Thus, the Jews were essentially the bankers for the farmers.[99] The more prosperous Eichtersheim Jews traveled across the region, trading in the markets in Mannheim and Heidelberg.[100] The less prosperous of the traders remained closer to Eichtersheim, trading with the local farmers[101] This relationship between the Jewish trader and the small-scale farmer helped develop the livestock business in Baden and helped farmers successfully sell their livestock and grain through the markets opened by the Jewish trader.[102]

Life was hard for Jews in these small towns, but the Revolution of 1848 provided hope for the Jewish communities. In the wake of the revolutionary events of February 1848 in France, civil unrest broke out in the German lands.[103] In February 1848, every town in the Grand Duchy of Baden demanded that the Grand Duke grant the people the freedom of the press, trial by jury, the right to bear arms and to meet in public, and a popular legislative assembly.[104] And Jews were seeking emancipation, "giving them equality of status with the rest of the citizens of the State in respect of political and civic rights."[105] Still, Jews experienced incidents of persecution, particularly in the rural regions, likely tied to opposition to the possibility of Jewish emancipation.[106] Such incidents may have also been connected to the worsening economic situation during this period, beginning with crop failures in 1846 and 1847, which had caused Jewish cattle and grain dealers and money-lenders to charge higher rates of interest and to call in loans.[107] In Baden, during this period, 22 anti-Jewish riots took place.[108]

During the Revolution of 1848, Jakob Heppenheimer was engaged with the leading members of the Jewish community in Eichtersheim in support of the revolution, hoping to gain greater rights for Eichterheim's Jewish residents. [109] Known as the Eichtersheim Volksvereins (the Eichtersheim People's Association), this group met regularly at the "Zum Lowen," a tavern on Hauptstrasse (the town's main street). This group took orders from the revolutionary committee in Mannheim, distributing leaflets and encouraging soldiers to leave the Grand Duke's army.[110]

A parliament was established in Frankfurt in late April and early May 1848, but their efforts at change failed, and the revolution was finally quashed.[111] The revolt actually ended in Baden, where the revolutionaries were defeated by Prussian troops on July 23, 1849.[112] For Jews living in the Baden urban centers of Mannheim, Karlsruhe, and Heidelberg, there was much support for Jewish emancipation, but the Jew as creditor to the peasant farmer made the Jew an easy scapegoat for the agrarian crises, sparking riots against Jews during the Revolution of 1848.[113] These anti-Jewish riots in rural areas in 1848 also reflected the opposition of the German rural population to Jewish emancipation.[114] The failure of the 1848 Revolution effectively postponed full Jewish emancipation in Germany for another generation, although the Jews' position in German society did improve in the years following the 1848 Revolution. [115] But the efforts for Jewish emancipation in the Revolution of 1848 laid the groundwork for Jewish equality a few decades later, so that Jakob Heppenheimer's children would enjoy the freedoms he had fought for as a member of the Eichtersheim Volksvereins.

While Jakob engaged in activities to support the 1848 Revolution, his primary responsibility was to support his family, and like his father and grandfathers, Jakob was a grain trader. Jakob owned a house in Eichtersheim before the 1848 Revolution, although we do not know when the house was purchased or where it was located. And while we do not know how successful his trading business was before his 1848 Revolution activities, Jakob experienced some business challenges just after the Revolution was quashed that put his home and business at risk.

At the end of 1849, Jakob purchased spelt at an auction conducted by the Stifschaffnei Sinsheim, the church's administrative arm.[116] The Stifschaffnei managed large portions of the farmland in and around Sinsheim, the district that included Eichtersheim.[117] In the mid-nineteenth century, spelt was the principal grain grown in southern Germany and was used primarily for baking bread.[118] But spelt was an inefficient grain with a hard husk, and the removal of the husk significantly reduced the amount of spelt for milling.[119] After Jakob's purchase of the spelt, he left behind the spelt husks and refused to pay for the husks. The husks were re-sold at auction and the Stifschaffnei Sinsheim sued Jakob for the losses resulting from the re-auction. The Stifschaffnei Sinsheim determined that Jakob had the means to pay the claim, since he was a handelsmann, and the Stifschaffnei Sinsheim was awarded judgment against Jakob in 1850. The Stifschaffnei Sinsheim, however, was concerned about executing on the judgement, since it could mean the loss of Jakob's house (which the Strifschaffnei described as "little") and could also drive Jakob out of business. The Stifschaffnei Sinsheim ultimately agreed to settle for a discount of what was owed.

It is difficult to determine from available records whether Jakob Heppenheimer was a successful handelsmann. Eichtersheim's archives contain records showing that Jakob also owed money for grain purchased in 1849 and 1854. It is not clear whether the amount Jakob agreed to pay the Stifschaffnei Sinsheim represented a hardship for his business and whether the monies owed in 1849 and 1854 reflected business troubles, or whether this was simply the manner in which business was conducted during this period. But despite these business losses, Jakob was able to purchase another (and perhaps larger) home in 1853. In that year, Jakob purchased a house in Eichtersheim from Katharina Bender, a Christian woman.[120] Jakob's house was located on Heidelberger Strasse 11 at the edge of town.[121] The arrow points to the house in the map below:

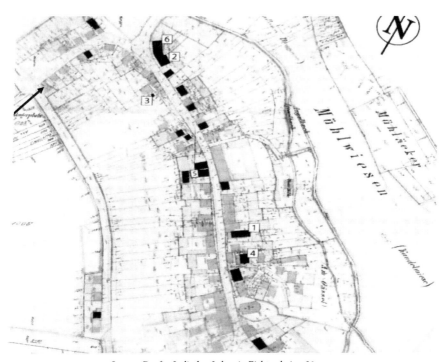

Source: Dorfer, Judisches Leben in Eichtersheim, 81.

By the time Jakob purchased his second home, Eichtersheim had a well-established Jewish community. While some cities and villages in the German lands forced Jews to live in concentrated communities, in most communities in this time period, Jews lived in mixed neighborhoods with their Christian neighbors,[122] and such was the case in Eichtersheim. The above map shows the key Jewish facilities scattered along Hauptstrasse (the main street). The map shows, for example, a kosher butcher shop at #3, the synagogue with the letter "S", and the schoolhouse and mikvah at #2. And on Jakob's street, he was neighbors with Jews, Catholics and Protestants.[123] In addition, in the 1840s, the community opened its own cemetery just west of town.[124] The number of Jews living in Eichtersheim reached its peak in 1848, when 160 Jews lived in Eichtersheim, reflecting 16% of the total population of the town.[125]

2.

Leaving Eichtersheim

akob Heppenheimer's ancestors had lived in Eichtersheim for generations. Residency restrictions had kept the family in Eichtersheim through
the eighteenth and early nineteenth centuries, although even with the easing
of restrictions following the issuance of the Jewish Edict, it would have been a
challenge for Jakob to move with his family to another town. And Jakob, who
owned a house and a grain trading business, may have been content with his
life in Eichtesheim and saw no reason to leave. But after Jakob's death in 1856
and Babette's death in 1862, their six children would all leave Eichtersheim.

The key driver in the decision for some of Jakob's children to leave
Eichtersheim was likely the continued challenge of marrying in Eichtersheim.
The Matrikel was still in place for Eichtersheim's Jews, so that the eldest child
stood the best chance (and for some families, the only chance) at marriage.
As the eldest, Maier was granted permission to marry in 1867 when he was
25 years old.[126] At the time of his marriage, Maier was a handelsmann, likely
trading in grain, like his father and grandfather,[127] and had been earning
enough of a living that the Synagogue Council granted his request to marry.
Maier married his first cousin Hanchen, who was the daughter of Maier's
uncle, Liebmann (Babette's brother). Maier and Hanchen had five children:
Jacob (born June 18, 1868); Leopold (born September 15, 1870); Berta (born
April 26, 1873); Ludwig (born October 10, 1874) and Adolph (born April
25, 1878).[128] When Hanchen died in 1879, Maier married her sister Jette and

they had two children: Sally (born on March 11, 1880) and Selma (born on May 17, 1885).[129] Jette died in 1886.

While Maier was able to marry, the family likely did not have sufficient resources to allow for any of Maier's other siblings to marry in Eichtersheim. Obtaining permission to marry would have always been a challenge for Maier's younger siblings, and that challenge only increased with the deaths of both parents.[130] In fact, likely just after Babette's death, her children sold the family's house.[131]

Maier's sisters were the first to leave Eichtersheim, and they emigrated to America. German Jews began to emigrate to America around 1820.[132] Eichtersheim, as well as neighboring villages, saw a steady exodus of young men to America in the earlier years, so that Jewish women soon began to outnumber men,[133] making it difficult for Jewish women to find spouses. Moreover, dowries were still required for marriage,[134] and with no living parents, there may have been little money for a dowry for either Johanna or Rebecka. Both sisters emigrated to America around 1868, just after Maier's wedding.[135]

The next sibling to leave was Hirsch, who left in 1870, but he remained in the German lands. Hirsch moved to Frankfurt am Main, about 70 miles north of Eichtersheim, and married Sara Hammel on October 26, 1870.[136] It is curious that Hirsch (and later his brothers Joseph and Lazarus) chose to move to Frankfurt rather than Mannheim. As traders, the Heppenheimer family would likely have had strong connections to Mannheim, the closest large city to Eichtersheim. Hirsch's decision to move to Frankfurt may have been based on two factors. First, Frankfurt had become a major center for Reform Judaism, having opened the Philanthropin, a Jewish school with a secular curriculum, in 1804, and educating the leading members of the Reform movement.[137] After living in a community that rigidly controlled worship, the freedom of Frankfurt may have been appealing for Hirsch, who did not appear to remain religiously observant once he moved to Frankfurt.

Second, and perhaps more important to Hirsch (and to his brothers, who would soon arrive), Frankfurt had become the financial center of Germany.[138] And because Frankfurt's economic dominance owed much to Jewish financial and commercial enterprises,[139] Hirsch likely saw greater opportunity for an ambitious Jew in Frankfurt than in Mannheim.

When Hirsch first moved to Frankfurt, he lived in the Altstadt (the old city), where most of Frankfurt's Jews lived.[140] Jews who moved to Frankfurt at the end of the nineteenth century tended to locate near the old Judengasse (the former Jewish ghetto) in the Altstadt, where housing was cheaper, but which was also near the synagogues and Jewish schools.[141] The map, below, shows the Alstadt and the surrounding neighborhoods, where Hirsch (and his brothers) would move to in later years:

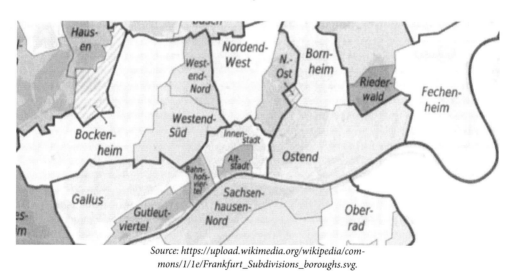

Source: https://upload.wikimedia.org/wikipedia/com-mons/1/1e/Frankfurt_Subdivisions_boroughs.svg.

(The heavy line below the Altstadt and the Ostend is the Main River.)

The year after Hirsch left Eichtersheim, life changed dramatically for all Germans, including German Jews. In August 1870, Prussian Prime Minister Otto von Bismark provoked a war with France and defeated Napoleon

III.[142] Unification of the 36 German principalities soon followed, with King Wilhelm I of Prussia now Kaiser Wilhelm I, the Emperor of the newly unified Germany.[143] In 1871, the new German Parliament passed an emancipation law recognizing Jews as equals, outlawing all restrictions on civil and political rights based on religious differences.[144]

Hirsh's brother Joseph was next to leave Eichtersheim. (Joseph was my husband's great-grandfather.) Unlike Hirsch, Joseph was no longer restricted by the Matrikel, and so likely moved to Frankfurt to take advantage of the new freedoms offered by Jewish emancipation (he would start Gebruder Heppenheimer, a scrap metal business, with Hirsch in 1877, as discussed more fully in the next chapter). Joseph married Mina Flegenheimer on November 1, 1875 in Wiesloch, a town just outside Eichtersheim, and moved to Frankfurt after the wedding.[145] When Joseph and Mina moved to Frankfurt, they moved in with Hirsch and his family. Joseph and Mina's first child, Bertha, was born on October 18, 1876 in Frankfurt. Joseph and Mina had four other children: Johanna (born December 18, 1877), Jacob (born January 1, 1879), Benny (born July 23, 1882), and Max (born October 31, 1888) (Max was my husband's grandfather).

The move of both brothers to Frankfurt around the time of German unification and Jewish emancipation proved to be one of good timing, particularly for those as ambitious as Hirsch and Joseph. German unification gave a sudden and dramatic boost to German industry and the German economy, and German Jews became critical to this economic expansion.[146] And German Jews were a critical part of German industrialization, financing all aspects of the industrial sector.[147] German Jews also helped integrate Germany into the world economy, which further cemented Germany's place as a world power.[148] As one writer has noted, "[t]here probably was no other European country where Jews played so diverse and prominent a role as in Germany."[149] Germany's rapid industrialization, along with Jewish emancipation, thus enabled German Jews to make rapid economic progress, becoming "the most upwardly mobile social group in Germany."[150]

Hirsch and Joseph did not achieve financial success overnight. Hirsch first appeared in the 1872 Frankfurt Address Book, but not as a trader; instead, he was a baker, perhaps the only job he could find in this new city.[151] Over the next few years, he changed occupations, becoming a tradesman and then a shopkeeper. After Joseph moved to Frankfurt in 1875, the brothers likely worked to establish their scrap metal business, which they opened in 1877. And as explained in the next chapter, this venture proved to be a success for both brothers.

At around the time that Hirsch and Joseph moved to Frankfurt, the number of Jews in Frankfurt had reached 11.74 percent of the population.[152] At the same time, the city was growing significantly in population, and the constant influx of new residents constrained the available housing and led to overcrowding.[153] By 1895, most residents of Frankfurt were living in apartments of three or fewer rooms.[154] The severe housing shortages thus led to the development of housing outside the Altstadt.[155] The Ostend (or East End) emerged as a population center for Frankfurt Jews, helped along by favorable planning policies at the end of the nineteenth century.[156] Through this planning, spacious 3-6 room apartments were built in the residential areas of the Ostend, becoming the residential area of middle and upper class Jewish families.[157] The Ostend was enhanced by the move of the zoological garden from the Westend to the Ostend in 1874.[158]

Taking advantage of this new and more modern housing (and likely resulting from the fact that Gebruder Heppenheimer was doing well financially), Hirsh and Joseph moved their families to the Ostend in 1880. Significantly, Joseph moved his family to their own apartment in the same apartment building as his brother's family.[159] Joseph continued to live in the same apartment through the 1880s and early 1890s, while Hirsch moved several times with his family during this period, including to apartments in the North end of Frankfurt.

Joseph's wife Mina died on November 17, 1892 at the age of 38, leaving him a widower with five young children. Likely recognizing the need for a spouse to care for his children, Joseph married Emma Baer, on May 2, 1894. Emma was from Biebrich, a town about 20 miles from Frankfurt and was the daughter of Seligmann Baer, a renowned Biblical scholar and teacher of religion.[160] Emma was 34 years old at the time of her marriage, so that her marriage prospects were likely limited and marrying a man with five children (the youngest was not yet 6 years old), but one with adequate financial resources, may have seemed a sensible choice.[161] Joseph and Emma had two daughters, Alice , born on July 4, 1896, and Selma, born on July 20, 1900.

In 1892, Hirsch moved to Ostendstrasse 70 in the Ostend. He emigrated to America that year, but his family remained in that apartment until they moved to America the following year. Joseph then moved into Hirsch's apartment on Ostendstrasse in 1894. Joseph and his family had lived at Bergerstrasse 18 since 1882, but perhaps Emma, newly married to Joseph, preferred to start her married life in a new apartment. Joseph's growing family may also have influenced the choice to move. Through the remainder of the nineteenth century, the family lived in three other apartments, all in the Ostend. All three were near the zoo in the more fashionable part of the Ostend.

While many of Frankfurt's Jews moved to the Ostend, Jewish life continued to revolve around the old Judengasse in the Altstadt during this period. The Reform synagogue on the Judengasse was preserved following the razing of most of the houses, and a new Orthodox synagogue was built on the southern end of the Judengasse in 1882, in what had been the Judenmarkt (Jewish Market).[162] In 1885, the Judengasse was renamed Bornestrasse and the Jewish Market was renamed the Borneplatz—both in honor of Ludwig Borne, a renowned Jewish writer born on the Judengasse who later converted to Christianity.[163] While fewer Jews lived near the old Judengasse, Bornestrasse and Borneplatz remained important Jewish centers of commerce.[164] Moreover, Borneplatz remained an important outdoor market until replaced by the Grossmarkthalle in the Ostend in 1928.[165]

Lazarus, the youngest of the brothers, moved to Frankfurt just around the time his brothers Hirsch and Joseph were moving to the Ostend neighborhood as successful scrap metal dealers. Lazarus appears for the first time in the Frankfurt Address Book in 1882 as a tradesman in the scrap metal business following his marriage to Auguste Schott in 1880. Lazarus and Auguste had five sons: Jacob (born on December 5, 1880); Gustav Arthur (born on June 13, 1885); Hugo (born on October 8, 1890); Robert (born on May 19, 1893); and Berthold (born on November 2, 1895). Lazarus was living across the Main River from his brothers in the Sachsenhausen section of Frankfurt. Unlike his brothers, Lazarus and his family were living in a poor and mostly non-Jewish neighborhood. Lazarus and his family remained in the Sachsenhausen neighborhood until 1888, when they moved to the old Judengasse neighborhood. Lazarus and his family continued to live in the poorer parts of the city.[166]

Maier, the eldest, was the last of the brothers to leave Eichtersheim. Maier's first wife died in 1879 and he married her sister Jette. After Jette's death, Maier moved to Frankenthal, a town located just outside of Mannheim, in 1887. Frankenthal seems a strange choice for someone seeking opportunities beyond a small rural town, since Frankenthal was just slightly larger than Eichtersheim.[167] But following Jewish emancipation, the number of Jews in Frankenthal increased from 246 in 1871 to a peak of 371 in 1900.[168] This contrasts with Eichtersheim's Jewish population, which was shrinking rapidly even before Maier left. While Maier chose to move his family to a smaller town than Frankfurt, he likely saw in Frankenthal a growing Jewish community and increased economic opportunity.[169]

While Jewish emancipation presented great opportunities for the Heppenheimer brothers, they likely remained wary of continued anti-Semitism. The brothers knew what it was like to have restrictions on marriage and livelihoods, and the reminders about the continued challenges of being Jewish in Germany came soon after the Jewish emancipation law was passed. In October 1873, the German stockmarket crashed and some blamed the Jews.[170] Wilhelm Marr, who coined the term "anti-Semite" in 1879 and headed the organization "The League of Antisemites," fought to overturn Jewish emancipation in Germany.[171] Marr was unsuccessful in his efforts, but these waves of anti-Semitism would continue. In fact, government-encouraged anti-Semitism occurred in 1881, followed by a second wave of anti-Semitic actions by the German government through discriminatory policies in 1893.[172] Still, such actions did not deter Jakob Heppenheimer's sons from pursuing opportunities as full German citizens.

3.
The Heppenheimers and the Scrap Metal Business

The Heppenheimer family had been grain traders in Eichtersheim for generations. However, by the 1860s, there was a reduction in the grain and livestock trade businesses in and around Eichtersheim.[173] After Jakob Heppenheimer's sons left Eichtersheim, they remained traders, but decided to trade in a different product. Whether responding to a reduction in the grain trading business or recognizing an emerging opportunity, each of the brothers entered the growing business of scrap metal trading.

Following unification, Germany experienced its first industrial revolution.[174] Increased production of metals was needed to build up the various sectors of the rapidly growing German economy, such as railways, bridges, steamships, and the armaments industry, and later the automobile industry.[175] At the same time, technological changes in steelmaking allowed for the increased use of scrap metal to make steel.[176] Through the addition of scrap, German steel production grew explosively from 1 million metric tons in 1885 to 10 million in 1905 and to 19 million in 1918.[177] By 1893, Germany became the world's second largest producer of steel, just behind the United States and just ahead of Britain.[178]

Jews had been important metal traders for virgin (new) metals, even before emancipation. Germany produced more zinc than it needed, and became the largest exporter of zinc in the world.[179] While Germany also had sufficient resources to meet its entire iron demand, Germany was poor in other mineral ores as compared to its needs, and so was forced to import a substantial portion of metal from other countries.[180] Jews served as the middlemen, engaging as metal traders to buy metal or to act as selling agents.[181] The three largest firms in the German metal trade for virgin metals were all started by Jews: Metallgesellschaft, Aron Hirsch & Sohn, and Beer, Sondheimer & Co.[182]

German Jews were well positioned following emancipation to take advantage of the growing scrap metal business. Jews had long been involved in the scrap field, traveling as peddlers from village to village, particularly during periods when Jewish settlement was restricted. Sorting and re-selling useful scrap material was the basis of the traditional scrap industry, trading new goods for rag, bone, old metal, and other worn-out objects from households.[183] In Germany, such traders were known as "Naturforscher," or naturalists, and generally specialized in a particular product (rags, glass, bone, metal, etc.).[184] The attraction of the scrap business to marginalized groups held true for the Jews in Germany, where scrap firms were often owned by Jews.[185] German Jews were thus attracted to the scrap metal business, where Jewish scrap metal traders soon represented nearly half of all scrap metal traders.[186]

The four Heppenheimer brothers may have chosen the scrap metal industry because the scrap trade required little initial capital. They may also have chosen the scrap metal business because it was an easy transition from the grain trading business. Grain dealers acted as middlemen, essentially serving as representatives of the modern capitalist economy to the German farmers.[187] After emancipation, it was easy for Jews like the Heppenheimer brothers to gravitate to the scrap metal business, where they could excel in their role as middlemen.[188]

Leaving Eichtersheim allowed Hirsch and Joseph to test their business acumen without the earlier constraints, and both proved to be ambitious and able businessmen. Hirsch and Joseph established Gebruder Heppenheimer ("Heppenheimer Brothers" in German) as a scrap metal business in 1877.[189] In the early years of the business, the brothers sold whatever they could to make money, as reflected in the following advertisement in the Orthodox Jewish paper for the sale of a modern matzo maker ("mazzen maschine"), which they promoted for its ease of use:

Source: http://sammlungen.ub.uni-frankfurt.de/cm/periodical/
pageview/2515361?query=gebr.%20heppenheimer.

Initially, Hirsch and Joseph operated Gebruder Heppenheimer out of their shared apartment. In 1879, Gebruder Heppenheimer opened a facility at Heiligkreuzgasse 18, just north of the old Judengasse.[190] In 1881, the business was relocated about a third of a mile northwest to Elephantengasse 15, as reflected in the above advertisement. By 1890, the company had moved a few blocks south to Grosse Friedbergerstrasse 38. In 1891, the business made its first purchase of a building, which was located on Kleine Eschenheimerstrasse

32 and had four tenants (although Gebruder Heppenheimer remained at the Grosse Friedbergerstrasse location).

Hirsch and Joseph had early successes in their new business, but the scrap metal business was still a challenging business. While entering the scrap metal business may have required little start-up capital, to be successful, the business required significant working capital. The scrap metal dealer always paid for scrap in cash, but would often need to warehouse the scrap until the dealer had sufficient stock to sell to the customer.[191] This need to balance the collecting and distributing of scrap metals made the economics of the business challenging.[192] And while the scrap metal dealer would gather metals in the hopes that prices would rise, the scrap metal dealer also risked financial losses should the prices fall while the dealer warehoused the metals.[193] Like their days as grain dealers, Hirsch and Joseph assumed the financial risk for both the purchase and sale of scrap.

In 1892, Gebruder Heppenheimer sold the building on Kleine Eschenheimerstrasse and purchased two connecting buildings on the corner of Dominikanergasse and Klostergasse, and moved their business there. The buildings, located at Dominkanergasse 3/5 and Klostergasse 12, had previously housed a brewery and eating establishment.[194] Unlike the previous places where Gebruder Heppenheimer was located, the move to Dominikanergasse was a move to the heart of the Altstadt and the heart of Jewish life in Frankfurt.

The move to Dominikanergasse was also significant because, for the first time, Gebruder Heppenheimer had the means to purchase the building in which the business was located. The company also purchased a building much larger than its needs, and was landlord to the other businesses. The Dominikanergasse building had a ground floor occupied by Gebruder Heppenheimer, plus three stories rented to other businesses and the Klostergasse building had a ground floor and two stories. According to the 1893 Frankfurt Address Book, there were nine other tenants in the

Dominikanergasse building and seven tenants in the Klostergasse building. A map from 1894, below, shows the new Heppenheimer facility (the arrow points to the two connected buildings):

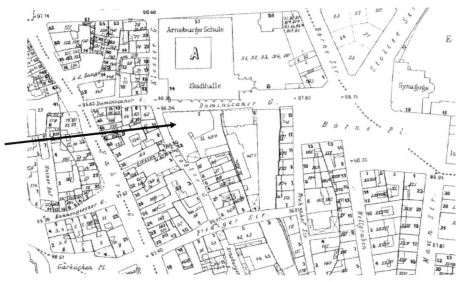

Source: *Der Borneplatz in Frankfurt am Main, Hans-Otto Schembs, Verlag Waldemar Kramer, p. 98 (1987)*

In addition to the connected buildings, Gebruder Heppenheimer also owned the space in the rear of the building, which they used as a scrap yard and warehouse. There is an alley between Dominikanergasse 1 and 3/5, which allowed for access to the scrap yard from the street. The business was located just off the Borneplatz—also the location of the Orthodox synagogue—and just a short walk to the Reform synagogue on the Bornestrasse. This location would remain part of the business until Gebruder Heppenheimer was forced to sell the buildings at the end of the 1930s.

Gebruder Heppenheimer's new office was located in the old part of the city, with narrow streets and older structures. To fully appreciate the narrowness of these streets, the picture below was taken in 1902 and shows a beer house that was located at the south end of Klostergasse (the corner of Klostergasse and Predigerstrasse—Prediger Str. on the above map).

Source: https://commons.wikimedia.org/wiki/File:Frankfurt_Am_Main-Fay-BADAFAMNDN-Heft_09-Nr_098-1902-Eckhaus_der_Predigerstrasse_u_Klostergasse_2.jpg

One can imagine the challenges in navigating these narrow streets to collect and deliver scrap iron and metal.

Hirsch emigrated to America on April 10, 1892 to begin a scrap metal business in New York, H. Heppenheimer & Sons.[195] His wife Sara and their younger children emigrated to America the following April. Having just made a significant investment in two office buildings in Frankfurt, it seems strange that Hirsch would decide to emigrate to America with his family. But, based on this investment, as well as the continued connection of both families in the businesses in both Frankfurt and then New York, it appears that Hirsch did not intend to fully sever ties with Gebruder Heppenheimer.

While Hirsch left for America with most of his family, his oldest sons Jacob and Adolph remained in Frankfurt, and were partners in Gebruder Heppenheimer with Joseph.[196] At the same time, Joseph's oldest son Jacob moved to New York in 1897 and worked for his uncle Hirsch. Hirsch's son Adolph visited New York in 1907, noting that the visit was for business.[197] Joseph also visited New York in both 1903 and 1906, and while we do not know what the purposes of those visits were, we can assume that two visits in a relatively short period of time likely included a business component. With such strong ties between the families and their businesses, it may be that Hirsch and Joseph aspired to be like the highly successful German Jewish metals business— Metallgesellschaft—with connected businesses in Germany and America.[198]

While Hirsch's business was developing in America (Hirsch changed his name to Henry when he emigrated to America, and is referred to hereafter as Henry), Gebruder Heppenheimer remained at the Dominikanergasse address and continued to grow as a business, helped by German policies favoring German businesses. Germany was becoming the leading industrial state on the Continent, and this industrial expansion was achieved partly by vigorous state intervention, including states policies to help grow the German scrap metal businesses.[199] Cartels in the heavy industries were encouraged, so that by 1900, 275 cartels were in operation in Germany.[200] Before World War I, the international zinc cartel was essentially the three largest German Jewish metal traders (Metallgesellschaft, Aron Hirsch & Sohn, and Beer,

Sondheimer & Co.), and they controlled world production quotas and fixed prices.[201] In fact, collusion among the three companies, as well as with the producers through international cartels, enabled these three, as well as the other German firms, all essentially Jewish-owned, to dominate the international trade in metals and minerals before the first World War.[202]

The years 1905 and 1906 were significant years for the Heppenheimer scrap metal businesses on both sides of the Atlantic. In 1905, Gebruder Heppenheimer opened a zinc and lead smelter facility in Mainkur (a suburb of Frankfurt), which it now owned in addition to the original facility on Dominikanergasse.[203] The following is an invoice from the Gebruder Heppenheimer's new smelter facility:

Source: Institut Fur Stadtgeschichte, Hospital zum Keiligen Geist Nr. 2393, Seite 21.

The invoice shows a smelter facility, as well as an attached house and office. [204] The facility had direct access to the railway, which allowed for increased trading.[205] In 1906, Joseph's son Jacob returned to Germany from New York and became a Prokurist[206] of Gebruder Heppenheimer (and would become a full partner around 1910), and the company was trading in both scrap iron and scrap metals at the two facilities.[207]

In the same year that Joseph opened the smelter facility, Henry opened a second American business, the National Copper Company, to smelter copper and brass refuse.[208] That business had a plant in New Jersey and offices at 101 Beekman Street in New York.[209] Henry then incorporated the scrap metal business in 1906, and that company had a plant in Brooklyn and offices also located at the 101 Beekman Street address.[210] Henry was the President of the businesses, while his sons Leo and Max were Treasurer and Secretary, respectively, of both businesses. Moreover, Henry's daughter Hedwig (who changed her name to Hattie) married Adolph Keller (who proved to be extremely important to the Heppenheimer family members still living in Germany in the 1930s), and Adolph became part of the family business.[211]

In 1906, things looked promising for the Heppenheimer brothers on both sides of the Atlantic. In fact, Henry's scrap metal smelting and refining businesses were among the largest in the New York metropolitan area.[212] But in 1907, there was a significant drop in the price of copper, which caused financial problems for both of Henry's businesses, since the copper business and the scrap metal business were tied together financially.[213] Fortunately for Adolph Keller, he had left Henry's company in 1907 to start his own scrap metal company.[214] Unable to weather the financial storm, Henry was forced to file for bankruptcy in 1908 and all of his facilities were ultimately sold.[215] We do not know whether the Heppenheimers in Frankfurt lost any money as a result of the collapse of Henry's businesses in New York, although none of the Frankfurt businesses seemed to have been affected by the U.S. bankruptcy.[216]

While the American scrap metal and smelting businesses may have failed, in the years leading up to World War I, Gebruder Heppenheimer in Germany remained a successful company. Gebruder Heppenheimer continued to operate its two facilities: the zinc smelter and metal handling facility in Mainkur and the main warehouse and office on Dominikanergasse in Frankfurt. Gebruder Heppenheimer was also engaged in international scrap metal trade. For example, it was noted in the March 29, 1914 and April 5, 1914 editions of Moniteur des Intérêts Matériels, a leading financial journal published in Brussels, Belgium, that Gebruder Heppenheimer was selling bronze chips and waste and wrought iron from the Mainkur facility and iron, steel and cast iron from its headquarters in Frankfurt.[217]

Joseph's ambitions extended to technological enhancements to his smelter facility, and to profit from such enhancements. In 1913, Gebruder Heppenheimer submitted a patent application, along with Viktor Slotosch,[218] for a procedure at the Mainkur smelting facility. The following is a description of the process: "The lid of the crucible, which serves to produce cones of constant volume, as used to rapidly determine the composition of alloys (e.g., the tin content in tin lead alloys), has a sprue having a knife-like edge and moves like a scissors to the crucible."[219]

While he also lived in Frankfurt, Joseph's younger brother Lazarus was not a part of Gebruder Heppenheimer. Lazarus began his rags and scrap metal business just after he moved to Frankfurt in 1880. He soon added wood and coal to his business, but was trading only in scrap metal by 1902. There is no evidence that Lazarus ever worked with his brothers Henry and Joseph.

We can surmise that Lazarus was not as successful as his brothers, because he continued to live with his family in the poorer parts of the city. Still, until 1903, he had maintained a business address separate from his home address. That changed in 1903, when he listed his home address as his business address in the Frankfurt Address Book. One can assume that Lazarus closed his office because he could no longer afford a separate office for his scrap metal business. This assumption is strengthened by the circumstances of his death at the end of 1903.

Lazarus drowned in the Main River in December 1903, at the age of 49. It seems unlikely that anyone would be on the Main River for pleasure in December, so Lazarus' drowning may have been intentional. Lazarus's business may have been failing by 1903, and it likely did not help that Henry and Joseph had developed successful metals businesses, and Lazarus was not part of those businesses. The prospect of failing while surrounded by successful brothers may have proven to be too much for Lazarus. Lazarus' death left his wife to raise their five sons, with the three youngest being 13, 10, and 8.

Lazarus' eldest son Jacob, who was 23 years old at the time of his father's death, took over his father's business. Jacob had likely been working for his father for a number of years, and he became the primary support for his mother and siblings.

The scrap metal trade always had a reputation for straddling the legitimate and the black economies.[220] There is no evidence that any of the principals at Gebruder Heppenheimer ever engaged in illegitimate activities, but that was not the case for Lazarus' eldest son. Being responsible for his family at a relatively young age, Jacob may have felt the pressure to cross that line between the legitimate and black economies. In 1907, Jacob was caught selling stolen metals to his cousin Adolph Heppenheimer at Gebuder Heppenheimer's Mainkur facilty.[221] Jacob was sentenced to one year in prison and 6 years of loss of civil rights.[222]

Since Jacob was the main source of income for his family, his imprisonment likely created another financial hardship for the family. Jacob's brother, Gustav Arthur, who was about 23 years old when Jacob went to prison, was now responsible for supporting the family.

Lazarus' son Jacob moved to Strasbourg in Alsace in 1910,[223] and we can assume that he moved there immediately after his release from prison. Perhaps seeking a fresh start in a city where he was unknown, Jacob started a scrap metal business in Strasbourg. Jacob was doing well enough in Strasbourg that he was able to provide some support for his mother and brothers back in Frankfurt. Jacob's other brothers also became scrap metal dealers. While Gustav Arthur appears in the Frankfurt address book as a businessman in 1911, he was likely a scrap metal dealer, since that was his profession after World War I. Lazarus' son Hugo also became a scrap metal dealer by 1913, and was joined by his brother Berthold when he graduated the eighth grade.

Joseph's brother Maier had a late start in the scrap metal business. In 1887, Maier moved to Frankenthal, a town just outside Mannheim, and started a scrap iron and metal business called M. Heppenheimer. The 1898/99 Frankenthal Address Book contained the following advertisement for Maier's scrap metal business:

Source: Frankenthal Addressbuch 1898/99, p. 219, https://
www.dilibri.de/rlb/periodical/pageview/1004414.

The business was doing well enough to have a separate office from Maier's home address, and dealt in metals, iron, paper and used machinery. Maier registered his business as an Offene Handelsgesellschaft (OHG)[224] in 1902.[225] Maier's son Leopold and son-in-law Moses (also known as Max, who had married Maier's daughter Berta in 1901) became shareholders of the company in 1904.[226] Maier opened a branch office of M. Heppenheimer in Mannheim in 1910, and Leopold ran that branch of the business.

Maier died in 1913, and the company was dissolved.[227] Maier's son Leopold opened his own scrap iron and metal treatment business at the same location as M. Heppenheimer's Mannheim office. Moses established a sole proprietorship in Frankenthal, but retained the name of his father-in-law's business, M. Heppenheimer. Moses' wife Berta was involved in the business, and was responsible for bookkeeping and other financial matters.[228] Berta and Moses' son Walter also worked in the business.[229]

Maier's other sons left Frankenthal and became scrap metal dealers. Maier's oldest child, Jacob, emigrated to America on August 10, 1891, married Jenni Wreschensky in 1894, and became a metal dealer. Maier's son Adolph emigrated to America in 1905, and worked as a scrap metal worker for his brother Jacob.[230] Maier's sons Sally and Ludwig moved from Frankenthal to Worms in 1894.[231] Ludwig established Ludwig Heppenheimer as a scrap iron and metal business, and registered the business in 1895.[232] Sally joined Ludwig Heppenheimer and became a personally liable partner on July 1, 1919.[233]

4.

Life Around the Turn of the Twentieth Century

L eading up to the turn of the twentieth century, Germany saw increases in both Jewish population and Jewish wealth. Jewish population in all of Germany grew from 512,000 in 1871 to 615,000 in 1910,[234] while Frankfurt, which attracted entrepreneurial Jews like the Heppenheimers, saw its Jewish population rise from 10,009 in 1871 to 21,974 in 1900.[235] Germany's total wealth increased from 200 thousand million marks in 1895 to over 300 thousand million marks by 1913, with Jews playing an important role in this economic growth.[236] The comparative wealth of German Jews can be seen by the taxes paid, for example, by Frankfurt's Jews—in 1900, almost 6,000 Jewish citizens paid 2,540,812 Marks in taxes, while almost 35,000 non-Jews paid just 3,611,815 Marks.[237] In fact, just prior to World War I, German Jews earned five times the income of the average Christian.[238]

Taking advantage of these new opportunities for German Jews, the men of Gebruder Heppenheimer grew wealthy. And free from the constraints of second class status, the Heppenheimer family, like all Jews in Frankfurt, enjoyed all aspects of life available to full citizens of Germany. The Heppenheimer family had enough income to make charitable donations, such as, for example, a donation in 1903 to support a new hospital being built in Jerusalem, Shaare Zedek.[239] The Heppenheimers also experienced, for the first time, religious choices, as well as enhanced educational opportunities. Living in Frankfurt around the turn of the century were Joseph and his family, Lazarus' family, and Henry's son Adolph.[240] And Maier and his family, living in and around Frankenthal, were also enjoying the benefits of Jewish emancipation.

Life in Frankfurt's Ostend

At the turn of the century, almost 45% of Frankfurt's Jews were living in the Ostend.[241] Joseph and his family had been living in the Ostend since 1880. But their move to Roderberg Weg 30 in 1914 truly signaled their achievement of upper middle-class status.[242]

Roderberg Weg was one of the larger streets in the Ostend and was considered quite fashionable, as can be seen from this postcard photo taken in 1910:

Source: Ostend: Blick in ein Judisches Viertel, p. 16.

The apartment was likely more luxurious and modern than any of the family's previous apartments. The building had been built in 1905, and when Joseph moved into the building, the ground floor housed a Jewish boarding school for 12 young women.[243] Given that the ground floor was large enough for a school, its twelve students, and the two women that ran the school, the Heppenheimers' apartment, which encompassed the entire first floor of the building, must have been quite large. We do not know whether the apartment had electric lighting—only 6.32 percent of all households in Frankfurt had electricity in 1910—but it was likely equipped with gaslights.[244]

The apartment on Roderberg Weg was also just a few blocks from the Zoological Garden (the arrow on the map below points to the location of the apartment):

Source: https://www.wikiwand.com/de/Bernhard-Grzimek-Allee

Around the time the Heppenheimers moved to Roderberg Weg, the Zoological Garden was one of the most important sights in the city, and residents enjoyed concerts on summer evenings. This advertisement from 1891 shows the range of activities for families at the Zoo:

Zoologischer Garten

zu

Frankfurt am Main.

Täglich von Morgens 7 Uhr an geöffnet.

Reichhaltige Sammlung lebender Thiere.

Anmuthige Parkanlage.

Aussichtsthurm mit herrlicher Rundschau nach dem Taunus und in das Mainthal.

Täglich Nachmitttags 4 Uhr und Abends 8 Uhr:

CONCERT

von der Capelle des Gartens unter Leitung des Capellmeisters Herrn Louis Keiper.

Grossartiges Gesellschaftshaus.

RESTAURATION ERSTEN RANGES

von Thoma & Steger.

Vorzügliche Küche. Ausgewählte reine Weine.

Besondere Salons für separate Diners und Soupers.

Bierhalle — Lesezimmer — Billards.

Seewasser-Aquarium

mit lebenden Thieren aus Meeren und Flüssen.

Eintrittspreise:

für den Zoologischen Garten 1 Mk., Kinder 50 Pfg.; für das Aquarium 50 Pfg., Kinder 20 Pfg.

Monats-Abonnement für Fremde.

Source: Frankfurt in Fruhen Photgraphien 1850-1914, p. 60.

According to the advertisement, in addition to the Zoo and the Aquarium, visitors to the Zoological Garden could enjoy restaurants, a beer hall, billiards room, and concerts.[245] The zoo offered daily musical performances and regular symphony concerts, beauty competitions, and balls.[246]

One important aspect of Jewish life in Frankfurt at the turn of the century was the cafe, and the Jews of the Ostend frequented Café Goldschmidt.[247] Located at the north end of the old Judengasse, the café was open from 6 am until 11 pm.[248] The café had multiple rooms, catering to traders and fruit and vegetable wholesalers, as well as a gaming hall for the more well-to-do.[249] There was a more elegant room for fancier service, as well as a ladies salon.[250] Café Goldschmidt was known for its cheesecake, as well as its cigars.[251] This advertisement for Café Goldschmidt provides a sense of the size and scope of the facility:

Source: http://web.nli.org.il/sites/NLI/Hebrew/digitallibrary/pages/viewer. aspx?presentorid=NNL_Ephemera&DocID=NNL_Ephemera700346596&Print=true

The café was known as "Café Jonteff" (holiday in Yiddish), given the number of Jews that frequented the establishment.[252] One can imagine the Heppenheimer family enjoying coffee and pastries in the cafe, or the Gebruder Heppenheimer's partners conducting business in the billiards room or over cigars. And it was not uncommon for the cafes popular with Jews to be open on Saturday and to extend "credit" to those who did not want to pay on the Sabbath.[253]

Frankfurt had an extensive tramway system, and by 1904, the horse-drawn trams had been converted to electric trams.[254] By the time Joseph and his family had moved to Roderberg Weg, it was easy for them to take electric trams to work or to the many other offerings in the city. The map from 1914, below, shows the tracks for the electric trams near the offices of Gebruder Heppenheimer (identified by the arrow):

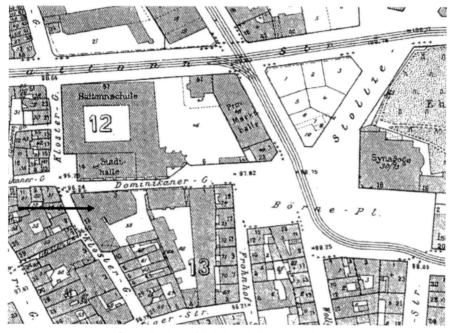

*Source: Der Borneplatz in Frankfurt am Main, Hans-Otto
Schembs, Verlag Waldemar Kramer, p. 111.*

The Ostend, planned to include a mix of residential and industrial elements, began to see further changes around the time Joseph and his family moved into the apartment on Roderberg Weg. First, the general development plan of 1909/1910 included the construction of the eastern harbor (the Osthafen), which enhanced industry in the Ostend.[255] Second, less religious or more economically successful Jews were moving out of the Ostend to other parts of the city, and were being replaced by Eastern-European Jews who found work in the new industrial plants in the Ostend.[256] With such changes, Joseph and his family began to see their neighborhood become less desirable, although Joseph and Emma would remain in the Ostend. But such changes would cause the next generation of Heppenheimers to leave the Ostend and seek fancier housing, as will be discussed in Chapter 6.

Religious Life

Jews living in Germany's towns were members of "Gemeindes" until World War II—Jewish communities that acted as the official representative of Jews to the Gentile world.[257] In Eichtersheim, the Synagogue Council was the Gemeinde and had a strong hold on virtually all aspects of the lives of the Jewish community, deciding where Jews could go to school, how they could pray, and whether and when they could marry. By law, all Frankfurt Jews belonged to the Gemeinde, but the Frankfurt Gemeinde was less restrictive than the Eichtersheim Synagogue Council, both because of Jewish emancipation and because Frankfurt was more religiously pluralistic.[258]

Around the turn of the twentieth century, the Frankfurt Gemeinde administered four synagogues (two Reform and two Orthodox), the Philanthropin (the more secular institution) and an Orthodox Yeshiva.[259] Reform Judaism had develop as an alternative to traditional Judaism, but also as an antidote to the growing number of conversions to Christianity.[260] The Frankfurt Gemeinde built the Hauptsynagoge (Main Synagogue), a Reform synagogue, around 1860.[261] The Hauptsynagoge incorporated the changes promoted by the Reform movement at the time, including the addition of an organ and changes in the liturgy.[262] The Hauptsynagoge had 1,020 seats, but continued to separate the sexes, so that the 504 seats in the upper gallery were for women.[263] A second Reform synagogue was built in the Westend (the "Westend Synagogue") in 1910 to serve the more affluent Jews that had moved to the western and northwestern parts of Frankfurt.[264] Frankfurt's Orthodox community remained a presence in the city, and an Orthodox synagogue was built on the Boerneplatz in 1882.[265] A second Orthodox synagogue, which had been built in 1874, was added to the responsibility of the Gemeinde when Bockenheim was classified as a district of Frankfurt in 1895.[266]

Before Henry and Joseph moved to Frankfurt, they had limited options in terms of religious observance. In Eichtersheim, there was one synagogue and the Jews were required to follow the strict rules of that synagogue. The brothers' move to Frankfurt, at the time of Jewish emancipation, provided them with options they never had, beyond just economic freedom. We do not know for certain what their religious practices were, but we can guess that they were Reform Jews, based on their financial contributions to the Philanthropin and the fact that, as discussed in the next section of this chapter, all of their children likely attended the Philanthropin.

Moreover, the life of a businessman in Frankfurt around the turn of the century would have forced Joseph to compromise on his religious practices. In 1905, the Frankfurt City Council passed a law requiring the closure of businesses on Sunday.[267] Any Jewish businesses that had closed on Saturday to observe the Sabbath would have found it impossible to close their business for two days.[268] Thus, few Jewish businesses closed on Saturday after 1905, and that was likely the case for Gebruder Heppenheimer.[269]

The Heppenheimers found themselves in Frankfurt at a critical time for the Reform movement. Attendance in the Reform synagogues was lagging and the Gemeinde brought in Rabbi Caesar Seligmann in 1902 to renew interest in religious life, especially among the youth.[270] Rabbi Arnold Lazarus was hired by the Gemeinde in 1904 to be the second Reform rabbi in Frankfurt, and together these two rabbis pushed for a new synagogue (which would become the Westend Synagogue) that would have seating for men and women on the same floor (but seated on separate sides) and would have prayer books in both German and Hebrew.[271] A third Reform rabbi, Geor Seligmann, was added to the Gemeinde payroll after the opening of the Westend Synagogue. The Westend Synagogue drew so many congregants that, by 1918, an additional service in the auditorium of the Philanthropin was required during the high holidays.[272] The Westend Synagogue even had bat-mitzvah ceremonies for girls, although they were not performed in the Hauptsynagoge.[273]

Education in Frankfurt

In Eichtersheim, there was a single school for Jews, and it is likely that the Heppenheimer children did not attend school past their early teens. On the other hand, Frankfort afforded more educational opportunities for families like the Heppenheimers. Towards the end of the nineteenth century, the German school system had three types of schools: the Gymnasium, the Realschule and the Oberrealschule.[274] The Gymnasium was an elite school that prepared students for the university, while the Realschule and the Oberrealschule were secondary technical schools.[275] The latter two schools were primarily for the children of the nascent industrial bourgeoisie and upper strata of the skilled working class, but the Realschule was more rigorous in its academic requirements than the Oberrealschule.[276] After completing the Realschule, the student could work or continue vocational training.[277]

Joseph's children attended the Philanthropin, which was a Realschule.[278] Beginning in 1880, Joseph began contributing during fundraisers to support the Philanthropin. Joseph's oldest son Jacob graduated from the Philanthropin in 1896 at the age of 16, listing his profession as businessman.[279] Joseph's youngest son Max also graduated from the Philanthropin in 1904 at the age of 15 years and listed as his profession businessman. Max, himself, contributed to the school during a fundraiser in 1908. Joseph's oldest daughter Bertha also attended the Philanthropin, but she had to leave school at the age of 14 to help take care of her younger siblings after her mother's death in 1892.[280]

The Heppenheimer support of the Philanthropin reflected their interest in education following emancipation, although the Heppenheimer family did not take full advantage of the opportunities available in higher education, as did other Jews in Germany. By 1900, Jews were 1 percent of the German population, but were 10 percent of all students.[281] Jews became doctors, lawyers, journalists, and academics.[282] Still, more than half of the Jewish population received only an elementary education at the time, and generally opted for independent commercial opportunities rather than academics.[283] That seemed to be the case for Joseph's sons, who all attended the Philanthropin and chose not to attend a university; instead they followed in the "family" business of scrap metal trading.[284]

Joseph's sons may have chosen to end their education at the Philanthropin, but that was not the case for one of Joseph's daughters. In the late nineteenth century, daughters in Jewish middle-class families tended to work in the home, or in a family business, until marriage.[285] This was likely the case for both Bertha and Johanna, Joseph Heppenheimer's daughters from his first marriage, who married in 1898 and 1902, respectively. But times were also changing for Jewish women in Germany, and it seems that Alice, Joseph's older daughter from his second marriage, was able to take advantage of the changing times.

As advances in the food and consumer industries began to reduce homemaking tasks, daughters of the middle-class no longer needed to work in the home.[286] Moreover, after finishing their schooling at sixteen, Jewish girls faced six to ten years before they were ready to marry.[287] Discouraged from earning a living, many of these girls prevailed upon their parents to allow them to pursue advanced studies.[288] German universities officially admitted women in the first decade of the twentieth century.[289] I do not believe that Alice attended a university, but I believe that Alice did attend an arts and crafts school, based on her occupations in the 1920s and 1930s.[290] And this would mean that she was the first of Joseph's children (and likely the only one) to attend a higher educational institution following graduation from the Philanthropin.

Between 1903 and 1913, there were a rising number of technical and vocational schools in Germany.[291] Arts and crafts schools opened for the first time in Germany in the late nineteenth century.[292] Applicants to the school would have needed to have some level of proficiency in their proposed course of study, as well as proficiency in drawing, and the course of study would generally last three years.[293] Around the time Alice would have attended an arts and crafts school, the following courses were generally offered: architectural designing in wood and metal, metal engraving, modeling, steel engraving and etching, design for fabrics, pattern designing, artistic embroidery, decorative painting, enamel painting, designing, and painting figures and plants.[294] Women interested in the arts and fashion would have attended arts and crafts schools.[295]

Alice likely attended an arts and crafts school in Nuremberg. Alice graduated from the Philanthropin around 1912, when she was 16 years old. Alice married Ludwig Adler in 1920 in Nuremberg; Alfred was from Nuremberg. Alice opened an arts and crafts studio in Nuremberg in the 1920s. One of the few arts and crafts schools in Germany accepting women at the time Alice graduated from the Philanthropin was the Nuremberg School of Applied Arts.[296] Since Alice married in Nuremberg in 1920, did not have family in Nuremberg, and since the arts and crafts school in Nuremberg was one of the few schools that accepted women students, it seems plausible that she attended the school following her graduation from the Realschule, met Alfred while living in Nuremberg, and married Alfred after her graduation from the Nuremberg School of Applied Arts.[297]

Even though only one of Joseph's children attended a higher educational institution, Joseph was still interested in education. Gebruder Heppenheimer contributed financially to an organization whose focus was to protect the German youth from so-called "trash fiction." The organization, Frankfurter Verband Zum Schutz der Jugend Gegen die Schundliteratur (or Frankfurt Association for the Protection of Youth Against the Trash Literature), had its start in 1910. Its purpose was to educate the populace against "trash" and to supply readers with better quality reading material.[298] Gebruder Heppenheimer made contributions to the organization in 1913 and 1914.[299] And Joseph Heppenheimer's interest in ensuring that the youth had adequate reading materials continued into World War I. In April and May of 1918, Joseph donated money to the Rhine-Main Association for Public Education to provide reading materials for the troops of the 18th Army Corps (his son Max was in the 18th Army Corps).[300]

Life in Germany for Maier's Family

Unlike his three brothers, when Maier Heppenheimer left Eichtersheim in 1887, he moved to Frankenthal. While all of his children initially moved with him, only his daughter Berta and her family remained in Frankenthal. Maier's oldest son, Jacob, emigrated to America in 1891. Next to leave Frankenthal were Ludwig and Sally, who moved to Worms, about 7 miles from Frankenthal, in 1894.[301] The Worms Jewish community was larger than Frankenthal and likely represented greater opportunities for Ludwig and Sally to establish and grow a scrap metal business.

Maier's son Leopold moved to Mannheim, about 9 miles from Frankenthal, between 1895 and 1900, first to operate a branch of his father's scrap metal business and then to open his own scrap metal business following his father's death. Leopold was the only one of Maier's sons to have an ownership interest in Maier's scrap metal company (along with Leopold's brother-in-law Moses) before it was dissolved.[302]

Maier's youngest son from his first marriage, Adolph , was the last son to leave Frankenthal. He was 27 years old and unmarried, and was not a partner in the family business. So, in 1905, Adolph decided to emigrate to America and moved in with his brother Jacob in New York. Adolph worked for his brother in Jacob's scrap metal business. We do not know how life was for Adolph in New York, but we can guess that it may not have been the success that he had hoped for. By 1910, Adolph was a lodger in a stranger's apartment, likely still working for his brother as a scrap metal dealer and still unmarried. Adolph returned to Mannheim, Germany around 1914. Having lived in America for almost ten years, and having seen his other brothers marry and prosper, Adolph may have decided that he would do better in Germany. Or Adolph may have returned to Germany from America simply to fight for Germany in the war.

Assimilation and Intermarriage Before World War I

Jewish emancipation brought more than just economic prosperity to German Jews. It also allowed for increased assimilation and, with it, intermarriage, particularly when, in 1875, marriage between Jews and Gentiles in Germany was legalized.[303] Between 1900 and 1930, the percentage of German Jews marrying non-Jews nearly tripled, from 8 to 22 percent.[304] The Heppenheimer family appears to have avoided this outcome of Jewish emancipation, at least in terms of the children of the three Heppenheimer brothers who remained in Germany at the turn of the century and at least in terms of those marriages occurring before World War I.

Joseph's children from both of his marriages all married Jewish partners, with the older children marrying before the first World War. Bertha married Marcus Marx on June 3, 1898. At the time of their marriage, Marcus had his own business, but soon joined Gebruder Heppenheimer.[305] Joseph's second daughter, Johanna, married Isidor Wolfsheimer in 1902.[306] Both Marcus Marx and Isidor Wolfsheimer were named Prokurists of Gebruder Heppenheimer on August 7, 1922. Jacob married Johanna May on December 24, 1908.[307]

Maier's children who married also married Jewish partners, all before World War I.[308] Maier's daughter Berta married Moses Schwarz. Leopold married Helene Eichtersheimer in Eichtersheim on May 4, 1905.[309] Ludwig married Franziska Mayer on October 26, 1902.[310] Sally married Berta Mayer (Franziska's sister) on October 24, 1909.[311]

In terms of Lazarus, three of his sons married just before the war, and those sons married Jewish women. Jacob married Rosalie Weil sometime before 1914.[312] Gustav Arthur married Jettschen Grunebaum on April 8, 1910. Hugo married Pessa Klapper on December 20, 1913 in Frankfurt.

5.

The Heppenheimers During and Immediately After World War I

B y the early 1910s, Heppenheimer family members had built successful scrap metal businesses and were enjoying life as German citizens during a period of peace that had existed since German unification in 1871. But alliances among European powers were being threatened by political instability in the Balkans and concerns about German attempts to enhance its global empire.[313] The assassination of Archduke Franz Ferdinand in Sarajevo, Bosnia on June 28, 1914 by a Serbian nationalist triggered the start of World War I.[314] With Germany's support, Austria-Hungary declared war on Serbia, Germany then declared war on Russia and attacked Russia's ally France, which brough Great Britain into the war on the side of France and Russia.[315]

The outbreak of World War I was greeted in Germany with a new sense of patriotism, particularly for Germany's Jews. On August 5, 1914, two days after Germany's declaration of war, Jews throughout the Reich heeded the emperor's call to devote the day to special prayers on behalf of Germany.[316] One author described best what this war meant to the Jews of Germany: "The intense and almost universal identification with the German cause in those initial days of the war was borne by a sense that the longed for moment had arrived when German Jews would finally be fully accepted as fellow citizens."[317] At no time were Jews better able or more willing to prove their commitment to Germany than during World War I.[318] And Jews were able to play a prominent role in the war, where, for the first time, Jews were made officers in the army, and where prominent Jewish businessmen helped in the war effort.[319] Even Jews who had emigrated to Palestine returned to fight for Germany.[320]

The Heppenheimers Respond to the Call for Soldiers

The Heppenheimer family showed their strong sense of commitment to Germany in their response to the call for soldiers. There are no records documenting Jewish enlistments; the only available records are for soldiers who were wounded or killed in action. Still, we know that Maier, Joseph and Lazarus all had sons who fought in the war.

Joseph sent at least two sons to war. Benno enlisted, although he was discharged early in the war after suffering heat stroke. Max also enlisted, and may have served all four years of the war. Soldiers from Frankfurt fought in the 18th Army Corps in either the 21st or the 25th Division,[321] so Max would have been posted to one of those two divisions. Both divisions participated in battles on the Western Front, beginning in 1914.[322] The 25th Division remained on the Western Front, while the 21st Division went to Russia to fight the Russians in April 1917.[323] The 21st Division returned to France in October 1917, just before an armistice was signed between Germany and Russia on December 15, 1917.[324] Max earned the Iron Cross 2nd Class at the end of 1917, either for acts performed in Russia with the 21st Division or on the Western Front with the 25th Division.[325]

Both divisions of the 18th Army Corps enjoyed victories in the Spring of 1918 in France, but the tide turned in favor of the Allies (which now included American troops) beginning in July 1918.[326] For the next four months, the Allies engaged in the "hundred days offensive," pushing the German army back to the battle lines of 1914.[327] Max's unit engaged in battles with Allied soldiers in the early part of September, but he was given leave for the last two weeks of September.[328] During this rest period, Max was able to enjoy some time in the old fortress town of Le Quesnoy in northern France and took the following photograph doing the mundane task of brewing coffee:

The lace stripes around Max's collar indicate that he was a non-commissioned officer.[329] By the time this photograph was taken, Germany was losing the war and was about to begin negotiating an armistice with the Allies.[330] An armistice was signed on November 11, 1918, and the war was over.[331]

Maier's son Jacob was living in America, and Jacob's sons actually fought for America in the war. But Jacob's brothers fought for the Kaiser. Leopold spent three years fighting in Russia,[332] and Sally was drafted into a Worms garrison troop.[333] Adolph, who had been living in America with his brother Jacob and may have moved back to Germany in order to fight for Germany, joined the 69th Reserve Infantry Regiment in early 1915.[334] Adolph's unit fought initially on the Western Front, and the unit suffered considerable losses in 1915.[335] In May 1917, Adolph's unit was transferred to the Eastern Front (to Galicia) to fight against Russia.[336] Adolph's unit suffered heavy losses in July and August of 1917. Adolph survived his unit's heavy losses on the Western Front, but was not so lucky after his unit was transferred to the Eastern Front. He was killed on August 3, 1917; he was 39 years old at the time of his death.[337] Adolph's siblings posted the following notice of his death in the Frankfurt paper:

Source: Frankfurter Zeitung, August 28, 1917, at http://sammlungen.ub.uni-frank-furt.de/periodika/periodical/zoom/7011577?query=heppenheimer

As for Lazarus' sons, Hugo served in Landwehr Infantry Regiment 17.[338] This unit was part of the 85th Landwehr Division, and served on the Eastern Front.[339] Unlike the Reserves, in which his cousin Adolph had served, the Landwehr was responsible primarily for occupation and security duties rather than heavy combat.[340] Nevertheless, the unit did see some combat and Hugo was killed on September 5, 1917 while fighting on the Eastern Front.[341] Hugo's brother Gustav Arthur went to war in 1915 and was wounded in September 1917. And Berthold also served in the army, and was wounded five times.

By the end of the war, nearly 100,000 Jews had served in the Kaiser's armies, with 12,000 dying in action and 35,000 decorated.[342] But as was the case in earlier years, anti-Semitism remained an issue even during the war. By 1916, following a half million German casualties in the war, disillusionment set in, and Jews became the scapegoat.[343] This scapegoating resulted in the Prussian Minister of War ordering a "counting of Jews" in response to a claim that Jews were shirking their duties. This census of 1916 found, instead, that Jews were overrepresented as a population in the war, and a disproportionately high number of Jews fought as common soldiers at the front.[344] In fact, a later analysis found that 80,000 Jews had fought at the front.[345] Still, the "Jewish census" poisoned the atmosphere among the troops, and also fueled prejudice on the home front against Jews.[346]

The Scrap Metal Business During the War

While German Jews played an important role as soldiers in the war effort, German Jews also played an important role in the management of the war. German Jews had a history of war contracting, providing support for Otto Bismarck during the wars of 1866 and 1871.[347] During World War I, German Jewish entrepreneurs were suppliers to the armed forces, providing food, uniforms, and weapons.[348] But it may be that the most important role for German Jews (other than as soldiers) was in securing metals during the war, including scrap metals.

Before the war, Germany had the world's largest metal trading companies (principally the Jewish-founded companies Metallgesellschaft, Aron Hirsch & Sohn, and Beer, Sondheimer & Co.), controlling much of the world's metal trading markets.[349] But while Germany was the leading trader of metals, it lacked sufficient raw materials. Raw materials for critical metals such as copper, lead and tin were in short supply in Germany before the war, with 46.5% coming from overseas sources.[350] Only zinc was produced in Germany in large enough quantities before the war.[351] Zinc was essential for munitions purposes during World War I, being used in cartridge and shell cases, die castings for shell fuses, tanks and aircraft components, and as dust for smoke screens.[352] Copper was also critical in the manufacture of ammunition, and Germany imported large amounts of copper prior to 1914.[353]

When the war began, the British government immediately instituted a blockade that threatened to cut off the overseas metal supply, causing a sudden rise in demand and the potential for hoarding.[354] With an immediate shortage of metals caused by the blockade, scrap metal traders like Gebruder Heppenheimer enjoyed increased interest from companies unable to secure virgin metals.[355] To ensure that sufficient metals would be available for the war effort, the Jewish Industrialist Walther Rathenau established the War Raw Materials Department, and created a series of war corporations to coordinate with private industry to manage raw materials.[356] Among the war corporations was the Kriegsmetall-AG (K.R.A.), founded on September 2, 1914, which encouraged the metal trading firms to make arrangements for importing metals from abroad, and then purchase the metals when they arrived in Germany.[357] By late fall of 1914, faced with increasing prices due to metals shortages, price controls were implemented on copper, nickel, antimony, brass, tin and aluminum.[358] By March 1915, Rathenau had laid the foundations of a system controlling both the prices of metals and their supply to the war industries that had received contracts from the German government.[359]

Even with the K.R.A. in place, Germany continued to face metals shortages, particularly with regard to copper and zinc.[360] By the fall of 1915, these two metals were in such short supply that the government began requisitioning materials that were made of either metal.[361] The K.R.A. promoted the collection of scrap metals and recorded all scrap metals collected.[362] The K.R.A. also sub-contracted with smelter facilities to produce metals for the war effort.[363]

Scrap metal trading was likely affected by the establishment of the K.R.A. With the government serving the trading function, trading was curtailed for many of the nonferrous (non-iron) metals. Scrap iron was not controlled by the K.R.A., and zinc and lead were only controlled later in the war. We do not know how these trading restrictions affected Gebruder Heppenheimer, but the company may have seen curtailments in their trading. All of the Gebruder Heppenheimer facilities remained open during the war, so they must have had enough demand to remain a functioning business. For example, on July 6, 1916, Gebruder Heppenheimer was seeking a warehouse clerk,[364] and the company continued to advertise through the war for scrap metal, such as in the following advertisement in 1917 for scrap zinc:

Source: *Frankfurter Zeitung, June 23, 1917, 6, at http://sammlungen.ub.uni-frank-furt.de/periodika/periodical/pageview/6950869?query=heppenheimer.*

In addition, since zinc smeltering remained critical to the war effort, it is possible that Gebruder Heppenheimer was a subcontractor for the K.R.A., particularly when the K.R.A. began to control the zinc market. We do know that the smelter facility was fully functioning as of the middle of 1915, since they had an accident that was significant enough that it was reported in a Baltimore, Maryland German newspaper: on April 11, 1915, a 60 year-old worker sustained life-threatening injuries in the Gebruder Heppenheimer's smelter plant while loading an iron carrier.[365]

Regardless of the impact the K.R.A. may have had on German metal traders in general, Gebruder Heppenheimer remained a healthy company through the war, as can be seen through the significant financial contribution the company made to the German war effort in 1917. Germany financed most of the war through the issuance of war bonds. Through the issuance of nine bond series between 1914 and 1918, the government borrowed 98 billion marks from its citizens, covering around 85 percent of the war costs.[366] Most of the bonds were purchased by wealthy investors, who saw the bonds as long-term investments that would be paid out with revenue from taxation or war reparations.[367] Moreover, the bonds could be used as collateral for bank loans, making them no different than other liquid assets, and thus providing additional value to those investors purchasing war bonds.[368]

Gebruder Heppenheimer purchased 500,000 marks worth of war bonds in the seventh war bonds sale in September 1917.[369] This was the company's first significant purchase of war bonds, and such a large purchase (about $1.6 million in current dollars) came just after the retirement of Joseph from the business in June 1917.[370] The company had previously contributed to the war effort by purchasing war bonds, but the purchases were in the 200—500 mark range. The purchase of such a large amount of war bonds shows both the financial health of the company and its commitment to the German war cause, but also likely reflects a change in approach by the new leadership in the company. As discussed later, with Joseph's retirement from the company, the partners of Gebruder Heppenheimer became more ambitious in terms of their company's growth. Unfortunately, it is likely that Gebruder Heppenheimer was unable to recoup any of the value of their war bond investment. While Gebruder Heppenheimer may have used it as collateral to make early purchases after the war, the coming hyperinflation period, as discussed later, essentially wiped out the value of the war bonds.[371]

Notwithstanding the efforts of German companies like Gebruder Heppenheimer to support the war effort, Germany continued to struggle with securing sufficient raw materials. The K.R.A. engaged in requisitioning, such as issuing a demand on March 1, 1917 that church parishes hand over their church bells and pipe organs.[372] Still, such efforts proved insufficient as Germany was forced to increase its imports from neighboring neutral countries such as Denmark and the Netherlands.[373] While scrap metal dealers like the Heppenheimers likely played an important role in the war effort, there was simply not enough metals (new or scrap).[374] Some historians believe that the Germans lost the war, in part, because they had an inadequate supply of raw materials, including the critical metals for armaments.

The Immediate Aftermath of the War

World War I destroyed the old governmental and social structure of Central and Eastern Europe, and left Germany badly damaged.[375] Following the loss of the war and Germany's surrender to the Allies, Germany's Kaiser Wilhelm II abdicated.[376] Germany lost all of her colonies, lost control of Upper Silesia, Alsace, Lorraine, and the Saar Basin, and lost more than 14 percent of her cultivated land.[377]

Recognizing that Alsace had a strong Germanic culture and concerned about the influence this could have on the integration of Alsace into the rest of France, the government decided to expel German nationals that had immigrated to Alsace after 1871.[378] Approximately 300,000 people had immigrated to Alsace and Lorraine after 1871, and about half were ultimately forced to leave, beginning in 1918.[379] Many of those who left came to Frankfurt, which saw an average of 10,000 a month arriving in the city during the first half of 1919. Among those forced to leave was Lazarus' son Jacob, who left in 1919, leaving behind his wife and daughter.

Germany was forced to sign the Treaty of Versailles in the summer of 1919, which imposed on the Germans the payment of an extraordinary amount in reparations and placed constraints on economic recovery.[380] The French expulsion campaign in Alsace and Lorraine officially ended in 1920 after the Treaty of Versailles was signed, which formalized the transfer of Alsace and Lorraine to France.[381] But this action was too late for Jacob. His wife and daughter soon joined him and he purchased a home at Kettenhofweg 119 in the Westend section of Frankfurt. While most of those expelled were forced to forfeit their homes and property,[382] that seemed not to be the case for Jacob, who had sufficient resources to purchase a home in the fashionable Westend.

The Scrap Metal Business Following the End of the War

The outbreak of World War I had marked the end of a long period of sustained growth for the iron and steel industry in Germany.[383] Production fell in the first two years of the war because large number of workers had been drafted into the army.[384] Following the end of the war, the metals industry suffered as production had to be converted from a wartime to a peacetime economy.[385] Steel production remained low in the first few years following the end of the war.[386] Inflation was also on the rise, with both wages and material costs increasing by a total of 73% in 1918.[387]

While the iron and steel industry suffered following the end of the war, the scrap metal industry saw an initial boon. When the war ended, tremendous amounts of scrap metal were made available to German blast furnaces, and these quantities were augmented by the destruction of arms, ammunition and war material of all sorts required by the disarmament clauses of the treaty.[388] Approximately 300,000 tons of scrap metal was available to the scrap metal industry at this time.[389] In addition, the iron and steel producers began hoarding scrap in anticipation of a future ore shortage, so that scrap increased in price from 67.50 marks a ton in January 1919 to 2200 marks a ton in February 1920.[390] By 1922, scrap iron had become so scarce that it was commanding a higher price than foundry pig iron.[391]

Gebruder Heppenheimer had survived the war, and may have even prospered through arrangements for the use of its smelter facility. Joseph retired from the company just before the end of the war, on June 7, 1917. Joseph had started the company with his brother Henry forty years earlier, and was able to grow the business into a successful business with two facilities: the zinc smelter and metal handling facility in Mainkur and the main warehouse and office on Dominikanergasse in Frankfurt. Joseph was ambitious, but conservative, successfully employing his sons, nephews, and sons-in-law.

Joseph's son Jacob and Henry's son Adolph had been partners of Gebruder Heppenheimer, but with Joseph's retirement, they were now in charge.[392] And following the end of the war, they decided to take advantage of the apparent opportunities available to the scrap metal industry and expand the footprint of the company.

One of the first actions taken by this next generation of Gebruder Heppenheimer partners was actually begun during the war. Gebruder Heppenheimer purchased a smelting facility in Rheinau, a district of Mannheim, likely in 1915, since Gebruder Heppenheimer, as owners of the Rheinau facility, appeared for the first time in the 1916 Mannheim Address Book. Gebruder Heppenheimer did not appear in the Address Book again until 1918, when Gebruder Heppenheimer was identified as the owner of the Rheinau facility, suggesting that the Rheinau facility did not become operational until 1917 or 1918. The smelter had 8 smelting furnaces and processed 150 tons of lead, zinc, and brass per month.[393] Gebruder Heppenheimer had long been structured as an Offene Handelsgesellschaft (OHG), or an open trading company.[394] When they purchased Metallschmelzwerk Rheinau, they initially structured the new business as an OHG, and the company became a subsidiary of Gebruder Heppenheimer.[395]

Gebruder Heppenheimer added a new storage facility around 1918, which was located on Daimlerstrasse in the Osthafen (East Harbor) along the Main River. The Osthafen, located in the eastern portion of the Ostend, had been planned as a purely industrial area along the Main River and had opened in 1912.[396] A rail line was connected in 1913 to the harbor, allowing increased access for the facilities located at the harbor.[397] Gebruder Heppenheimer may have made the decision to open this new facility because of improved access to the Main River, although they only kept the facility for a few years. By 1921, Gebruder Heppenheimer had closed this storage facility, perhaps concluding that there were not any increased benefits from direct access to the Main River.

Instead, around 1920, Gebruder Heppenheimer purchased two connecting buildings at Untermain-Anlage 8/9 in the Bahnhof section (the area of Frankfurt where the main train station was located), and made this new location their main office. Untermain-Anlage was a beautiful street with a large median that separated the left and right sides of the street. Across the street from this new headquarters of Gebruder Heppenheimer was the Schauspielhaus, the main theater for Frankfurt. The following photo (which shows the Schauspielhaus) demonstrates the grandeur of this new location, as well as the magnificent view from Gebruder Heppenheimer's new offices:

*Source: https://commons.wikimedia.org/wiki/Category:Schauspielhaus_*
Frankfurt?uselang=de#/media/File:Schauspielhaus.jpg.

This purchase was a significant investment for Gebruder Heppenheimer, and likely signaled their belief that they had truly achieved what Joseph and Henry had set out to accomplish when they left Eichtersheim. Building 8 had a ground floor and three upper floors and building 9 had a ground floor and four upper floors. The offices not used by Gebruder Heppenheimer were rented to other businesses.[398] This is how Untermainanlange 8/9 looks today, and it is likely how it looked when Gebruder Heppenheimer purchased the buildings:

*Source: https://commons.wikimedia.org/wiki/File:Frankfurt_*
Untermainanlage_9.Gutleutstra%C3%9Fe_1.20130404.jpg[399]

The Hauptbahnhof (the main train station) had opened in 1888, and between 1893 and 1913, new streets were paved and commercial and residential buildings were constructed.[400] Given its proximity to the main train station, this new neighborhood had hotels, inns, restaurants, taverns, cafes and entertainment establishments.[401] This move by Gebruder Heppenheimer may have reflected the younger generation's efforts to modernize the business and have its main office away from the old and dated Jewish neighborhood. The original office on Dominikanergasse was still retained and was converted to a second office and warehouse.

Gebruder Heppenheimer thus had three facilities in Frankfurt by the early twenties (the original office and warehouse on Dominikanergasse, the smelter and iron and metal handling facility in Mainkur, and the new office on Untermain Anlage), as well as the smelter facility in Rheinau. Adolph Heppenheimer, Joseph's nephew, who had been living at the Mainkur smelting facility during the war, was now living in Frankfurt, and Joseph's son Benny had moved to the house at the Mainkur facility.

The purchase of the Rheinau facility was significant for Joseph's youngest son Max, since it was Max who was placed in charge of running the facility after it became operational. Before the war, Max worked as a chemist for Gebruder Heppenheimer.[402] After he was discharged from the army and married,[403] Max was sent to Mannheim to run the Rheinau facility. Max received his citizenship card (which may have been required for his move) in October 1919, and that card was stamped by the Mannheim district office in November, likely the month he moved to Mannheim. This is his photo from the citizenship card:

Max, as the youngest of Joseph's sons, was likely always in the shadow of his older brothers. However, based on what we know about what happened to the Rheinau facility in the 1920s, it seems likely that Max was a reluctant participant in this expansion of the family business. Max had completed his schooling at age 15 with his graduation from the Philanthropin. He had become a chemist, but this was likely through apprenticing in his family's smelter facility or another facility, since, as far as we know, Max had no formal education after his graduation from the Philanthropin. He had contributed science equipment to his old school, suggesting an interest in the sciences. And we know that his family believed that he was more of an "intellectual" than a businessman. [404] It may be that Max had wanted to attend a university, but was forced by his family to abandon any academic pursuits and instead enter the family business. All of Joseph's other sons and sons-in-law had done the same. After four years of fighting for Germany, Max may have wanted to pursue a different life. He also may not have wanted to leave his family in Frankfurt and run a factory in another city. But dutiful Jewish sons followed the wishes of their family, and Max moved with his new wife to Mannheim.

Gebruder Heppenheimer also sought to expand into other businesses. Gebruder Heppenheimer entered into a contract in August 1919, along with J. Adler Junr, one of the largest scrap metal dealers in Southern Germany, to purchase Chemische Fabrik Grieschein-Elektron A.G., a chemical plant that made explosives during the war. [405] Under the contract, some of the buildings to be purchased were to be demolished, so it is possible that the intent of the purchase was to obtain the land and the buildings and convert it to another use. The deal ultimately failed and IG Farben, the giant German chemical company, purchased Chemische Fabrik Grieschein-Elektron in 1925. [406]

Gebruder Heppenheimer also made investments in at least one non-metal related venture, investing in Rohpappen-Fabrik Aktiegensellschaft, a corrugated cardboard company located in Worms. The company was first registered in 1921, [407] so the investment likely was made around that time as well. Unfortunately, by 1922, the investment appeared to have been a loss for Gebruder Heppenheimer. But this investment, as well as the other purchases or potential purchases, reflected a shift in approach with the retirement of Joseph from Gebruder Heppenheimer. While Joseph was conservative in how he grew the company, his sons and nephew were interested in growing the company and growing it fast.

The end of the war also saw changes with respect to the scrap metal businesses of Lazarus' sons. Before the war, Hugo and Berthold had been in business together. Following Hugo's death in World War I, Berthold joined his brother Gustav Arthur (who went by the name Arthur) in founding the scrap iron and metal handling company A&B Heppenheimer.[408] The business was registered with Frankfurt's Commercial Register on April 23, 1920, with both Arthur and Berthold as personally-liable partners. Berthold left A&B on January 27, 1921 and Arthur became the sole owner of A&B,[409] although Berthold did not register his own scrap iron company, Berthold Heppenheimer Co., until 1924. As discussed earlier, Jacob was forced to moved back to Frankfurt from Alsace, and he joined his brother Arthur's company on August 9, 1921.[410]

6.

The Family During the Weimar Republic

G ermany's loss in World War I saw an end to the German Empire. A new constitution was adopted on July 31, 1919, and Germany became a democratic republic with universal suffrage.[411] With the establishment of the Weimar Republic (named after the town where the government was formed), Jews saw unprecedented integration into every sphere of German life, and Jews like the Heppenheimers flourished.[412]

As was the case during earlier periods in German history, the Jewish people, making up less than 1% of the population, made an outsized contribution to German life during the Weimar Republic. Jews made up 13% of all doctors and 16% of all lawyers, and owned one-fifth of all private banks and four-fifths of all department stores.[413] Jews became important writers and scientists, making their mark in both the natural sciences and the humanities.[414] And Jews were highly active in the theater, where 50 percent of the 234 theater directors in Germany were Jewish.[415]

The German Jewish population also became more urban during the Weimar period. While 20 percent of all German Jews resided in metropolitan areas in 1910, by 1933, more than 70 percent of Germany's Jews lived in cities whose populations exceeded 100,000, and only 15 percent of Jews lived in villages of under 10,000.[416] During the Weimar period, most of the Heppenheimers were living in Frankfurt and Mannheim, with just a few living in Worms and Frankenthal. No Heppenheimers were left in Eichtersheim.

Still, anti-Semitism remained a challenge for German Jews. The foes of this new German Republic termed it a "Jews Republic," and called the Weimar flag "the Jews banner."[417] Walter Rathenau, the prominent Jewish businessman who was responsible for German raw material during World War I and who then became the Minister of Foreign Affairs during the Weimar Republic, was assassinated in 1922 by German nationalists, likely, in part, because he was Jewish.[418] But such actions did not deter German Jews like the Heppenheimers from pursuing the enhanced opportunities during the Weimar period and feeling strongly connected to their community. For example, the Jews living in Frankfurt (like the Heppenheimers) considered themselves "Frankfurt Jews" and saw themselves "at the cutting edge of Jewish thought and reform, modern, urbane and sophisticated."[419]

The Heppenheimer Businesses During the Weimar Period

The increased use of scrap metal after the war enabled Germany to begin to return to pre-1913 production levels for steel.[420] By 1920, business had improved for German industry, and German businesses were optimistic.[421] Such optimism likely encouraged Gebruder Heppenheimer to make some significant investments just after the war, as discussed in the previous chapter. However, this was probably the worst time to make any significant investments.

The Treaty of Versailles imposed conditions that essentially prevented Germany from repairing the war damage.[422] In April 1921, the Reparations

Commission fixed Germany's total liability for the war at 132,000 million gold marks, and the first payments were made in June 1921.[423] But Germany could not possibly meet the reparation obligations, and the value of the mark began to fall.[424] The German economy was already experiencing inflation by the end of the war and that inflation turned into hyperinflation by the middle of 1922.[425] When Germany failed to meets its reparation obligations in January 1923, French and Belgium troops invaded the Ruhr Basin to force Germany to pay their obligations; instead of achieving its goal of forcing payment of reparations, the occupation caused a near shut-down in the industrial heart of Germany.[426] Hyperinflation reached its peak in 1923, and was ended only by a radical revaluation of the German currency.[427]

As was the case with other companies during the hyperinflationary period, Gebruder Heppenheimer experienced financial challenges. The war bonds they had purchased in 1917 and likely used as collateral for their investments following the war had lost virtually all of their value. The company also lost its investment in the cardboard factory, which was likely related to the hyperinflation period. In the fall of 1923, the company appealed a tax bill issued by the municipality of Fechenheim for the Mainkur business.[428] The tax authorities issued a bill based on a profit of 65,378,755 marks, but also included a tax of 400,000,000 marks for inventory.[429]

Because of hyperinflation, it is difficult to conclude whether the numbers reflect a healthy company or a struggling company. But the tax appeal itself is interesting because it included the following price list for Gebruder Heppenheimer scrap iron and metals, which shows the significant changes in prices between 1921 (pre-hyperinflation) and 1922, the year in which hyperinflation began:

Preistabelle 1921/22 (per kg).		
	1921: (31.12.)	1922: (31.12.)	Durchschnitt: (nach § 33a)

Eisen:

	1921: (31.12.)	1922: (31.12.)	Durchschnitt: (nach § 33a)
Maschinenguss	3.--	135.--	20.--
Kernschrott	2.40	145.--	20.93
Stahlschrott	2.40	150.--	21.60
Späne	2.10	105.--	15.40
Blechschrott	1.20	80.--	11.45
Ofenguss	2.10	120.--	17.40
Martinschrott	2.25	135.--	19.50
Hochofenschrott	2.15	130.--	18.80
Rohrschrott	2.25	135.--	19.50
Träger	2.50	185.--	26.60
Hartguss	2.30	145.--	20.85
Brandguss	1.95	125.--	17.95
Katzguss	2.15	130.--	18.75
Nutzeisen	2.20	180.--	25.50
Walzensinter	-.10	40.--	5.35
Scherenschrott	1.50	100.--	14.33
Schlacken	-.30	60.--	8.10
Pfannenreste	-.30	50.--	6.76

Metalle:

	1921: (31.12.)	1922: (31.12.)	Durchschnitt: (nach § 33a)
Rotgusspäne	30.--	1 400.--	206.65
Altblei	15.--	750.--	110.--
Hartblei	13.50	675.--	99.--
Altzink	13.--	800.--	115.35
Remelted-Z.	14.--	1 000.--	142.65
Alum.Blech	20.--	700.--	106.65
Kupfer	45.--	1 800.--	270.--
Rotguss	35.--	1 500.--	223.30
Messing	25.--	1 250.--	183.35
Messingspäne	22.--	1 100.--	161.35
Zinkasche	4.--	350.--	49.35
Bleiasche	3.50	325.--	45.65
Stangenmessing	18.--	1 600.--	225.35
Kartuschen	30.--	1 500.--	220.--
Tombak	30.--	1 400.--	206.66
Alum.Späne	2.50	800.--	105.--
Komposition I	60.--	4 800.--	680.--
Lötzinnasche 100%	90.--	4.800.--	700.--
Komposition II	30.--	1 200.--	180.--
Nickel	45.--	2.500.--	363.33

Source: Institute Fur Stadtgeschichte, Frankfurt am Main, Signatur 681.

This price list is also interesting because it shows the scope of the Gebruder Heppenheimer's trading business. While we know that Gebruder Heppenheimer engaged in the trading of both ferrous and nonferrous metals, the price list shows the range of such trading.

We do not know what the outcome of the appeal was, although the company claimed that it had no money to pay any part of the assessed taxes.

During this period of hyperinflation, many businesses chose to delay payment of their tax obligations, since the longer they waited, the smaller their obligation would be.[430] Any resulting payments Gebruder Heppenheimer may have made would have been relatively small in relationship to its earlier tax obligations, and it is possible that Gebruder Heppenheimer paid none of the taxes owed.

The Frankfurt Heppenheimers were not the only Heppenheimers to struggle during the hyperinflation period. The scrap metal company Ludwig Heppenheimer, owned by Ludwig and Sally Heppenheimer (Maier's sons), also requested that its tax obligations for the year 1923 be significantly reduced. The company complained about the general shortage of money, which prevented its customers from buying scrap.[431] But it also explained that its main customers were in Rhineland and Westphalia and, because of the occupation of the Ruhr Basin by the French, it was unable to sell its stock.[432] It is certainly possible that Gebruder Heppenheimer had similar customers in the Ruhr Basin, given that this region was the industrial heart of Germany, and were unable to sell its stock because of the occupation.

In April 1924, an agreement known as the Dawes Plan was reached that reset the reparations payments to more sustainable levels (increasing over time as the German economy improved) and required that the foreign troops leave the Ruhr Basin.[433] The plan provided for a large capital influx and a new currency was adopted, which helped to end hyperinflation.[434] Following the hyperinflation period, Germany was able to regain some of her competitive advantage as a producer of iron and steel products.[435] And by 1925, Germany had recovered sufficiently from the Ruhr occupation that steel production had returned to its pre-1913 levels, and that production continued to grow.[436]

While the Gebruder Heppenheimer's Frankfurt business may have struggled during the hyperinflation period and the occupation of the Ruhr basin, and lost some of the company's value and investments, the company survived the hyperinflation period.[437] In fact, the 1925 Jahrbuch der

Frankfurter Bürgerschaft (Frankfurt Citizenship Yearbook) noted that Frankfurt was one of the most important places for the scrap metal trade in Germany and that Gebruder Heppenheimer was one of the top scrap metal trading companies in Frankfurt.[438] It was also noted in the Yearbook that Gebruder Heppenheimer was the only one of the top scrap metal companies in Frankfurt to engage in both smelter and trade.[439] And beginning in 1927 and continuing through the remainder of the decade, Gebruder Heppenheimer appeared to be doing very well, at least in terms of their Frankfurt businesses, as reflected in increases in the income taxes paid in those years to the city of Frankfurt.[440] According to Rudolph Henninger, a long-time employee of Gebruder Heppenheimer, the partners in the company were earning at this time between 25,000 and 30,000 RM annually.[441] Since the typical German worker earned about 2,400 RM a year and a middle class family earned approximately 6,000 RM a year,[442] the partners of Gebruder Heppenheimer were all doing quite well.

As Germany was beginning to experience the hyperinflation period, Gebruder Heppenheimer made an important decision about Metallschmelzwerk Rheinau, their smelter facility in Mannheim. The facility had been structured initially as a subsidiary of Gebruder Heppenheimer, with the partners fully liable for any losses from the facility. On May 28, 1922, Gebruder Heppenheimer converted the smelter company to an Akitengesellschaft, or a joint-stock company. This conversion into a joint-stock company allowed Gebruder Heppenheimer to limit its liability.[443] Under the terms of the new company, Adolph Heppenheimer, Jacob Heppenheimer, Benny Heppenheimer, and Max Heppenheimer owned equal shares, and Louis Vollweiler, a Prokurist for Gebruder Heppenheimer who had been with the company since at least 1910, owned a smaller share in the company.[444] A Supervisory Board was established, comprised of Adolph, Benny and Jacob, as well as the company's lawyer Fritz Ettlinger and banker Hugo May, with Adolph as Board Chairman and Jacob as Deputy Chairman.[445] Max was not included as a board member. Instead, Max and Louis Vollweiler were appointed as supervisors of the smelter facility.[446]

There are two things that are striking about the manner in which the Rheinau facility was established as a joint-stock company, and both things suggest how Max was viewed by the rest of the Gebruder Heppenheimer partners. First, while Max was a full and equal owner of the facility, he was initially excluded from the Supervisory Board of the company and never served on the Board.

Second, while Max had been living in Mannheim since 1919 and was in charge of running the facility, when the joint-stock company was established, the rest of the Gebruder Heppenheimer partners decided to make Louis Vollweiler a supervisor of the facility as well. When the Rheinau facility first became operational, Louis Vollweiler had been named Prokurist of the facility, but Louis remained in Frankfurt and Max was the direct supervisor of the facility.[447] Based on what we learn later about Max's inadequacies as a businessman, it seems likely that Louis was sent to Mannheim to help Max operate the facility. Louis, who had been a Prokurist for Gebruder Heppenheimer in Frankfurt, was given an ownership interest in the Rheinau facility under the terms of the joint-stock corporation, likely as an incentive for the move he would make with his family to Mannheim. Louis moved to Mannheim in 1923 or 1924 to assume his new responsibilities as a co-supervisor of the Rheinau facility.

In terms of the other Heppenheimer scrap metal businesses, the scrap metal company Ludwig Heppenheimer (which had been owned by Maier's sons Ludwig and Sally) recovered after the hyperinflation period. Ludwig had died in 1921, but his widow continued the scrap metal business with Sally, becoming a personally liable partner.[448] Sally's wife Bertha also worked in the business.[449] Ludwig's daughter Johanna (Hanna) had married Kurt Goldschmidt and both worked in the business.[450] Ludwig Heppenheimer had two facilities: an office and a warehouse and scrap yard along the Rhine

River. In addition to the family members, Ludwig Heppenheimer employed two additional persons in the office (including a bookkeeper), a driver, and at least 1-3 persons in the warehouse.[451] In addition, Sally's son Willi, who had been training in the scrap metal industry in Mannheim since April 16, 1928 (perhaps with his uncle Leopold), returned to Worms on April 1, 1931, to join the family scrap metal business.[452] The business was doing well enough in the 1920s that Sally purchased a fancy car and employed a chauffeur.[453] During the 1920s, Ludwig Heppenheimer was the largest scrap metal dealer in Worms and the surrounding area.[454]

Maier's other son Leopold, who was living in Mannheim, also appeared to be doing well. According to the 1925 Mannheim Address Book, his scrap metal business had two locations, and he had those same two facilities in 1930.

Maier's daughter Berta, however, may have been doing the best financially of all of Maier's children. Berta's husband Moses worked with Maier in M. Heppenheimer scrap metal in Frankenthal, and established a new scrap metal business after Maier's death. According to Berta's son Walter, this new company, M. Heppenheimer, was considered one of the leading businesses in the industry.[455] The company had annual sales of about 500,000 RM (approximately $4 million in today's dollars), had ten employees, and two facilities (an office and a warehouse).

Lazarus' sons Jacob, Arthur, Robert, and Berthold were all living in Frankfurt following the war—Hugo had died in the war. Jacob had been forced to leave Alsace in 1919, but he left with enough resources to purchase a home in the Westend section of Frankfurt. As previously discussed, Jacob joined his brother Arthur as a partner in A&B Heppenheimer on August 9, 1921.

Jacob's goal was to return to Strasbourg. The French government began to encourage immigration to make up for the serious deficit in the male population as a result of the war.[456] Jacob took advantage of such encouragement, selling his Frankfurt home and returning to Strasbourg with his family in 1924. France changed its laws in 1927, making it easier for immigrants to obtain French citizenship,[457] at which point Jacob became a French citizenship.

Jacob resumed his scrap metal business upon his return to Strasbourg. His business grew quickly, and Jacob was able to purchase a large home, which he filled with beautiful furniture, valuable objects, and great art. Jacob purchased a large car, and hired a driver, maid and cook. This picture of Jacob with his daughter Gertrude, along with his driver and car, is from around 1925, and shows a man clearly enjoying his success as a businessman:

Source: Jean Horgen

In terms of Lazarus' other sons, according to 1923 Frankfurt Address Book, Robert was a scrap metal trader, and according to his daughter, he remained a scrap metal dealer until he was forced to escape Germany for political reasons in the mid-1930s.[458] Arthur appeared to be doing well in the 1920s, with two facilities. Berthold had incorporated as a scrap metal dealer, earning about 15,000 RM (about $120,000 in today's dollars) per year in the 1920s.

While virtually all of the Heppenheimers remained focused primarily on building and maintaining their scrap metal businesses, the arts did find its way into one family business. As discussed earlier, Joseph Heppenheimer's daughter Alice was living in Nuremberg when she married businessman Ludwig Adler on May 25, 1920.[459] In November 1926, Alice registered with the Nuremberg business registry to open an applied arts studio.[460] The studio likely opened in 1927, since the business appeared for the first time in the Nuremberg Address book in 1928. We do not know whether the studio was for Alice's own crafts or whether she was selling for others. In 1927, Alice registered with the Nuremberg business registry for a ladies' hat factory, and in 1929, she registered as a business in the textile trade.[461] Alice still listed her business as an applied arts studio in the 1929 and 1930 Address Books, and listed her business as a women's handbag business in 1931. Alice may have continued her applied arts studio through this period, and as she concentrated her business on hats, handbags, and other textiles in the late 1920s, she likely used her background in the applied arts in these endeavors.

Where They Lived

When Henry and Joseph Heppenheimer first moved to Frankfurt, they settled in and around the Altstadt, where Jews had lived in Frankfurt for hundreds of years. As they became more financially successful, they moved their families to the Ostend. The map of the Frankfurt neighborhoods in Chapter 2 shows these districts.

When Joseph moved to the Ostend, there were more Jews there than in any other district in Frankfurt. But as the next generation of Frankfurt Jews became more affluent and less religious, they became more interested in moving to other sections of the city, such as the Westend.[462] Joseph died in 1923, and his widow Emma remained at Roderberg Weg 30 throughout the 1920s. Joseph's daughter Bertha moved in with her step-mother after the death of her husband in 1925. But Joseph's son Jacob and his nephew Adolph would move into more fashionable neighborhoods.

Adolph had been living with his family at the house connected to the Mainkur smelter facility. But with the retirement of Joseph from Gebruder Heppenheimer and the decision to have Joseph's son Benny move into the house at the Mainkur facility around 1920, Adolph purchased a large four-story single-family home across the Main River at Steinlestrasse 34 in the western part of Sachsenhausen.[463] The wealthy were flocking to this section of the city, and building villas to reflect their newly acquired wealth.[464] Adolph filled the home with antiques and enjoyed the trappings of wealth.

Adolph's cousin and business partner Jacob joined him in the western section of Sachsenhausen in 1927, purchasing a home at Passavantstrasse 24. Until that time, Jacob and his family had been living in the Ostend. Jacob may have decided to wait until the economy stabilized after the hyperinflation period before he purchased his home. Interestingly, when Jacob finally left the very-Jewish Ostend, he chose a neighborhood that was wealthy, but decidedly not Jewish. Just 2.1 percent of the population of the neighborhood where both Adolph and Jacob chose to purchase their homes was Jewish.[465]

Lazarus' widow Auguste had moved to the Ostend in 1912, and was living at Bergerstrasse 16 through the 1920s. She remained in this apartment until her death in 1930. Her sons, however, moved out of the Ostend by the early to mid-1920s. But instead of moving to the Westend or other fashionable neighborhoods, the three sons still living in Frankfurt (Arthur, Robert, and Berthold) chose to live just north of the old Judengasse, in the Innenstadt (or downtown) neighborhood. We do not know the quality of these residences, although it is unlikely that they were even close to the size or grandeur of Joseph's apartment on Roderberg Weg or Adolph's home in the Sachsenhausen section of Frankfurt.[466] After Auguste's death in 1930,

Arthur and Berthold both moved back to the Ostend. Both would remain in the Ostend with their families until Arthur died in 1936 and Berthold emigrated to America in 1937.

When Max moved to Mannheim, he rented an apartment at Richard Wagner Strasse 9 in the Oststadt (east city) section of Mannheim. At the time, the Oststadt was one of the most affluent sections in Mannheim[467] The family lived on the fourth floor, sharing the floor with just one other tenant. Large apartments were common in the Oststadt,[468] and we can assume that Max and his family lived in a large apartment. The Oststadt was just outside of downtown Mannheim, and it was easy for Max and his family to enjoy the opportunities available to the young and affluent family. In fact, they lived just two blocks from the iconic Mannheimer Water Tower and Friedrichsplatz, where they could enjoy a stroll on a Sabbath afternoon, as shown in the picture below:

*Source: https://commons.wikimedia.org/wiki/Category:Friedrichsplatz_*
(Mannheim)#/media/File:Mannheim_-_Friedrichsplatz.jpg

Max's arrival coincided with the largest number of Jews living in Mannheim—in the 1925 census, 6,972 Jews (or 3% of the total population) were living in Mannheim.[469] And Max's neighborhood was particularly Jewish, with Jews representing 6.9 percent of the population by the 1930s.[470]

Leisure Time and Community Support

Before the Weimar period, Jewish families tended to spend summer vacations in the homes of parents and relatives in rural areas. But as German Jewish families became more urban, they no longer needed to go back to their villages.[471] Thus, during the Weimar Republic, German Jewish families began to travel to hotels and tourist facilities for their vacations, although they tended to restrict their destinations to Jewish-friendly resorts.[472] And German Jews tended to vacation at resorts that focused on maintaining health.[473]

Bad Kissingen, a spa resort just south of the Rhoen Mountains in Bavaria, was very popular with affluent Jews, who came to the resort to "take the cure."[474] Joseph and some of his family visited Bad Kissingen in August 1919, and sent the following postcard to Joseph's son Max in Mannheim:

Source: Carol Harvey

The postcard contained the following messages from Joseph and Emma:

> Dear children!
> In memory of my Cure in Kissinger I send a photograph of me
> and Benny to you.
> Hope you are well and lively. Your father
> Greetings from me as well, and also from Selma, I will send you a
> letter soon. Your mother.

Joseph, newly retired from Gebruder Heppenheimer, took advantage of the health facilities at Bad Kissinger, while Benny and Selma, who were both single at the time, likely joined their parents to enjoy the resort's other amenities, which included swimming and hiking.

In addition to vacationing in the mountains, German Jews also vacation at the North Sea, particularly at Nordernay, which was often referred to as the "Jewish bath."[475] Some of Joseph's children and grandchildren vacationed together in the summer of 1923, and Alice sent the following postcard to Max:

Source: Carol Harvey

Alice and her husband Ludwig are the couple to the right and Benny and his wife Margot are to the left of Alice. Benny's brother Jacob's children Melanie and Ernst are to the left of Benny, and the woman to the far left is Jacob's wife Johanna. The woman to the far right is likely a sister of Margot. Alice sent the following message to Max:

My dear brother:

A small recording of the "Michpoche." ["family" in Yiddish] But we're not as fat as in the picture yet. We have been here for a week now and the weather is wonderful, far too hot for me. We were very sorry that we couldn't meet. We had the honest intention to come to you, but it would have been too complicated. The journey was already terribly exhausting because of the heat. But postponed is not canceled, child. Warm regards to everyone, your Alice.

With Benny on vacation, Jacob may have needed to remain in Frankfurt to run the business rather than vacation with his family.

Greater disposable income during the Weimar Republic allowed Germany's Jews to enjoy their leisure time, but also provided them with the means to continue their support of the Jewish community. Many civic institutions, including hospitals, libraries and museums, were established in the Weimar period by Jewish philanthropy, particularly from the Rothschild family.[476] The Jewish hospital on the Gagernstrasse opened in 1914, and became the most modern hospital in Frankfurt during the Weimar period.[477] Frankfurt University, which was established in 1914 primarily by Jewish donors in the hopes of providing a university that was more open to Jewish students and Jewish professors, continued in importance as a Jewish educational institution through the 1920s.[478]

Marriage and Divorce

Intermarriage continued to be a challenge for the German Jewish community during the Weimar Republic, with nearly 37 percent of all marriages involving Jewish partners being of mixed unions.[479] In Frankfurt, the proportion of marriages between Jews and non-Jews between 1919 and 1931 grew from 10 percent to 35 percent.[480] While the Heppenheimer family appeared to have avoided this issue in earlier years, intermarriage in the Heppenheimer family living in Germany occurred for the first time during the Weimar period.

Maier's children who married were all married to Jewish spouses before World War I. Joseph also avoided intermarriage among his children, including those who married after the war. Benny married Margot Klara Lebrecht on May 6, 1921. Their son Hans (later Herb) was born on April 3, 1922 and their son Werner (later Bill) was born on March 7, 1926. Max married Recha Lehmann on June 20, 1919.[481] Their first son Kurt (later Curtis Heppen) was born on March 29, 1920 and their second son, Alfred (later Fred), was born on January 29, 1923. In terms of Joseph's daughters from his second marriage, Alice had married Ludwig Adler in 1920 and Selma married Lippmann Lewin in 1929.[482]

But the changing times caught up with Lazarus' two youngest sons, who both married non -Jews following the war. Berthold married Martha Kleixert, on June 10, 1924, although she converted to Judaism at some point after their marriage. Robert married Margarete Auelmann on October 21, 1921, although they divorced in 1927.

The Weimar Republic represented a period of political, social and cultural changes, and this was particularly the case for women, with the Republic granting equal rights and suffrage to women in 1919.[483] Alice clearly took advantage of these new opportunities, opening her own arts and crafts studio in Nuremburg. But these changes also impacted Alice in a different way, giving her the courage to divorce her husband Ludwig Adler.

Alice was likely the first Heppenheimer to divorce when she divorced her husband in the early 1930s and moved back to Frankfurt.[484] While divorce was rarely sought in Germany, the divorce rate had been rising—from 24.6 per 100,000 inhabitants in 1913 to 62.9 per 100,000 inhabitants in 1921.[485] Still, obtaining a divorce was difficult even during the Weimar period, since the only grounds for divorce were adultery, attempted murder, gross neglect of marital duties, abandonment, or mental insanity.[486]

During the Weimar period, women were also less interested in having children, so that by 1933, Germany had the lowest birthrate in Europe.[487] Both Alice and her sister Selma would follow this trend, since neither had children.

Religion

During the Weimar period, Frankfurt experienced a growth in the Jewish community in terms of both Orthodox and Reform Jews. Unlike the rest of Germany, Frankfurt's Orthodox Jewish communities grew between 1910 and 1925.[488] In fact, the Frankfurt Gemeinde began plans in 1928 for the construction of a new Orthodox synagogue with 1,000 seats in the northwest section of Frankfurt.[489] The number of Reform Jews also increased in Frankfurt between 1910 and 1925,[490] with that growth likely coming from German-born Jews like the Heppenheimer family.

Joseph was likely a Reform Jew, but how Joseph chose to be buried shows just how far he had come from the orthodoxy of his youth. As German Jews became more intertwined in Germany society, their gravestones started to look more like Christian gravestones.[491] When Joseph died in 1923, he was buried in the Jewish cemetery on Rat-Beil-Strasse in Frankfurt. Rather than a simple marker, Joseph chose a substantial gravestone, perhaps to emphasize the financial success he achieved in his life. There is also no Hebrew lettering on the stone, as can be seen in the photo, below:

Source: http://grabsteine.genealogy.net/tomb.php?cem=4721&tomb=7536&b=H&lang=de.

The gravestone simply reads "Josef Heppenheimer, 14 Aug. 1851—18 Febr. 1923." Joseph's nephew Jacob (Henry's eldest child) is buried in the same cemetery, but more than two decades earlier, and his gravestone contains his Hebrew name in Hebrew letters. Two decades later, Joseph's gravestone looks no different than any Christian's gravestone. Only its presence in a Jewish cemetery is how we know that Joseph had been Jewish.

While we can guess that Joseph was less religious, in terms of the younger generation of principals of Gebruder Heppenheimer, we know that those living in Frankfurt were all Reform Jews. Benny's family, living at the smelting facility in Mainkur, attended Frankfurt's Hauptsynagoge, the Reform synagogue that was built in 1860.[492] And Adolph Heppenheimer, another member of Gebruder Heppenheimer, also attended the Hauptsynagoge.[493]

By 1927, Joseph's oldest son Jacob had moved across the Main River and relatively far from the Orthodox synagogues (and far from Jewish neighborhoods), which he would not have done had he been an observant Jew. Curtis Heppen remembered that Jacob's son Ernest did a poor job during his bar mitzvah, suggesting that Jacob's family were not just Reform Jews, but likely indifferent Jews. Moreover, Jacob and Benny did not observe the Sabbath, and often conducted business meetings with customers in their downtown office on Saturdays.[494] In fact, Jacob and Benny and their cousin Adolph were reflective of a general movement in Germany away from religious observance. During the Weimar period, the religious community complained about low attendance at services, even on the High Holy days.[495] In Frankfurt, for example, the average attendance on the High Holy Days during the 1920s was just 41 percent.[496]

While his brothers and cousin in Frankfurt were Reform Jews, Max and his family were more observant and were members of the Klaus Orthodox synagogue in Mannheim. The Klaus synagogue had a long history in Mannheim, having been founded as a learning center for the study of the Talmud.[497] At the time Max moved to Mannheim, the city was experiencing an influx of Jews from eastern Europe, and those Jews, coming from an Orthodox tradition, attended the Klaus synagogue.[498] It is odd that Max, new to the city, would choose a synagogue that was attracting non-German Jews. But Max's choice of the Klaus Synagogue may have had to do with the synagogue's dynamic rabbi, Isak Unna, who had received a PhD in philosophy.[499] Rabbi Unna was the founder of an organization promoting unity among the various Orthodox factions and had founded an Orthodox newspaper.[500] As an intellectual, Max may have been interested in a synagogue that promoted the discussion of ideas, while maintaining traditional practices. For example, Max's family kept a kosher home. And Rabbi Unna must have been successful in his outreach, since reconstruction of the Klaus Synagogue in 1930 increased the number of seats in the sanctuary from 230 to 500.[501] The Klaus Synagogue was located on what is now Kurpfalz Street in downtown Mannheim, and would have been about a 20-minute walk for Max from his apartment. But while the family was observant and kept a kosher home, they did not allow their observance to influence their social circle, so that many of their friends, while still Jewish, did not keep a kosher home and were not religious.[502]

Education

During the Weimar period, Jewish education was enjoying a renaissance, with Jewish families sending their children back to Jewish schools.[503] By 1928, most Jewish children in Frankfurt received their primary education from one of the community religious schools, either the Philanthropin, with 407 students (growing to 900 in 1930), or the IRG's Samson Raphael Hirsch elementary school, with a total of 651 students.[504] The total number of Jewish students at various Jewish community schools in Frankfurt numbered 2,175 versus Jewish students at the city's public schools, which numbered 1,419.[505]

Unlike other Jewish families who may have sent their children to non-Jewish schools before the Weimar period, Joseph Heppenheimer's children attended the Philanthropin, and that tradition continued for some of his grandchildren. Bertha's daughter Bettina, Jacob's son Ernst (later Ernest), and Benny's son Werner (later William) attended the Philanthropin for all of their school years.[506] But several of Joseph's grandchildren bucked the trend of increased attendance at Jewish schools, choosing to attend more rigorous non-Jewish high schools that would better prepare them for university. Jacob's daughter Melanie attended the Viktoriaschule for high school, graduating in 1929 at the age of 19.[507] Benny's older son Hans (later Herb) attended the Philanthropin for his elementary school years,[508] but transferred to a public school for high school, the Reform Real Gymnasium.[509]

While Max and his family attended an Orthodox synagogue, Max did not feel compelled to enroll his oldest son Kurt in a yeshiva, or another Jewish school. Instead, Kurt attended the Karl-Friedrich-Gymnasium, a humanistic high school and the oldest high school in Mannheim, which was a short walk from the family's apartment. Max did not attend university after he graduated from the Philanthropin just shy of his sixteenth birthday, but he believed that education was important for his son, and ensured that he was educated in a school that would prepare him for a university. In fact, Kurt was planning to become a doctor. While Kurt did not attend a yeshiva, he did attend six years of Hebrew School at the Klaus Synagogue, where he received a rigorous Jewish education.

Jewish education was important for Germany's Jewish youth, but Jewish education for Germany's adult population was also seen as important. There was a concern among Jewish thinkers that assimilation into German society was resulting in a loss of Jewish connections. In late 1919, a number of Jewish leaders established the Free Jewish House of Learning (or Lehrhaus) in Frankfurt and the well-known Jewish philosopher Franz Rosenzweig was asked to be its director.[510] The term "free" meant that the Lehrhaus was free to all for study (although tuition was charged so that the course of study would be taken seriously) and the study of Jewish texts would be at the heart of the program.[511] The objective of the Lehrhaus was to win back to Judaism those educated Jews who found their spiritual and intellectual home outside of Judaism.[512] The Lehrhaus was to be a school of lifelong learning.[513] The school enticed enrollment through famous lecturers, including Martin Buber, Rabbi Nobel, the sociologist Franz Oppenheimer, and the Jewish feminist Bertha Pappenheim.[514] At its peak in 1922-23, its fourth academic year, the Lehrhaus had an enrollment of eleven hundred students.[515] Unfortunately, enthusiasm for the Lehrhaus waned and the school was forced to close in 1927.[516] Still, between 1920 and 1926, the school offered 90 lecture courses and 180 study groups.[517]

Growing Troubles for the Jewish Community and for Gebruder Heppenheimer

The Weimar Republic represented a high point for the Jewish people in German history,[518] and a high point financially for the Heppenheimer family. Both Adolph and Jacob had purchased large homes in a wealthy part of Frankfurt. And while Benny was living at the house connected to the smelter facility and owned by the business, he had a live-in maid and cook.[519] Maier's son Sally and Lazarus' son Jacob employed chauffeurs to drive their fancy cars.

When the U.S. stock market crashed in 1929, it brought economic disaster once again to Germany. Like most industries, the metals industry was impacted, with the price for three key metals—copper, lead, and zinc—falling 40 percent between 1929 and 1933.[520] The three largest German metals trading companies—Metallgesellschaft, Aron Hirsch & Sohn, and Beer, Sondheimer & Co.—had lost significant investments following World War I, and then were negatively impacted by the hyperinflation period.[521] The depression that followed the stock market crash proved too great a challenge for Aron Hirsh & Sohn and Beer, Sondheimer & Co., and those companies were liquidated in 1929 and 1930, respectively.[522]

The resulting depression also presented a challenge for the scrap metal industry, including Gebruder Heppenheimer, although the company had been experiencing problems with the Rheinau smelter facility even before the hyperinflation period. Louis Vollweiler had been sent to Mannheim to help Max Heppenheimer run the facility, likely because the business was struggling under Max's leadership. Unfortunately, Louis died on January 24, 1926, just two years after moving to Mannheim. While it is unclear how well the facility was functioning before Louis' death, the facility was losing money following Louis' death.[523] For the years 1927 and 1928, the joint-stock company lost a combined RM 43,574 and lost RM 8,343 in 1929. Max blamed these losses on increased competition, as well as the severe economic depression beginning in 1929. While the stock market crash likely increased the challenges for the smelter facility, it seems likely that the losses before the crash resulted from Max's inadequacies as manager of the facility, since the Mainkur smelter facility continued to make money during the same time period. Concluding that there was no possibility that the joint stock company could recover, Gebruder Heppenheimer voted to dissolve the company on April 10, 1930.

Max Heppenheimer was appointed liquidator of the Rheinau business, and over the next two years worked to close the facility. The smelter business was not sold to another entity, and there was no explanation in the records of why the business was not sold. By 1930, the only outstanding debt was owed to Gebruder Heppenheimer—in the amount of RM 40,334, and when the company was finally closed in August of 1932, that debt had not been repaid. While the Rheinau facility was structured as a joint-stock company to limit its owners' liability, the only money owed by the company by the time it closed, as it turned out, was to Gebruder Heppenheimer.

Unfortunately, the impact of the depression on Gebruder Heppenheimer did not end with the closure of the Rheinau facility. Feeling the effects of the world financial crisis, Gebruder Heppenheimer was forced to close its main office on Untermain Anlage in 1930, although it continued to own the connecting buildings. And perhaps feeling pressure to turn around their recent financial losses, Gebruder Heppenheimer speculated in the lead and copper markets in 1931, likely stockpiling lead and copper in the hopes that prices would rise. [524] Instead, the bottom fell out on both metals. Reflecting the losses to the company from those speculations, Gebruder Heppenheimer had no taxable income in 1931 or 1932. Finally, the company was forced to close the smelter facility in Mainkur. Likely facing bankruptcy, Gebruder Heppenheimer entered into a financial settlement in 1932 in order to resolve the issues with its creditors.[525]

The impact of the financial settlement on the owners of Gebruder Heppenheimer was likely significant. As discussed earlier, the company was structured as an OHG, so that Adolph, Jacob, Benny, and Max were personally liable for all losses to the company. Although we do not know the extent of the losses, we know that Jacob was forced to sell the house he had purchased in 1927. The house was sold in 1932, and he and his family ultimately moved to a rented apartment in the Westend. The losses to the company also took a toll on Adolph's finances. While he was able to weather the hyperinflation period (he had purchased his large home around 1920), the failure of Gebruder Heppenheimer caused Adolph to rent out his home beginning in 1931; he sold it sometime after 1935.[526] But Adolph did not live like a pauper even after the failure of the company—he rented a seven-room apartment on Beethovenstrasse 5 in the Westend.[527] And Benny and his family, who had lived in the house attached to the smelter facility, moved to an apartment in the Westend section of Frankfurt in 1933. The house was rented to businesses in 1934 and 1935, and sold to one of those businesses in 1936.

Having learned first-hand the financial risks of owning an OHG company (and aware of the benefits of having the Rheinau smelting facility organized in a way that limited financial exposure, at least in theory), Jacob and Benny formed Gebruder Heppenheimer G.m.b.H., a limited liability company, on November 10, 1933.[528] But they did not include any other Heppenheimer in this venture, although Rudolf Henninger, who had worked for the OHG company since 1899, was hired to work for the G.m.b.H. company. The OHG company, run by Joseph, had been a family company. After Henry left for America, his sons Jacob and Adolph worked for the company. Joseph's three sons all worked for the company, as did two sons-in-law. After Joseph retired in 1917, the company remained a family business, but the company experienced four significant financial challenges after Joseph's retirement—first, hyperinflation; second, the stock market crash, followed by the depression; third, the liquidation of the Rheinau smelter facility (which the family may have blamed on Max); and fourth, the financial settlement with creditors following the copper and lead speculation failures.

After the speculation failures and the failure of the Rheinau facility, something may have happened among the brothers and cousin that caused Jacob and Benny to incorporate on their own. It is possible that only Jacob and Benny wanted to create the new limited liability company and the other principals wanted to start their own scrap metal companies, although that seems highly unlikely given that they were in the middle of the depression. It seems more likely that Jacob and Benny chose to exclude the others from this new venture, and that, for the other family members, parting ways was not voluntary. Adolph had been Chairman of the Board of the Rheinau joint-stock company, and one can assume that he held similar stature in Gebruder Heppenheimer, which Jacob and Benny may have resented. It may also have been that Adolph, who had purchased a large villa in 1920 just after Germany suffered a devastating loss in the war and was experiencing severe inflation, had been somewhat reckless during his years at the helm of Gebruder Heppenheimer, which may have included the disastrous copper and lead speculations that brought down the OHG company.[529] And Jacob and Benny likely saw Max as a drain on the company, particularly after the loss of the Rheinau facility. The OHG company remained as a registered company and continued to own the properties connected with the business (the Mainkur property, the Rheinau property, the Untermain Anlage build-ings, and the Dominikanergasse buildings), but it does not appear that any scrap metal business was conducted through the OHG company after the creation of the G.m.b.H. The G.m.b.H. company, however, did operate out of the Dominikanergasse office. But Max, Adolph, and Isidor Wolfsheimer (Joseph's son-in-law who had worked for Gebruder Heppenheimer since his marriage to Johanna) were not employed by the new enterprise.

Following the closure of the Rheinau facility in 1932, it seems likely that Max continued to work for the OHG company. According to Rudolph Henninger, an employee of Gebruder Heppenheimer, Max worked as a self-employed scrap metal dealer, although his business was overseen by Gebruder Heppenheimer. In both the 1929 and the 1934 German Reich Directory for Industry, Commerce and Trade, Jacob, Benny and Max are all listed as the owners of Gebruder Heppenheimer, with the address listed as Dominikanergasse in Frankfurt, so it appears that Max remained a mem-ber of Gebruder Heppenheimer and that his trading business was part of Gebruder Heppenheimer, at least for as long as the OHG business continued to function as a scrap metal business. Once the G.m.b.H company was estab-lished at the end of 1933, however, Max no longer worked as a member of Gebruder Heppenheimer. Since his son Kurt (later Curtis) only knew of his father as a scrap metal dealer, it seems likely that Max started his own scrap metal business in Mannheim beginning in 1934.

Like Max, Adolph was also excluded from this new G.m.b.H. company. After the OHG company ceased functioning, Adolph opened his own scrap metal trading company.[530] Adolph had been with Gebruder Heppenheimer since before the turn of the century, and like his cousin Max, had only ever worked for his family's scrap metal company. At the age of sixty, after having been the head of a successful and important scrap metal company, Adolph was on his own for the first time in his life.

Prior to the closure of the OHG company, Isidor Wolfsheimer earned a comfortable living as a Prokurist for Gebruder Heppenheimer.[531] His salary for 1929 was nearly 10,000 RM, and he continued to do well in 1930, earning a salary of 8493 RM.[532] Isidor continued to work for Gebruder Heppenheimer through 1933, although his salary that year was 5,400 RM, likely reflecting the collapse of the company.[533] Isidor opened his own scrap metal trading business in 1934—I. Wolfsheimer Eisen und Metalle en gros—but the company never did well.[534] His highest earning year was 1937, when he earned approximately 3,800 RM, and he was forced to rely upon his son-in-law, Franz Neumeier, for financial support through the 1930s.[535]

Gebruder Heppenheimer was not the only Heppenheimer scrap metal business to feel the impact of the stock market crash. Berthold Heppenheimer, Lazarus' youngest son, had a small scrap metal business, employing three workers by the end of the 1920s.[536] The company, however, failed in 1930, and was deregistered on January 5, 1931.[537] Berthold's brother Arthur also experienced financial hardships beginning in the early 1930s. Arthur had been making a comfortable living in the scrap metal business, earning more than 10,000 RM in 1930.[538] But beginning in 1931, his income dropped, and in 1932, his wife Henny sought permission to trade in non-precious metals.[539] The company continued to trade, but it never earned the money it had earned in the 1920s, and it appears that Henny was operating the company on her own after 1932 (perhaps because Arthur was sick and unable to work).

Ludwig Heppenheimer (the business started by Ludwig and Sally, Maier's sons) also struggled because of the stock market crash. Sally had purchased shares on credit a few weeks before "Black Friday" and continued to hold onto them following the stock market crash, suffering significant losses.[540] Moreover, Sally had purchased a considerable quantity of scrap and continued to hold onto it as its value continued to fall. The company lost about 20-30,000 RM as a result of these business failures. While these business miscalculations caused the business to suffer, Ludwig Heppenheimer recovered somewhat and continued to remain a viable business through the mid-1930s.

The various Heppenheimer scrap metal businesses had faced challenges to their financial health during the hyperinflation period. And as those businesses worked to recover from the 1929 stock market crash, the family was about to face renewed anti-Semitism. Unfortunately, unlike previous anti-Semitic actions, this new round of anti-Semitism would raise existential questions for every member of the Heppenheimer family.

7.

Stay or Leave?
The Heppenheimers
in 1930s Germany

The Heppenheimer family had faced anti-Semitism since Jewish emancipation, but extreme examples of anti-Semitism, especially during the Weimar Republic, were rare.[541] Across the street from Gebruder Heppenheimer's office on Dominikanergasse was the Henninger Brewery, which had a large assembly hall that was a popular meeting place for right-wing and national-socialist groups during the 1920s.[542] While this likely served as a reminder that anti-Semitism persisted even during the Weimar period, the Heppenheimers could co-exist with such extremist groups.

Unfortunately, by the early 1930s, the situation had changed. Jewish prominence during the Weimar Republic had already served to link Jews with a democratic order that fell into disfavor because of its association with the unpopular Treaty of Versailles.[543] And while there was a period of relative prosperity following the hyperinflation period, the American stock market crash in 1929 led to the Great Depression in Europe, which hit Germany harder than any other European country.[544] At the same time, chauvinistic forces were in play in Germany -- the doctrine that the German people were biologically superior, which became popular at the beginning of the twentieth century, began to be taught in the 1920s in German schools and universities.[545] This combination of economic challenges and feelings of racial superiority led many Germans to become disillusioned with the Weimar Republic and to turn towards anti-democratic parties that blamed Jews for their plight.[546]

In the July 1932 elections, the National Socialist German Workers Party (the Nazi party) captured 230 out of 608 seats in the Reichtag (the German parliament), becoming the largest party in the legislature.[547] Adolf Hitler, the leader of the Nazi party, was appointed Chancellor on January 30, 1933.[548] Upon German President Paul von Hindenburg's death on August 2, 1934, the offices of the president and chancellor were merged under the title Leader and Chancellor (Furer und Reichskanzler), cementing Hitler's position as dictator of Germany.[549]

Anti-Semitism in the Early Years of Nazi Control

With the seizure of power by the Nazis, a systematic campaign of anti-Semitic measures began against German Jews. On April 1, 1933, two months after Hitler's appointment as chancellor, a one-day boycott of Jewish stores took place.[550] Kurt Heppenheimer (later Curtis Heppen) had his bar mitzvah one week after the boycott and remembered what should have been a joyous event as a very sad day, coming on the heels of the boycott. In April 1933, the Nazis enacted a law against the overcrowding of German schools and colleges that severely limited the number of Jewish students in public schools.[551] In that same year, legislation was enacted that forced the termination of all non-Aryan government employees.[552]

Following the Nazi rise to power, Jewish businesses in Frankfurt were immediately impacted. Trade went down sharply in Jewish stores, with a number going bankrupt, and many Jewish-owned enterprises were sold to non-Jews.[553] In the period from March to October 1933, 536 Jewish business enterprises in Frankfurt were closed.[554] Frankfurt's Economics Office was so concerned about the impact of these measures on the economic health of the city that it issued a Memorandum on February 17, 1934 warning of the difficulties that could be experienced by Frankfurt as a result of the measures taken against "non-Aryans."[555]

Any concerns about the impact anti-Jewish measures could have on the Frankfurt economy (or the German economy as a whole) clearly had no effect on the implementation of such measures by the Nazi government. Additional measures against the Jews followed those initial actions. The Nuremburg Laws of 1935 stripped Jews of their German citizenship.[556] Following the 1933 boycotts and the 1935 Nuremburg laws, many Jewish firms were forced to close, although the larger of the Heppenheimer scrap metal businesses were able to continue to trade, as discussed below.

Other aspects of life also changed for the Heppenheimers during this time. Benny Heppenheimer and his family had been great patrons of the arts, with subscriptions to the symphony and the opera. After 1933, they could no longer attend the symphony or the opera. Instead, they attended concerts performed by the newly founded Jewish Cultural League, which could only perform in synagogues.[557] Still, the Heppenheimer family continued to celebrate religious milestones. For example, Bertha Marx's (Joseph's eldest daughter) grandson Walter Hirsh had his bar mitzvah at the Westend Synagogue in November 1933.[558] Benny's son Hans (later changed to Herb) had his bar mitzvah in the spring of 1935 at the Hauptsynagoge.[559] But the Jewish population continued to shrink through the Nazi years, and its rabbis began to leave. While the Frankfurt community had three Reform Rabbis during the Weimar Republic, by the end of 1932, a single rabbi, Rabbi Salzberger, served both Reform synagogues.[560]

Jewish Scrap Metal Businesses and German Rearmament

With 20,000 Reichmarks in capital, Jacob and Benny Heppenheimer established their limited liability company Gebruder Heppenheimer GmbH on

November 16, 1933. Like the OHG company, the GmbH company traded in scrap metals. The new company began to advertise almost immediately, as reflected in the following ad, which states that they are cash buyers of all types of scrap, specialize in the demolition of shutdown businesses, and have an extensive warehouse of iron:

Source: Neueste Zeitung, December 17, 1933, 11, at http://sammlungen.ub.uni-frank-furt.de/periodika/periodical/zoom/3433484?query=heppenheimer.

The new limited liability company appeared to be viable in its early years of operation, allowing the partners to earn about 20,000 RM a year, although this was much less than what they had earned while the larger OHG company, which had included the two smelter facilities, was still operating. While the main office and warehouse on Dominikanergasse were the only facilities being used by the company, Gebruder Heppenheimer GmbH was still successfully trading in scrap metals and, as it turns out, may have unwittingly helped the German rearmament efforts.

At the same time that the Nazis were imposing restrictions on German Jews, the Nazis had decided to rearm the German military. Because of the restrictions in the Treaty of Versailles following World War I, Germany was without basic military equipment, and was limited to an army of not more than 100,000 men.[561] Hitler's first move after he became Chancellor in 1933 was to suspend payment on Germany's international debts and to prioritize rearmament.[562] Full scale rearmament began in 1934, although it was initially hidden from view because it violated the Treaty of Versailles restrictions.[563]

For Germany to rebuild its army, large amounts of steel and other metals were needed.[564] And scrap became an increasingly important element of steel production in Germany—while only 29% of the raw materials used in steel production in 1913 was scrap, by the 1930s, the average was above 40%.[565] Thus, as the Nazis began to rearm the German military, scrap metal dealers saw a major increase in their business.[566]

Jews in early 1930s Germany still dominated the scrap metal industry, and so found themselves a part of the rearmament effort and a beneficiary of this increase in business.[567] Until 1935, Jewish firms were still receiving contracts to do business with the Nazi government, so that Jews were reaping profits from the buildup of the Luftwaffe, the Wehrmacht, and the German navy.[568] As of 1935, Gebruder Heppenheimer in Frankfurt, Leopold Heppenheimer in Mannheim, M. Heppenheimer in Frankenthal, and Ludwig Heppenheimer in Worms were all still operating as scrap metal businesses, and any trading of scrap metal, at the time, necessarily meant some participation in the rearmament business. The fact that the Heppenheimer scrap metal businesses were likely providing metals to the rearmament efforts of a government that was working to undermine their very existence is a cruel irony that was likely not lost on the Heppenheimers (although they could not know, at the time, the full extent of such an irony).[569]

Some of the very large Jewish scrap metal dealers also found themselves providing indirect assistance to the growing rearmament of Germany. The fall in exports was causing a balance of payments problem for Germany, causing Germany to suspend in 1934 some repayment of long-term and medium-term foreign debts.[570] J. Adler Junr., a Frankfurt scrap metal company that was one of the largest in Germany (and had nearly been a business partner of Gebruder Heppenheimer following the first world war), had both a domestic and an international scrap metal business by the time the Nazis came to power.[571] In the early 1930s, Adler saw its domestic business begin to slow as more large German companies started to sort their scrap by means of company-owned departments.[572] Moreover, the stigma of a Jewish-owned enterprise also began to have an impact on its domestic business.[573] Seeing reductions in its domestic market, Adler increased its focus on its foreign business, buying and selling scrap in foreign markets.[574] Between 1935 and 1938, when the business was finally liquidated, Adler performed an important role for Germany as a foreign exchange importer, helping to balance the foreign exchange imbalances caused by the rearmament program.[575]

Jewish scrap metal businesses thus played a role in the Nazi armament efforts, both directly (as was likely the case for the Heppenheimer scrap metal businesses) and indirectly (as was the case with J. Adler). While these businesses were doing what they needed to do to survive, they were unfortunately helping to sow the seeds to their own destruction.

Nazi Impact on the Jewish Fashion Industry

Joseph Heppenheimer's daughter Alice had moved back to Frankfurt from Nuremberg in the early 1930s. Alice was not involved in the scrap metal business, having had an applied arts studio in Nuremberg. And when she moved back to Frankfurt, she continued to follow her own path, opening a fine ladies' dressmaking shop in Frankfurt. And swimming against the tide of anti-Semitic actions, Alice opened her dressmaking shop in the very year that the Nazis took power, 1933.

The clothing and fashion industry in Germany was dominated by Jews. When the Nazis took control of Germany, almost 80 percent of department and chain store businesses were Jewish-owned, as were 40 percent of wholesale textile firms, and 60 percent of wholesale and retail clothing businesses.[576] Once the Nazis came to power, they decided to target the clothing industry. They established the Federation of German-Aryan Manufacturers of the Clothing Industry (Adefa), whose mission was to permanently eliminate German Jews from the design, production, and sale of clothing and textiles.[577]

On July 17, 1933, Alice joined the Dressmakers Guild, one of the trade guilds in Frankfurt.[578] While Alice was an artisan in Nuremberg, she did not appear to be a professional dressmaker in that city. Alice could join the Dressmakers Guild in Frankfurt only after she passed an examination and met certain requirements.[579] A 1934 law required that all artisans such as dressmakers join a guild and, after 1935, artisans were required to pass a master's examination, which likely required Alice to retake her master's examination.[580]

That Alice would open a dressmaking shop at the very time Germany was beginning to openly attack the Jewish clothing industry and remain open even as increased hurdles were imposed on Jewish businesses suggests that Alice was a motivated and ambitious businesswoman. Alice chose to be a member of the Dressmakers Guild before such membership was required, and was able to maintain that membership through the 1930s.

Like all Jewish businesses during the Nazi era, Alice was forbidden from advertising in mainstream newspapers.[581] So Alice advertised her new shop in the Municipal Gazette of the Israelite Community Frankfurt am Main, a local Jewish paper, using her married name "Alice Adler." Alice married her second husband Alfred Falkenstein in 1936[582], and after her marriage, she advertised her women's shop using her newly married name Alice Falkenstein-Adler. Here are the ads that appeared in the 1933, 1934, and 1936 editions of the Municipal Gazette of the Israelite Community Frankfurt am Main:

Alice Adler	Alice Adler	Alice Falkenstein-Adler
BLEICHSTRASSE 70 I Telefon: 28218 Die Schneiderin der eleganten Dame. Beste Verarbeitung. — Billige Preise.	Bleichstr. 70¹ Tel. 28218 Feine Damenschneiderei Zeitgemäße Preise	jetzt: Kronbergerstr. 7, I. früher Töpfengasse 9, I Feine Damen-Schneiderei Tel. 792 03

Source: *Goethe University Digital Collections, http://sammlungen.ub.uni-frankfurt.de/.*

While the Germans worked to destroy the Jewish clothing industry through Adefa beginning in 1933, their efforts were not successful in the early years. German consumers in the urban centers, such as Frankfurt, continued to shop in their favorite department stores or fashion salons.[583] Even the wives of highly placed Nazi officials continued to frequent their favorite Jewish fashion designers.[584] Perhaps Alice was one of those coveted Jewish designers, since she stayed in business until 1938. However, when all Jewish businesses were forced to close at the end of 1938, Alice closed her shop as well.

Impact on the Mannheim Heppenheimers

Before the Nazis' rise to power, Max Heppenheimer and his family led a comfortable middle-class life. Max's wife Recha was in a bridge club and Max's older son Kurt attended a prestigious and rigorous high school, a Gymnasium. Kurt enjoyed the life of any typical teenager, going swimming and to the movies and to parties with friends, as well as reading and listening to the radio.[585] After the closure of the Rheinau smelter facility in 1932, Max became a scrap metal dealer in Mannheim, although his business was overseen by his brothers in Frankfurt through Gebruder Heppenheimer OHG. Thus, to the extent there were any problems in the business, Max would likely have been helped by his brothers.

That lifeline was lost when the new limited liability company was established at the end of 1933 and Max was excluded from his brothers' new business. Thereafter, Max was on his own as a businessman for the first time in his life. Here is Max around this time period, looking like the successful businessman he hoped to become:

But the reality was that, by 1935, Max's business was failing. The boycotts in 1933, followed by the dismissal of Jews in multiple sectors of the German economy, would have made it difficult for any Jew to start a business. But for Max, who had never before been in business on his own, and was, by all accounts, an ineffective businessman, the challenges were likely insurmountable. After more than a year on his own, it was probably clear to Max that he would not be able to provide for his family as a scrap metal dealer.

Max had served his country in World War 1. Many left the war damaged both physically and emotionally, and that may have been the case for Max. His son Kurt described him years later as cold and aloof, and that may have been the result of years fighting in the trenches. He may also have been forced to pursue a career he did not want (we know that he was interested in the sciences as a young man and was known in the family as an "intellectual") and certainly appeared ill-suited to follow in the path of his father and older brothers. Added to his financial concerns was his son Kurt being forced to leave school at the age of 15 in the spring of 1935 when all Jewish children were barred from attending public schools like the Gymnasium.[586] Kurt was academically driven and intended to become a doctor, perhaps fulfilling Max's own dream of a university education. For an intellectual who failed in business, the denial of his son's own intellectual pursuits, coupled with the continued anti- Semitic actions of the Nazi government, may have proved too much for Max. Approximately three months after his son was expelled from the Gymnasium, Max committed suicide.[587] Here is his gravestone from a Mannheim cemetery:

Source: Marchivum at https://www.marchivum.de/de/
juedischer-friedhof/g2-a-06-08-heppenheimer-max.

Kurt never went to the Jewish school following his father's suicide. Instead, he decided to emigrate to America. Kurt apprenticed at a paper manufacturing plant for two years to support his family while he waited for his visa to be approved. But life was hard for Kurt during these two years, where he often found himself the subject of taunts from fellow students at the trade school he was attending for his apprenticeship.

Following enactment of the Nuremberg Laws in 1935, the Nazi party increased its efforts to destroy the "Jewish economy" in Mannheim by forcing the closure or Aryanization of Jewish-owned businesses.[588] The Mannheim indoor pool, which had been funded by a Jewish businessman, was Aryanized and Jews were banned.[589] And as the Nazis worked to close Jewish businesses in Mannheim, the Nazis chose to make an example of Leopold Heppenheimer, Maier's son.

By 1937, Leopold had been in the scrap metal business for fifty years (he was 66 years-old at the time) and had a sales volume of 200,000 Reichmarks (about $1 million in today's dollars).[590] Between October and December of 1936, Leopold purchased approximately 600 kilograms of copper from an antiques merchant.[591] Leopold had previously done business with this merchant and he did not (and likely could not) know that the merchant did not have a license to engage in scrap metal sales.[592] In 1937, Leopold (and another scrap metal dealer, Sigmund Jentof, who had also purchased copper from the merchant and who was also Jewish) were charged with copper theft.[593] Both Leopold and Sigmund Jentof were convicted and both were sentenced to more than one year in prison.[594] In addition, both were prohibited from engaging in any work for three years.[595]

We cannot know for sure that Leopold's arrest and subsequent imprisonment occurred because he was Jewish. But Leopold had never been in legal trouble before and had been operating his own successful scrap metal business in Mannheim for approximately twenty-five years. Moreover, it was acknowledged during the trial that Leopold did not know that he was purchasing scrap from an unlicensed dealer. Given the times and the constraints being imposed on Jews, it seems likely that Leopold was arrested, convicted and sent to prison simply because he was Jewish. After he went to prison, his scrap metal business was Aryanized.

Early Jewish Emigration from Germany

The Nazis' anti-Semitic policies and actions were unlike anything the Heppenheimer family had experienced before. The great German Rabbi Leo Baeck announced in 1933, shortly after the Nazis took power, that "the end of German Jewry has arrived."[596] But Baeck and other Jewish community leaders concluded that emigration could save only a small minority of German Jews and committed to working with this new regime.[597] Thus, not surprisingly, in the early years of the Nazi regime, German Jewish emigres tended to be unmarried individuals between the ages of twenty and thirty with little to lose economically.[598]

The Heppenheimer family followed this early pattern of emigration. A few of Joseph's grandchildren left Germany following the rise of the Nazis. Joseph's daughter Bertha had two daughters—Erna and Bettina. Erna emigrated to the U.S. in 1932, working first as a governess for a family and then remaining in the United States.[599]

Joseph's son Jacob had two children: Melanie and Ernst. Melanie had attended a prestigious girls high school in Frankfurt. Upon her graduation in 1929, Melanie enrolled in the University of Munich to study chemistry.[600] Over the next two years, she also attended the University of Frankfurt and the Sorbonne in Paris. Melanie had to leave school in 1931 to work for her father's business because, according to Melanie, Jacob became ill. This is the year Gebruder Heppenheimer experienced serious financial difficulties, so it may be that Melanie was forced to leave school because of the collapse of the business and used "illness" as a way to avoid the embarrassment of a business failure. Melanie remained with her father's business until 1933, intending to return to her studies. However, by the time she was ready to return in the summer of 1933, she found that she could not re-enroll. Melanie decided instead to emigrate to Palestine. She married Paul Horn on March 2, 1934, and the two left for Palestine on March 5, 1934 and stayed.[601]

Jacob's second child Ernst attended the Philanthropin and graduated in 1932 at the age of 18.[602] He then became an apprentice in a textile firm.[603] Ernst recalled many years later why he decided to leave Germany:

> On Whitsuntide [a Christian holiday just after Easter] 1934 two friends and I wanted to take the same night trip to the Taunus mountains which we had taken the year before from Zeilsheim to the Feldberg.[604] Early in the morning at 4:30 am, dead tired, we arrived at the Feldberg and saw a magnificent sunrise. Around 9 o'clock we got to Dreisberg where we had stayed in a beautiful house the year before. We rang the bell and the lady of the house looked out the window. We asked if she would give us lodgings. Whereupon she called down "You are Jews and I don't take you." and closed the window shutters with a bang. We found lodgings somewhere else and I said to my friends "I will no longer stay here. We Jews don't have a future here."[605]

After he returned from his trip, Ernst informed his parents that he was emigrating to America.[606] He asked his American relative Adolph Keller (Henry Heppenheimer's son-in-law) for a sponsorship, took the sponsorship to the consulate in Stuttgart, and received his visa.[607] He arrived in New York on September 21, 1934.[608] Ernst later changed his name to Ernest Harvey.

The ebb and flow of Jewish emigration from Germany corresponded to the various phases of Nazi persecution. The brutal excesses of the early years of Nazi rule resulted in a large numbers of emigrations, mostly by young Germans.[609] This emigration slowed down during the calmer periods occurring between 1934 and 1937, perhaps reflecting hope that the Jewish community could survive Nazi rule.[610] In fact, some Jewish businesses benefited from an upswing in prosperity flowing from Germany's stabilization and economic expansion during Hitler's early years in power, which encouraged those Jewish businessmen to remain.[611] Emigration hit an early peak of 37,000 in 1933, then fell to 21,000 in 1935, rising a bit to 25,000 in 1936 in response to the Nuremberg laws, but falling once again in 1937.[612] In fact, the contradictory tactics of the Nazis served to mask the ultimate menace and confused Jews trying to decide whether or not to leave.[613]

A few Heppenheimers emigrated in those middle years, and they were also from the younger generation. Adolf Heppenheimer's nineteen year-old son Heinz emigrated to America in 1936. And Max Heppenheimer's son Kurt left Mannheim for America in 1937. By November of 1935, Kurt had secured a German passport.[614] Kurt and his family had lived for years on Richard Wagnerstrasse, but moved to Hugo-Wolfstrasse 10, which was further from the town center, likely because they could no longer afford the larger and fancier apartment.[615] Kurt submitted his application for a U.S. immigration visa to the American Consulate in Stuttgart, Germany on March 10, 1937.[616] Kurt paid for his own passage to America, and arrived in New York on April 13, 1937.[617] This is the picture attached to Kurt's visa:

Source: Kurt Heppenheimer Application for a U.S. Visa, Visa No. 10227.

Following passage of the Nuremberg laws, the number of anti-Semitic actions and anti-Jewish laws decreased.[618] The reasons had less to do with a change in attitude toward Jews in Germany, and more to do with a concern that continued actions towards Jews could jeopardize Germany's rearmament program and the Olympic Games in Berlin in 1936.[619] But this calm had the effect of slowing down emigration, including among the Heppenheimer family members. The remainder of the Heppenheimers who left Germany emigrated to the United States (rather than Palestine), and did not leave until the late 1930s or early 1940s. The Jews who did not emigrate told themselves that the Third Reich was just one more pogrom.[620] The Heppenheimers had seen themselves as part of the fabric of the German economy and German life and likely thought that this, like the other pogroms, would soon end. And the Heppenheimers—who had worked hard to develop successful scrap metal businesses—were likely concerned about the loss of wealth that would follow emigration and the loss of social status in their new country.[621] And so they remained.

By the end of 1937, a total of 129,000 Jews had left Germany.[622] Still, another 371,000 German Jews were still in harm's way.[623] Recognizing a growing crisis, 140 representatives from 32 nations, along with delegates from 40 private aid agencies, convened a meeting in Evian, France on July 6, 1938.[624] Following nine-days of discussions, only the Dominican Republic expressed a willingness to take a large number of refugees.[625] After the Evian conference, the German government concluded that it would need to take more drastic steps to make Germany "Judenfrei" (free of Jews).

Kristallnacht and its Aftermath

1938 began with new emigrations within the Heppenheimer family. Adolph Heppenheimer, Henry's son, who remained in Frankfurt when his family emigrated to America in the 1890s and became a partner in Gebruder Heppenheimer, emigrated to America with his wife on October 29, 1938.

Adolph had previously travelled to America at the end of 1936 on a temporary visa with his son Heinz, who had permanently emigrated to America. Perhaps Adolph, who returned to Germany in January 1937, had travelled to America to work with his brother-in-law Adolph Keller, who had sponsored Heinz, as well as Jacob's son Ernst (Ernest Harvey) and Max's son Kurt (Curtis Heppen), to sponsor other members of the Heppenheimer family in their efforts to escape from Germany.

For the Heppenheimers still left in Germany, and particularly those who still owned businesses, Kristallnacht ("the night of broken glass") on November 9 and 10, 1938 likely ended any doubts about the need to leave Germany. The assassination of a German official by a 17-year-old Polish Jew was used as pretext for launching a night of anti-Semitic mayhem.[626] The following telex was issued by the Gestapo[627] at 1:20 am on November 10th to police commanders throughout Germany:

> Actions against Jews, in particular against their synagogues, will very shortly take place across the whole of Germany. They are not to be interrupted. However, measures are to be taken in co-operation with the Order Police for looting and other special excesses to be prevented… The arrest of about 20-30,000 Jews in the Reich is to be prepared. Propertied Jews above all are to be chosen.[628]

Kristallnacht ultimately saw the destruction of 267 synagogues throughout Germany, Austria and the Sudetenland, as well as damage to 7,500 Jewish-owned commercial establishments.[629]

The Jews in Frankfurt had been experiencing assaults on their religious institutions before Kristallnacht. During the High Holidays in 1936, ordinary German citizens disrupted services in Frankfurt's orthodox Borneplatz Synagogue by throwing rocks through the sanctuary windows, forcing the congregants to leave the building.[630] Still, nothing could compare to Kristallnacht. In Frankfurt, three of the four synagogues were completely destroyed, including the Reform Hauptsynagoge and the Borneplatz Synagogue, and the Westend Synagogue was badly damaged.[631] Young Jews in Frankfurt were forced to cut up the Torah scrolls and burn them.[632] The Klaus synagogue in Mannheim, the synagogue in which Curtis Heppen had his bar mitzvah, also was destroyed. The Germans could have seized Jewish assets without destroying nearly every synagogue in Germany, but the intent of Kristallnacht was the public humiliation and abuse of Jews in every city and village in the Third Reich.[633]

Gebruder Heppenheimer continued to own the building on Dominikanergasse. One can imagine that Benny, still living in Frankfurt, was worried about his building the morning of November 10th, in light of the damage being done to Jewish-owned businesses. The building on Dominikanergasse was just a block from the plaza where the Orthodox synagogue was located, and word may have reached Benny that all of Frankfurt's synagogues were on fire. Had Benny visited his office building that morning, this is what he would have seen just steps from his office—the Borneplatz synagogue on fire:

Source: https://jfr.org/month-holocaust-history-jfr-november-2017/

There is no evidence that the Dominkanergasse building sustained any damage during Kristallnacht. Still Benny—and all Jews still left in Germany -- heard the message loud and clear that they were not wanted in Germany.

The impact of Kristallnacht on Maier Heppenheimer's granddaughter Johanna Bauernfreund (Maier's daughter Berta's daughter) and her husband is reflective of the impact that Kristallnacht had on all Jews who were still in Germany. Johanna, who had been born and raised in Frankenthal, had moved to Frankfurt in the 1920s and married Heinrich Bauernfreund. Beginning on the evening of November 10, 1938, and continuing for the next few days, 10,000 Jewish men throughout Germany were arrested by German SS and police and taken to the Buchenwald concentration camp.[634] Benny Heppenheimer was arrested, but because he had a hearing injury from the first world war, he was released.[635] Heinrich Bauernfreund, however, was not so lucky. On November 13th, several days after Kristallnacht, Heinrich was arrested and taken by train to Buchenwald, about 130 miles from Frankfurt. For the Jews arrested in Frankfurt like Heinrich, they were met at the train station by a crowd that jeered at them and attacked them with clubs and sticks.[636]

Buchenwald had only recently been built in 1937 in central Germany for male prisoners, and the conditions were primitive.[637] After their arrival, the men were required to line up for roll call, still in their suits and coats:

Source: https://www.ushmm.org/information/exhibitions/
online-exhibitions/special-focus/kristallnacht/historical-overview

Heinrich and the other Jews that arrived after Kristallnacht were then subjected to extraordinarily cruel treatment, working fourteen to fifteen hours a day—generally in the infamous Buchenwald quarry—and enduring abominable living conditions.[638]

The intent of the arrest and brutal treatment at Buchenwald was to encourage Jewish emigration.[639] Within a few months, virtually all were released after their families had made commitments to leave Germany.[640] Heinrich was released on December 9th after his family committed to leaving Germany.[641] From that moment on, Heinrich worked to get his family out of Germany.

The drive to rearm Germany had a huge impact on the financial health of Germany. In 1932, the Reich government had enjoyed a surplus, but by 1938, the Reich had a deficit of 9.5 billion Reichsmarks.[642] Jewish resources were targeted to make up for this deficit, with the flight tax imposed on Jewish emigrants bringing in 45 million Reichsmarks between 1935-36, 80 million Reichsmarks between 1937-38 and 342 million Reichsmarks between 1938-39.[643] But Kristallnacht proved to be an economic bonanza for the Nazis. Following Kristallnacht, a law was passed making the Jews liable collectively for all damages.[644] The collective fine was 1 billion Reichsmarks, and all Jewish taxpayers were ordered on November 21, 1938 to pay a fifth of all their assets, in four tax installments, by August 15, 1939.[645] In October 1939, the proportion was raised to a quarter on the grounds that 1 billion Reichsmarks had not been reached, although more than 1.127 billion Reichsmarks had already been collected at that point.[646] Moreover, all insurance payments to Jewish property owners for damages resulting from Kristallnacht—amounting to 225 million Reichsmarks—were confiscated by the state.[647] The total amount confiscated by the Nazis for the damages they caused during Kristallnacht reached well over 2 billion Reichsmarks.[648] And to add insult to injury, the owners of the destroyed shops were required to restore the appearance of the street, at their own expense.[649]

The Aryanization of the Remaining Jewish Businesses

On November 12, 1938, two days after Kristallnacht, the Decree on the Elimination of Jews from German Economic Life was passed, which closed off nearly all remaining possibilities for making a living.[650] And on December 3, 1938, a Decree on the Utilization of Jewish Assets ordered the closure of all remaining Jewish businesses.[651] Jews were thus forbidden to do business and had to sell or liquidate their businesses and properties under the supervision of a governmental trustee.[652]

Of the 5,000 businesses registered in the Frankfurt municipal economic office in 1935, 1,700 were Jewish-owned.[653] By June 1938, approximately 300 Jewish-owned businesses still existed.[654] The following chart shows the total numbers of takeovers (sale of the business) and liquidations in Frankfurt by year during the Nazi period:

Year	1933	1934	1935	1936	1937	1938	1939-1942
Number	116	62	89	100	152	653	458

Source: Nietzel, Handeln und Uberleben: Judische Unternehmer
aus Frankfurt on the Main 1924-1964, 161.

As the table above demonstrates, there were a steady number of takeovers and liquidations of Jewish businesses beginning in 1933, which surged in 1938 following the decision by the Nazi government to require the closure of Jewish businesses.[655]

Most Jewish businesses were liquidated rather than sold. In Frankfurt, for example, 70 percent of all Jewish businesses were liquidated.[656] But, at least with respect to the Heppenheimer scrap metal businesses, most of those businesses were sold. The businesses that remained viable had their names changed and were re-registered in the commercial register to hide the fact that they had been Jewish-owned,[657] and that was the case for the Heppenheimer businesses that were sold. Scrap metal had been valued by the

Nazi government, which may explain why the Heppenheimer scrap metal businesses stayed open as long as they did and why they were sold rather than liquidated.

Gebruder Heppenheimer GmbH, the newly-created limited liability company owned and operated by Jacob and Benny, was still operating as a scrap metal business in 1938. While Gebruder Heppenheimer continued to struggle under the Nazi regime, it was still making money. Gebruder Heppenheimer continued to advertise to purchase scrap metals through the 1930s, but in perhaps the last advertisement placed by the company, in 1936, one can see the writing on the wall for the business:

Source: Neueste Zeitung, April 30, 1936, 6, at http://sammlungen.ub.uni-frank-
furt.de/periodika/periodical/pageview/3441549?query=heppenheimer

Instead of seeking scrap metals to buy, in this advertisement, the company lists all the metals available for purchase "cheap to sell." Jacob and Benny each earned 13,477 RM (about $90,000 in today's dollars) in 1937 and 14,302 RM in 1938, but this income may have come from the sale of assets. By the end of 1938, after Kristallnacht and the passage of laws requiring the closure of Jewish businesses, Gebruder Heppenheimer GmbH was sold to Heinrick Birkenbach.[658]

Unlike the GmbH company, Gebruder Heppenheimer OHG was liquidated. The OHG company had not been operating as a scrap metal business
for years, but it was the entity that continued to own all the physical assets
and was likely responsible for collecting the rent from the tenants. The house
located at the Mainkur smelter facility had been sold in 1936. Untermain
Anlange 8 (one of the two connected buildings owned by the company in the
Bahnhof section of Frankfurt) was owned by a bank beginning in 1936 (we
do know the circumstances of that ownership). The Rheinau property was
sold in 1937, although we do not know for how much. But by 1938, the OHG
company still owned the land on which the smelter facility in Mainkur had
been located, as well as the main office and warehouse on Dominikanergasse,
the building connected to the Dominikanergasse building at Klostergasse
12, and Untermain Anlage 9 (the other building that had been the company's
headquarters during the 1920s).

A government-appointed trusted conducted the sale of the remain-
ing OHG properties. The trustee sold 2,878 square meters of the Mainkur
property to Diskus-Werke Maschinenbau in 1937 for 5 Reichmarks[659] and
27,242 square meters to Klotz & Co. for 32,518.50 Reichsmarks in 1941.[660]
The company's office in downtown Frankfurt (on Dominikanergasse 3/5 and
Klostergasse 12), along with inventory, was sold to Heinrick Birkenbach.[661]
Untermain Anlage 9 (which included a warehouse) was sold to Hermann
Noe.[662] The money from the sales of these properties was deposited into a
blocked account at a foreign exchange bank,[663] which meant that no principal of Gebruder Heppenheimer had access to the account.[664] Following
the sale of all of its the properties, the OHG company was extinguished
from the Frankfurt Commercial Registry on August 18, 1941.[665] After more
than sixty years in business as a successful scrap metal company, Gebruder
Heppenheimer was forced out of business.[666]

Ludwig Heppenheimer, the scrap business started by Ludwig and
Sally Heppenheimer (the sons of Maier Heppenheimer) in Worms was

also Aryanized. While Ludwig Heppenheimer had no real competition through the 1920s, by the early 1930s, there was a new scrap metal company, Ritzheimer & Co., and that company was an Aryan company.[667] Beginning in 1933, Ludwig Heppenheimer began losing customers to Ritzheimer, so that the business had essentially stopped functioning by 1937.[668] On April 4, 1938, the company was sold to Mauthe & Merz, a company comprised of former employees of Ludwig Heppenheimer.[669] Mauthe & Merz paid 5,000 RM to Ludwig's widow Franziska and to Sally; Sally's share was immediately confiscated by the Worms tax office.[670]

The Challenges in Emigrating to America after Kristallnacht

Before they could leave Germany at this late date, the Heppenheimers needed to overcome a number of hurdles, which only increased as the war approached. First, they had to pay a Flight Tax, which was levied at a rate of twenty-five percent on all taxable property.[671] They also had to pay the tax to pay for the damages caused by Kristallnacht, which was twenty-five percent of any remaining wealth.[672] They would need to obtain a passport, visas for each transit country, a ship ticket purchased through a German travel agency, a certificate confirming that no laws had been broken, and a tax clearance certificate certifying that all outstanding taxes had been paid.[673] Monies sufficient to establish a modest existence abroad were required to be deposited into an account in a German bank, with a heavy deduction imposed on those deposited funds; in October 1936, the deduction was eighty-one percent, by June 1938, the deduction was ninety percent, and after September 1939, the deduction was 96 percent.[674] Once the family had obtained all the required passports, visas, and tickets and then transferred the required amount of money (into a blocked account), they still had to pay a tax on personal belongings, which was set by the currency and customs office following inspection.[675] These various levies were intended to rob the Jewish population and effectively amounted to full-scale expropriation.[676] Often, the family left

Germany with no other resources other than the 10 Reichmarks (roughly $63 in 2010 dollars) they were allowed to carry to America.[677]

Emigrating to the United States was also challenging because the U.S. limited the number of immigrants that could come to the U.S. from Germany. Under the 1929 Immigration Act, the total annual quota of all immigrants to America was not to exceed 153,774.[678] During the first years of the Nazi regime, Jewish and political refugees fleeing Germany did not enter the United States in any appreciable numbers.[679] The annual quota for immigrants who were natives of Germany (25,957) remained largely unfilled.[680] But that would change following Germany's annexation of Austria in March 1938 and Kristallnacht.[681]

In 1939, the German-Austrian quota was filled for the first time. In late 1938, 125,000 applicants lined up outside the U.S. consulates to try to obtain one of the visas under the immigration quota, and that number increased to 300,000 by June 1939.[682] There were simply not enough visas available to those that needed them. The following is a chart showing the percentage of the German-Austrian quota fulfilled and the number of German and Austrian immigrants admitted to the United States between 1933 and 1944:

Year	Total Number	Percent of Quota
1933	1,450	5.3
1934	3,740	13.7
1935	5,530	20.2
1936	6,650	24.3
1937	11,520	42.1
1938	17,870	65.3
1939	27,370	100.0
1940	26,080	95.3
1941	13,050	47.7
1942	4,760	17.4
1943	1,290	4.7
1944	1,351	4.8

Source: Herbert A. Strauss, "The Immigration and Acculturation of the German Jew in the United States of America," 68.

By 1940, approximately 90,000 German Jews had been granted visas and allowed to settle in the United States.[683] Unable to secure U.S. visas, approximately 100,000 German Jews emigrated to other Western European counties, but many of them later fell victim to the Holocaust.[684]

The Last Heppenheimers to Leave Before the Start of the War

Following Kristallnacht, and just before the start of World War II, a few more Heppenheimers were able to emigrate from Germany. Joseph's son Jacob Heppenheimer and his wife Johanna emigrated to America on November 24, 1938, joining their son Ernst (now Ernest) in New York. They sailed from Hamburg, Germany. Jacob's widowed older sister Bertha Marx sailed from Bremerhaven, Germany to New York on March 4, 1939, joining her daughter Erna, who had already emigrated.

In October 1938, Max's widow Recha and her son Alfred left Mannheim and moved to Darmstadt, likely living with Recha's sister Frieda May. Frieda was a beloved aunt of Curtis Heppen's and the sisters were very close. Recha was waiting for the visas to America and likely knew that she would be receiving them shortly, and so may have decided to spend time with her sister before leaving Germany. On January 10, 1939, Recha and Alfred went to Stuttgart and received their visas. Knowing that she could not take money or valuables to America, Recha had used what money she had to purchase a number of antiques, as well as several small sculptures. When she returned from Stuttgart, Recha packed her antiques and small sculptures, along with a strand of valuable pearls hidden in a skein of yarn, in a trunk. The trunk was then checked by customs officials, and, fortunately, they did not find the pearls nor did they appreciate the value of the other items. On January 12, 1939, Recha and Alfred left Hamburg and sailed for America.[685]

Given the length of time it took to satisfy the numerous requirements for emigration, all the Heppenheimers who left before the start of the war had likely begun the work to emigrate before Kristallnacht. And with the start of World War II, which began with the invasion of Poland on September 1, 1939, emigration would become even more difficult for those Heppenheimers who were still in Germany.

8.
Life and Death

The invasion of Poland in September 1939 marked both the start of World War II and a new phase in German policy toward German Jews. Jews were now required to be registered and were dispossessed of their property.[686] Jews were not permitted on the street after 8 pm, and were subject to severe food rationing.[687] They were permitted to shop for their needs only one hour per day and were not allowed to use public transportation. [688] On March 4, 1941, an order was issued requiring all Jews to engage in forced labor,[689] although some forced labor had already begun. Beginning on September 8, 1941, all Jews over the age of six were required to wear a Star of David, which they were required to purchase from the Gemeinde, the Jewish community authority.[690]

The Nazis gradually took away all of the rights given to Jews following emancipation and imposed on them dehumanizing conditions. Still, the policies initially focused on encouraging Jews to leave Germany. Emigration was handled by the Reich Office of Migration, which was within the Ministry of the Interior and mostly staffed by officials who were not Nazis.[691] But by late 1938, responsibility for emigration had passed into the hands of the Gestapo, and they made it even more difficult for Jews to leave Germany.[692]

The Gestapo was assisted in their efforts to make Germany Juden frei (Jew free) by the Reichsvereinigung der Juden (the Reich Association of Jews in Germany), which was established by law on July 4, 1939.[693] The

Reichsvereinigung grew out of Reichsvertretung der Deutschen Juden (the Reich Representation of German Jews), which had been created in 1933 as an umbrella organization of Jewish organizations to support German Jews during the Nazi period.[694] The Reichsvereinigung, also operated by Jews, was created to prepare Jews for forced emigration and to spur such emigration.[695] At the end of 1939, there was a central office in Berlin, as well as forty branch offices, including a local Reichsvereinigung in Frankfurt, all working with the Gestapo to force Jewish emigration.[696]

The official position of the German government with regard to Jews was to force emigration even after the Gestapo took charge, although the barriers to emigration often made it difficult to leave Germany. But that official position took a dramatic turn in June 1941 during the invasion of the Soviet Union, where the decision was made for the first time to exterminate the Jews of Europe. As the German army marched east into the Soviet Union, tens of thousands of Soviet Jews were rounded up by the Einsatzgruppen (roving bands made up of SS, local police and auxiliaries) and shot.[697] In September 1941, Hitler approved a plan to carry out mass deportations of Jews from Germany, Austria, Czechoslovakia, and Luxembourg, and in a letter dated September 18, 1941, SS Chief Heinrich Himmler ordered that deportations should begin immediately.[698] German Jewish emigration ended in October 1941 when Germany formally banned such emigration.[699]

With this emigration ban, the function of the Reichsvereinigung changed. In May 1941, the six thousand Jews working for the Reichsvereinigung had been ordered to compile card files for all Jews still living in Germany, and by September 1941, the task had been completed.[700] Rather than helping to get Jews out of Germany, the Reichsvereinigung was now helping the Gestapo prepare the lists that would be used for the deportation of all remaining German Jews.[701]

While deportations of Jews had begun in some German states as early as 1939, the mass deportations did not begin until 1941.[702] In January 1933,

522,000 Jews lived in Germany.[703] Over half—approximately 304,000 Jews—emigrated during the first six years of the Nazi dictatorship, leaving approximately 214,000 Jews still living in Germany on the eve of World War II.[704] By the end of the war, the Nazis and their collaborators had killed between 160,000 and 180,000 German Jews.[705] Each of the Heppenheimer brothers who remained in Germany into the twentieth century— Joseph, Maier, and Lazarus—had family who made it safely out of Germany and family who died in the Holocaust. 1941 became the point of no return—for those who had not left Germany by the middle of 1941, escaping from Nazi Germany would be all but impossible.

The next three sections of this chapter are divided among the families of Joseph, Maier, and Lazarus. Of the six children of Jakob Heppenheimer, these three stayed in Germany to raise families. These three sent sons to fight and die in the first world war, and those sons who returned from the war continued to operate and expand the successful scrap metal businesses that also help to grow the German economy. By the start of World War II, Joseph, Maier, and Lazarus were long dead, but their hopes and dreams had lived on in their families, some of whom were still in Germany when World War II began.

PART I:
Joseph Heppenheimer's Family

Joseph had five children with his first wife Mina—Bertha, Johanna, Jacob, Benny and Max —and two daughters with his second wife Emma—Alice and Selma. In terms of Joseph's first family, Bertha's daughter Erna emigrated to America in 1932 and Bertha emigrated in 1939.[706] Jacob's son Ernest emigrated to America in 1934, his daughter Melanie and her husband Paul emigrated to Israel in the mid-1930s, and Jacob and his wife emigrated to America in 1938. Max had died in 1935, but his son Kurt emigrated in 1937 and Max's wife Recha and son Alfred emigrated in 1939.

But other members of Joseph's family were still in harm's way in 1941. Johanna and her husband Isidor Wolfsheimer (who had worked for many years for Gebruder Heppenheimer) were still in Frankfurt. Benny and his family were also still in Frankfurt, as were Joseph's second wife Emma and the daughters from that second marriage, Alice and Selma.

Johanna Wolfsheimer and her Family

By 1938, Johanna Wolfsheimer, her husband Isidor, daughter Martha and son-in-law Franz Neumeier had decided to leave Germany.[707] Sometime in 1938, Isidor and Johanna applied for a visa for entry into the United States, but their high number suggested that they would not gain entry until 1942. Still, they began to take the necessary steps to leave Germany. The Neumeiers had passports, but Isidor and Johanna did not yet have their passports. In order to obtain a passport, Johanna and Isidor needed a tax clearance certificate, and the tax clearance certificate would be issued only after the Reich Flight Tax and other required and overdue taxes had been paid.[708]

While Johanna and Isidor worked to obtain their tax clearance certificate, Martha and Franz decided to emigrate to Switzerland, at least temporarily. Franz had been a chemist and co-owner of a successful pharmaceutical manufacturing company, Fabrik Pharmazeutischer Präparate S. Neumeier. The company manufactured such items as throat lozenges and asthma powder. Franz and his business partner were forced to sell their company on February 28, 1938 to Curta & Co. GmbH, a subsidiary of I.G. Farben Industries. As part of the deal, Franz was prohibited from using the name "Neumeier" in any new business and could not find work as a chemist. Hoping things would be better for them in Switzerland, the Neumeiers left for Switzerland in September 1938.

In order to cross the border, the Neumeiers needed to pay a sum of money to the Swiss government called a "bail."[709] They then would receive a temporary residence permit. Their emigration was not intended to be permanent, nor could it be. In the early 1930s, the Swiss government had enacted legislation that made permanent asylum nearly impossible; the stay could only be temporary and was for the sole purpose of arranging for emigration to a third country.[710] And fearing a tide of refugees following Germany's annexation of Austria in March 1938, the Swiss government took the additional step on August 19, 1938 of closing its border to Jews who did not have visas.[711] The visas the Neumeiers held were only temporary Swiss residence visas, which required that the holder have in possession a visa for onward migration.[712] The Neumeiers did not have U.S. visas, and so they must have had visas for emigration to another country. Franz could not move money out of his German bank, since the proceeds from the sale of his business were placed in a blocked account, and he and his wife crossed the Swiss border with just 20 RM. Still, he likely had a Swiss bank account since he had enough money to pay the Swiss "bail."[713]

While the Neumeiers could not move money out of Germany following their emigration to Switzerland, Franz was still able to continue to provide financial support to his in-laws from his German bank account as his in-laws waited to obtain their tax clearance certificate. In late 1938, Franz was able to transfer to his in-laws 15,000 Reichmarks for their subsistence.[714]

The Wolfsheimers received their tax clearance certificate on November 21, 1940, and so were able to obtain their passports to leave Germany. However, at this late date, Lisbon was the only neutral and reliable transatlantic harbor left in Western Europe, and so the Wolfsheimers needed to get to Portugal.[715] The problem for the Wolfsheimers was that, in reaction to an influx of Jews escaping Germany, Portugal issued a directive on October 28, 1938 that Jewish emigrants needed a visa to enter Portugal.[716] Moreover, in order to obtain the Portuguese transit visa, the Wolfsheimers needed an exit visa from Germany, an entry visa into the French "free zone," a Spanish transit visa, and an entry visa for a destination country.[717]

The Wolfsheimers had hoped to obtain passage on a ship from Lisbon to New York. But fearing the long wait for the U.S. entry visa, the Wolfsheimers instead obtained an entry visa to Haiti, and then used that entry visa to obtain their transit visas to Spain and Portugal. For those unable to obtain the coveted American entry visa, like the Wolfsheimers, it was relatively easy to obtain a visa to a Caribbean country like Haiti, and then try to obtain the American entry visa once they reached Lisbon.[718] And getting to Lisbon was critical, since it was only from there that the Wolfsheimers would be able to sail to America.[719] The Wolfsheimers had the Haiti entry visa and the transit visas to Spain and Portugal in hand by February 1941.

The Wolfsheimers had hoped to take the special train for Jews traveling to Lisbon. The Reichsvereinigung in Berlin worked with an official German travel agency to send Jews with proper documentation by train out of Germany, with the Joint Distribution Committee ("JDC") subsidizing the cost of the trains.[720] As many as 15,000 Jews in 1940 and 6,000 Jews in 1941 took these trains out of Germany and to Lisbon.[721] These trains were referred to as "sealed trains," since the Germans sealed the doors once all the Jews were on board.[722] While they were anything but luxurious, Jews were desperate to board these trains, since they facilitated transportation through the numerous check-points to Portugal.[723]

While the Wolfsheimers had transit visas to Spain and Portugal and an entry visa to Haiti, there was a catch to gaining passage on a sealed train: the JDC required a valid entry visa into the United States. Because they lacked a US visa, the JDC would not provide train passage to the Wolfsheimers. Mindful that their transit visas through Spain and to Portugal were about to expire, the Wolfsheimers' son-in-law arranged for a flight from Germany to Lisbon, paid for by a money wire from a Swiss bank account. Unlike many Jews still living in Germany, the Wolfsheimers had the good fortune to have a son-in-law who had the means to wire money for plane tickets (or who had friends willing to loan the money for the tickets). At the end of February

1941, with just two suitcases and 10 RM each, the Wolfsheimers boarded their plane and flew to Lisbon.

The Neumeiers also intended to emigrate to America. They knew they could not remain in Switzerland, but may have waited to leave until the Wolfsheimers were able to escape from Germany. In January 1941, the Neumeiers obtained Spanish and Portuguese visas. Since the Neumeiers did not have US visas and legal transit through Spain and Portugal was restricted to holders of visas for states outside Europe,[724] they may have obtained Haitian visas like the Wolfsheimers. The Neumeiers left Switzerland for Portugal in February 1941, traveling on a special train for Jews leaving Switzerland that was locked and guarded by Swiss police. It took them four days to travel through France and Spain, and the Neumeiers arrived in Portugal around the same time as the Wolfsheimers.

For refugees like the Wolfsheimers and the Neumeiers, the first thing they needed to do once they arrived in Lisbon was to find a place to live. They then began the task of obtaining their American entry visas, as well as securing any necessary extensions of their Portuguese visas.[725] Like many others who had Caribbean visas, the Wolfsheimers and the Neumeiers had no intention of going to Haiti.[726]

For German Jews in Lisbon, their days were spent waiting on long lines trying to secure their visas, and once the visas were secured, waiting on long lines to secure passage to America.[727] The procedure was a "nightmare of securing 57 varieties of visas—exit, entrance, transit, expirations, renewals, revalidations," requiring applicants to wade through a sea of red tape.[728] The Wolfsheimers and the Neumeiers likely frequented the cafes that now catered to German Jewish refugees, and the cafes sometimes served as places where one could secure ship's passage.[729]

The Wolfsheimers and the Neumeiers were finally issued entry visas to America on May 23, 1941. When the Wolfsheimers arrived in Lisbon, they were destitute, but the Neumeiers had money, and it is likely that such resources enabled the four to pay for their lodging and food in Lisbon, secure their visas, and pay for their passages to America.[730] The four obtained passage on the S.S. Nyassa, which set sail for America on June 3, 1941, and they had $2,200 with them when they arrived in America. It took nearly four months in Lisbon to secure entry visas into the U.S. and passage on a ship. The Wolfsheimers and the Neumeiers arrived safely in America on June 13, 1941.

Benny and Margot Heppenheimer

Benny watched as Heppenheimer family members left Germany, including his brother and business partner Jacob. But Benny's wife Margot had been reluctant for the family to leave Germany, believing that, in a land that produced Goethe, Shiller, Mozart and Beethoven, the Nazis could not remain in power. However, Kristallnacht changed her thinking, after which Benny and his wife Margot immediately applied for their U.S. visas.[731]

While the family waited for approval of their visa requests, Benny and his son Herb worked to support the family, with Herb (and perhaps Benny) working as forced laborers. On December 20, 1938, the Reich Unemployment Agency instructed regional labor exchanges to put Jews to work, to free up Germans for rearmament production.[732] With Jews now excluded from most jobs, they were forced to perform manual labor, such as excavation.[733] Following the sale of Gebruder Heppenheimer, Benny began to work for a dry cleaning establishment, which may have been a forced labor position. Herb had been forced to leave the Gymnasium in 1937 at the age of 15 and was apprenticing for a Jewish company.[734] But in 1939, Herb was sent to a farm outside of Berlin to pick potatoes, a forced labor position. Benny was able to secure a job for Herb over the winter at the dry cleaners, but Herb was assigned in April 1940 to a brick factory, another forced labor job. Since the brick factory work was seasonal, Herb returned to work in the dry cleaners in the fall of 1940.

Approximately six months after Kristallnacht, Benny's family was forced to move to another, smaller apartment. Their landlord had been fearful of inviting trouble by allowing Jews to remain in his building, and so told the family to leave. They moved to Telemannstrasse 18, an apartment still in the Westend. At the time, many Jews were required to leave their apartments and move to "Judenhauser" or Jewish Houses in the less fashionable parts of the city to free up Jewish apartments for Germans. [735] Benny's family was fortunate not to be forced to move to a Jewish House.

Benny was notified in 1940 that the family was eligible for their U.S. visas, but Benny did not have enough money to satisfy the funding requirement for their abroad existence.[736] Benny remained at the dry cleaners and Herb returned once more to the brick factory. Benny soon had enough money to satisfy the funding requirement, and the family went to the American Consulate in Stuttgart in May of 1941 to obtain their US visas.

Upon arriving in Stuttgart, the family was given the required medical exam. To her surprise, Margo was told that there was a spot on her lung x-ray and her visa application was rejected. Suspecting that the x-ray results were wrong, Margot immediately returned to Frankfurt and had herself x-rayed. The results were fine, but in the interim, all the American Consulates had been closed by the German government.[737] Margot thus could not obtain her visa. Knowing that there was no chance for Margot to secure a U.S. visa quickly, Benny and Margot made the difficult decision that Benny would take the boys to America without Margot.[738]

In preparation for their emigration to America, Benny and his family had loaded two or three steamer trunks with household goods and rugs, and those may have been sent ahead of time.[739] Unlike his cousins the Wolfsheimers, Benny and his sons had U.S. visas, and so were able to book transport with the Joint Distribution Committee on one of the "sealed trains" leaving Berlin. Benny and his sons left Frankfurt on July 27th, arriving in Berlin the next day. In Berlin, they received passport stamps and visas, including the Spanish and Portuguese visas. On July 30th, they were loaded onto a rail car attached behind the baggage car. The car had wooden benches for the approximately 160 Jewish passengers packed into the car and had windows from which to watch as they left Germany. The car had a single bathroom. After they were loaded into the car, the doors were locked. They crossed the German border into France, and travelled through both Vichy and occupied France. The doors remained locked until they arrived in Spain. At no point during their train trip did they consider themselves safe, since anything could happen along the way. When they finally arrived in Spain, they could breathe a sigh of relief. But it was bittersweet for Benny, since he had left his wife behind and he did not know when he would see her again.

Upon their arrival in San Sebastian, Spain, they were met by the Joint Distribution Committee, and remained in this city for several days. The JDC arranged for a hotel in Spain and for passage to Portugal by train. At the border between Spain and Portugal, the JDC arranged for a feast, and Benny and his sons were able to enjoy white bread for the first time in years, because of rations in Germany.

By the time Benny and his sons reached Lisbon, only a few passenger ships were still in service, and there were limited opportunities for the many refugees seeking passage to America. Up to this point, Benny only had a letter from the steamship line that the family could travel to New York on a particular ship, but did not actually have the tickets. Benny's father-in-law had some connections in the black market (since he was a wholesale wine merchant) and worked to secure passage for his son-in-law and grandsons. After waiting five weeks in Lisbon, the family was able to obtain their steamship tickets at a cost of $750 per person, and they left Lisbon for America on August 19, 1941.

After Benny and his sons left Germany, Margot was able to secure a Cuban visa, and when the family arrived in America, they worked to obtain ship's passage for Margot to Cuba.[740] But time was running out for Margot. On October 4, 1941, an order had been signed to deport 20,000 Jews from cities of the Reich to Lodz, a Polish city that had been annexed by Germany following the invasion of Poland.[741] The Gestapo requested a list of Jewish residents from the Reichsvereinigung.[742] But the Gestapo was also working to keep the upcoming transports a secret, so that on October 17, the Gestapo ordered the board of the Frankfurt Jewish community to deny rumors of transports in that week's Sabbath prayer services.[743]

The first deportation in Frankfurt was carried out by the Gestapo on October 19, 1941, with the assistance of the police and some seven hundred party members (SA[744], SS, and political leaders of the Nazi Party).[745] Between 6 am and 7 am, the Gestapo and their assistants showed up unannounced at the homes of 1,100 of Frankfurt's Jews, informing them that they had two hours to vacate their homes.[746] The 1,100 lived in the wealthier Westend neighborhood of Frankfurt, and this neighborhood was chosen since the apartments were coveted by Nazi officials.[747] After Benny left Germany, Margot and her mother had moved (or were forced to move) to Schumanstrasse 24, but the apartment was still in the coveted Westend. When the Gestapo arrived at Margot's apartment, she and her mother were directed to draw up an inventory of assets, which was left behind, and to make a cardboard sign containing personal information.[748] They were each told to bring 100 Reichmarks (50 RM to be paid to the Gestapo at the Frankfurt station and 50 RM to be paid in Lodz), 100 kilograms of clothing, and food.[749] All 1,100 Jews were then escorted by the SA, with the cardboard signs hanging from their necks, to the Grossmarkthalle, Frankfurt's wholesale vegetable market in the Ostend, for processing.[750]

The Gestapo had leased the basement of the Grossmarkthalle to use as an assembly for all deportations from Frankfurt, likely because of the ease of connection to the railway network,[751] as can be seen in the following photograph:

*Source: "Historic Grossmarkthalle," at https://www.ecb.europa.eu/ecb/
premises/intro/description/shared/img/1_3_2_img_002_big.jpg*

At the Grossmarkthalle, Margo and her mother registered at the check-in table, where their luggage and bodies were searched and their food ration cards were taken, and any remaining assets were identified and confiscated by the tax office.[752] They were then led to a table to pay the "travel costs" of 50 RM, checked against an attendance list for a second time, and had their ID card stamped "evacuated."[753] Finally, all 1,100 Jews were taken to an adjacent room to sit on mattresses and straw mats to wait for their deportation.[754] While all this was going on in the basement, business went on as usual in the wholesale market upstairs.[755] The following is a visual of the check-in process, with table 1 the check-in table, table 2 the luggage and body search table, table 3 the tax office, and table 4 the table in which the ID was stamped and the 50 RM was paid:

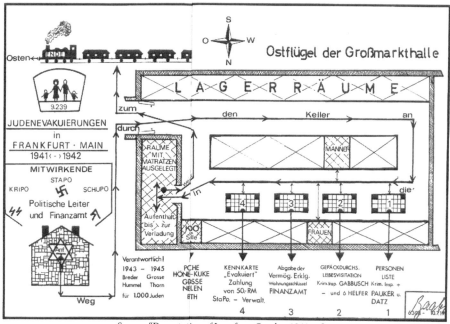

Source: "Deportation of Jews from October 1941 to June
1942," at http://www.frankfurt1933-1945.de.

The transport left Frankfurt that night for the Lodz ghetto, departing in the middle of the night (as was the case for all the transports of Jews leaving Frankfurt), so that no one would see the deportation of the Jews.[756] Many on the train—1,100 Jews in six unheated and cramped wagons—had no idea what their final destination would be, and were particularly concerned once they crossed the Polish border.[757] This was the first transport of Jews out of Frankfurt.[758] Even with the Cuban visa and Benny's efforts, Margo could not escape.[759] Here is Margot's name on the deportation list:

Hepner	Walther I.		31.10.41	
Heppenheimer Margot S. geb.Lebrecht		Schumannstr.24	18.6.99	Ffm.
			13.5.30	Ffm.

Source: http://www.statistik-des-holocaust.de/OT411019-22.jpg.

155

Lodz is located about 75 miles southwest of Warsaw, Poland, and was the second largest Jewish community in prewar Poland, after Warsaw. Before the war, 34 percent of Lodz's 655,000 inhabitants were Jewish and the city was an important center of Jewish culture in Poland.[760] The Germans renamed the city Litzmannstadt, after the German general who had captured the city during World War I.[761] In early February 1940, the Germans established a ghetto in Lodz, forcing the city's 160,000 Jews into an area of four square kilometers, and isolating them from the rest of the city by barbed-wire fencing.[762] Because Lodz had been a major industrial center in pre-war Poland, the Lodz ghetto became a major production center under German occupation, so that by August 1942, there were almost 100 factories within the ghetto.[763]

An overcrowded ghetto awaited Margot and her mother as they arrived in Lodz and were assigned housing. Margot was among the approximately 20,000 Western European Jews that were deported to Lodz in the fall of 1941.[764] These Western Jews arrived in Lodz in their furs, elegant clothes, and fancy footwear, and were disgusted by what they saw when they arrived.[765] The "Westjuden" like Margot and her mother found life in Lodz particularly challenging, since they did not speak Yiddish (the language spoken by the Lodz Jews), were used to living in comfortable quarters, and had difficulty finding jobs in the factories, and so received less food rations.[766] For these new arrivals, a soup kitchen meal soon became a luxury.[767]

Chaim Rumkowski, a Polish Jew, had been appointed by Nazi Germany to lead the Jewish Council of Elders in the Lodz Ghetto.[768] On April 29, 1942, about 15,000 of the Western European Jews received an eviction warrant, notifying them that they would be resettled.[769] Rumkowski actively cooperated with the German officials, and it has been suggested among historians that he played a large role in selecting Western European Jews for this "resettlement," since he found them to be uncooperative.[770] The notice, Proclamation No. 380, provided that those veterans who had been decorated with an iron cross during World War I or those currently employed would be exempt from the resettlement.[771] At the time, only about 3,000 of the approximately 17,000 Western Jews still alive in Lodz were employed.[772] Many submitted requests to the Office for Resettlement seeking an exemption from the resettlement, and approximately 4,500 were ultimately exempted.[773] At the same time, some who had received exemptions volunteered for deportation, believing that it could not be any worse than the conditions in Lodz.[774]

The resettlements began on May 4th, and all of the transports went to Chelmno.[775] It seems likely that Margot Heppenheimer and her mother were on that first transport to Chelmno. There is no record of Margot and her mother being deported from Lodz to Chelmno, and there is no record of their deaths. There is, however, a rations record in the Lodz archives, and the following notation was made for both Margot and her mother for May 4th: "ausw."[776] This notation meant that neither would be receiving rations since they had been deported.[777] Since no rations were available for Margot and her mother as of May 4th, they were likely on the May 4th transport to Chelmno.[778]

Margot and her mother had no way of knowing that Chelmno was the first Nazi camp where gassing was used to exterminate Jews on a large-scale basis, and was the first place outside the Soviet Union where Jews were slaughtered en mass as part of the "final solution."[779] Chelmno was created to serve as the extermination center for the Jews in the Lodz ghetto as well as those from the entire Warthegau region in Poland.[780] A run-down castle in Chelmno had been converted into a base camp, with barracks and a reception area added for the deportees.[781] The first group of victims arrived at Chelmno on December 7, 1941, with exterminations taking place the following day.[782]

On the afternoon of the day before each deportation from Lodz in May 1942, the deportees were escorted to one of several designated buildings, and remained there for the night.[783] They had been told to pack no more than 12.5 kilograms of belongings.[784] They were awakened early, given a loaf of bread, and escorted to the train, where they lined up in groups of ten in front of the compartment doors.[785] They were then instructed to drop all of their luggage and board the train, carrying only their bread.[786] The train was made up of seven passenger cars.[787] The train left at 7 am on the dot, returning to Lodz each night at 8 pm.[788] After the train left, all of the luggage was taken back to the Office for Resettlement in Lodz, where the items were stored in a warehouse.[789] Between May 4th and May 15th, twelve transports left Lodz taking 10,915 Western European Jews to Chelmno.[790] The cost for the transport was paid by the ghetto populations' production income, so that the deportees paid for their own final transport.[791] After the last of the transports left Lodz in May 1942, just 325 Jews from Frankfurt remained in Lodz.[792]

Chelmno was located 47 miles west of Lodz.[793] Since no railroad tracks reached Chelmno directly, the deportees were brought by the train to a station near Chelmno, and then loaded onto trucks that delivered them to the reception area at Chelmno. [794] They were told that they were being sent to a work camp, and thus had to wash up.[795] Groups of 50 were then sent to the building's ground floor, where they were told to undress—men, women, and children together.[796] Next, they were taken to the cellar, where they followed signs "To the Washroom," and were then forced down a ramp into a van.[797] The vans had been specially lined with tin and had airtight double doors to seal the van.[798] A pipe connected the inside of the van to the exhaust.[799] After the van was fully loaded, the driver locked the doors and turned on the motor.[800] After 10 minutes, the gas fumes had suffocated all those inside the van. [801] Margot Heppenheimer died a month shy of her 43rd birthday.

Alice and Alfred Falkenstein

Alice married Alfred Falkenstein, her second husband, in 1936.[802] That same year, Alfred's mother died and he was tasked with selling her home. At the time, Jews selling homes often had to accept far less than the fair market value of the property,[803] and Alfred's task in selling the home was made more difficult because of his arrest and incarceration at Buchenwald following

Kristallnacht. He returned from Buchenwald sick and unemployed, but he was finally able to sell his mother's house on December 20, 1938 for 24,000 RM. Alfred paid off his mother's 15,000 RM mortgage, and was left with his share from the sale of 4500 RM (Alfred's sister received the other 4500 RM).

The German government believed the house should have been sold for 27,000 RM and would not recognize the reduction in price. The German government thus assessed the Kristallnacht tax levy based on the 27,000 RM amount. Alfred challenged the levy, arguing that he did not have the resources to pay it, since he was not working. Alfred explained that he was attempting to obtain a tax clearance certificate, which he and Alice needed in order to obtain passports to leave Germany.[804] Alfred also noted that he and Alice had not worked since the end of 1938 (Alice had been forced to liquidate her business at the end of 1938) and had been selling furniture in order to survive. In July 1939, they were finally able to pay the taxes resulting from the sale of the house. However, in August 1939, the tax office assessed new levies on the Falkensteins of more than 2,000 RM, which included the new Kristallnacht levy.

At the same time that the Falkensteins were struggling to clear their tax obligations, Alfred was struggling with a separate and more frightening issue. On June 27, 1939, Alfred was arrested in Frankfurt and charged with racial defilement in violation of the Blood Protection Law. The Blood Protection Law, part of the Nuremberg Laws of 1935, prohibited marriages and extra-marital sexual intercourse between Jews and non-Jews.[805] According to the prosecutor, Alfred had engaged in a sexual relationship with Betti Herbst in January 1936 in Marktredwitz, a town near Nuremberg. Alfred maintained that he had only spoken with Miss Herbst and had given her a ring after she asked him for it (or perhaps demanded it). The Nazis had used the Blood Protection Law as a weapon of terror against Jews, even in the absence of any evidence of a relationship.[806] This may have been the case for Alfred, since, on October 13, 1939, the Nuremberg prosecutor dropped the charges against

Alfred. Alfred was released from the Frankfurt Detention Center on October 30, having spent five months in jail.[807] Still, the Falkensteins were required to pay the court 155 RM in fees, money the Falkensteins could ill afford to pay, since they were still struggling to pay their tax obligations.

In October 1939, Alfred and Alice received their quota number—11,196—for emigration to America. But their place in the queue would prove irrelevant for the Falkensteins. Following Alfred's release from jail, he and Alice faced an ever-expanding list of taxes and fees. As hard as they tried, the Falkensteins could not clear their ever-growing tax obligations, and thus could not obtain their passports.

Alice and Alfred had lived at Kronberger Strasse 71 in the Westend section of Frankfurt.[808] By January 1941, Alice and Alfred had moved to Oberlindau 108, also in the Westend. Alfred was working as an excavator for a nursery (likely a forced laborer position), earning a weekly salary of 30 Reichsmarks and Alice was receiving monthly support of 20 Reichsmarks from her sister Johanna Wolfsheimer, but they had no other income. [809]

Because of the laws imposed after Kristallnacht, Alice had to liquidate her dressmaking shop and was not employed. On January 20, 1941, Alice sent a letter to the Frankfurt Craft Guild requesting that she be allowed to work as a women's tailor for Jews.[810] The Gestapo had pressured all German municipal police offices to reject any petitions by Jews to practice the professions they had been forced to give up, since the Jews were needed for forced labor.[811] Thus, Alice's request was initially denied by the Frankfurt government in March 1941.[812] Still, the Frankfurt Craft Guild supported Alice's request in a letter dated June 14, 1941.[813] In the letter of support, the Guild noted that Alice had been a dues-paying member of the Dressmaker's Guild between July 17, 1933 and December 31, 1938 and was never the subject of a complaint regarding her work.[814] But in keeping with the directives from the Gestapo, the Frankfurt authorities denied Alice's request in September 1941, noting that she no longer needed to work as a dressmaker since she had already received a forced labor assignment.[815]

The first transport out of Frankfurt on October 19th (the transport that took Margot Heppenheimer and her mother to Lodz) was rather chaotic. The Germans worked to be more organized for subsequent transports, including limiting participation to Gestapo personnel and forty to fifty police criminal investigators, finance office officials, and employees of the Food Agency.[816] For each deportation, the Gestapo ordered the Reichsvereinigung to remove from their card files the names of all those in the area of the persons to be "evacuated," and then the Gestapo created a deportation list from this pool of names.[817] Rather than sending the SA to Jewish apartments unannounced, the Germans sent a deportation notification to those on the list three days before the transport date, which included an asset declaration form.[818] All valuables and precious metals, as well as the keys to the apartment and other important papers, were then turned over to German officials.[819]

On October 24, 1941, an order was issued to deport 50,000 Jews from sixteen cities in the Reich to the vicinity of Kaunas in Lithuania and Minsk.[820] That number included 2,042 Jews from Frankfurt.[821] Those transports from Frankfurt would be taking Jews to the Minsk ghetto on November 11th and to Kaunas on November 22nd.[822] Alice and Alfred were going to Kaunas, and likely received their deportation order, including their asset declaration form, on November 19th. On November 22, 1941, a Gestapo officer arrived at the Falkenstein home and reviewed the asset declaration form with Alfred.[823] Alfred placed all valuables and other assets in an envelope and handed it to the officer; he and Alice were permitted to keep their wedding rings and watches, provided they were not valuable.[824] The officer watched as they packed their suitcases (one each) to ensure that no valuables were placed in the suitcases, and then the suitcases were sealed shut.[825] Alice and Alfred were instructed to take one blanket each.[826] Upon leaving the apartment, the keys were given to the officer and Alice and Alfred each were required to wear a cardboard sign around their neck which contained their names, birthdates, and identification numbers, and were then escorted to the deportation site, the Grossmarkthalle in the Ostend.[827] Here are their names on the deportation list:

Falkenstein Alfred I.   Oberlindau 108   9.12.96 Ffm.
Falkenstein Alice S.   4.7.96 Ffm.
geb. Oppenheimer

Source: http://www.statistik-des-holocaust.de/OT411122-7.jpg

Alice and Alfred were put on a train bound for the ghetto in Kaunas, Lithuania. There were 991 Jews on this train.[828] The city of Kaunas had been under German occupation since June 25, 1941, and all the Jews had been ordered into the ghetto by August 15, 1941.[829] Fortresses had been built around Kaunas during tsarist times to protect the city, including the Ninth Fort.[830] In September and October of 1941, Lithuanian Jews had been taken from the Kaunas ghetto to the Ninth Fort and shot to death.[831] Alice and Alfred were likely unaware of these murders when they boarded their train in Frankfurt.

Alice and Alfred never made it to the Kaunas ghetto, but instead were taken to the Ninth Fort. There, on November 25, 1941, the Germans took everyone off the train. In the sudden realization of what was about to happen to them, a number of Jews fought back.[832] With the Jews standing in the freezing cold, the Einsatzkommandos shot and killed nearly 3,000 people that day, including Alice and Alfred and all those on their train. These Jews were buried in their clothes. The Einsatzkommandos returned to their barracks, many wounded and bleeding from the Jews who had fought back.[833] From November 16, 1941 until the middle of December 1941, approximately 20,000 Jews who were brought from Frankfurt, Berlin, Breslau, Vienna and other places were murdered in the Ninth Fort.[834] Alice was 45 years old and Alfred was 44 years old.

Selma and Lippmann Lewin and Emma Heppenheimer

Selma married Lippmann Lewin on March 14, 1929.[835] Lippmann was born on July 21, 1899 in Rogow.[836] Selma's mother Emma (Joseph Heppenheimer's second wife) moved in with her daughter and son-in-law after their marriage.[837] Lippmann, Selma, and Emma lived on Bohmerstrasse 60 in the wealthier Westend. Lippmann owned a wholesale coffee company, which he opened in 1930 but was forced to close at the end of 1938.

Lippmann and Selma's marriage was not a happy one. According to Selma's sister Alice, there were problems from the beginning, often relating to money, suggesting that Lippmann was not very successful in his wholesale coffee business. Before she married Lippmann, Selma had worked for Gebruder Heppenheimer, although she likely stopped working after her marriage.[838] According to Selma, Lippmann was such a poor provider that Selma was often forced to borrow money from family members to buy clothing. Having been raised in a relatively wealthy household and by a commercially successful father, it may have been hard for Selma to live in a household where money was a problem. And such frustrations may have affected Lippmann, as well, since he would throw household items at Selma. By the late 1930s, Selma and Lippmann were living in the same apartment, but sleeping in separate bedrooms.

In June 1939, Selma's "consultant" sent a letter to Lippmann advising him that Selma was contemplating divorce.[839] German Jews were told that divorced persons would be denied visas, since the divorced couple would be considered guilty of "moral turpitude."[840] Whether this was true or not, it served to encourage unhappy Jewish couples to wait until after emigration to divorce.[841] But it appears that Selma was not trying to emigrate, either because she chose to stay with her mother (who may have decided that she was too old to leave) or because she remained hopeful that things would change for the Jews in Germany. And by 1939, Selma wanted no more of Lippmann. Lippmann failed to respond to Selma's consultant, and Lippmann was informed in a letter dated July 7, 1939 that Selma would be filing for divorce.

Around the time that Selma informed Lippmann about her plans to divorce, Lippmann informed Selma that he intended to emigrate to Palestine, and that he would be going with his siblings and without Selma.[842] While Selma was not interested in emigrating with Lippmann, she was concerned that Lippmann would leave her without any resources once he emigrated to Palestine.

Lippmann's siblings began moving to Frankfurt around this time, likely to make it easier to emigrate with Lippmann.[843] In the fall of 1939, Lippmann sought approval from the customs office to ship items to Trieste, Italy for his passage to Palestine.[844] But Lippmann's requests to the customs office were repeatedly rejected. Frustrated by the denials, Lippmann arranged, in December of 1939, for a customs secretary named Wagner to come to Lippmann's apartment to inspect 6 suitcases and a crate for shipment. Wagner had no authority to inspect Lippmann's suitcases and no authority to approve their shipment to Trieste. Lippmann bribed Wagner with 250 Reichsmarks, and Wagner provided Lippmann with a seal of approval. Wagner did not file a formal statement regarding the luggage, so that no customs fees were assessed. In the luggage were men's and women's jewelry, silverware, household goods, men's and women's clothing, and 5,700 Reichsmarks (worth about $40,000 in today's dollars)—all items that would have been reject had the suitcases been legitimately inspected. And since Lippmann struggled financially, and because multiple watches, expensive jewelry, and ladies clothing were in the suitcases, it seems likely that his siblings had given him their valuables for him to ship to Trieste. This action is not unlike Benny sending the jewelry of his wife and sisters to a relative in Switzerland, to be later taken to America.

With the seal of approval, Lippmann was able to send the luggage to Trieste, Italy, to be held there until Lippmann and his siblings arrived later. Even with permission to enter Palestine, Lippmann and his siblings would still need to satisfy the numerous requirments to receive permission to leave Germany. Lippmann had successfully navigated one of those hurdles, having obtained a passport for emigration. Unfortunately, as Italy prepared to enter the war, it made the decision, in May 1940, to refuse to grant further transit visas to German Jews, to avoid having them stranded in Trieste when war broke out.[845] Lippmann and his siblings were unable to complete the necessary requirements to emigrate from Germany. As it turns out, it would not have mattered, since no refugee ships sailed from Trieste to Palestine after December 1939, the very month Lippmann's suitcases were sent to Trieste.[846] Lippmann's window to emigrate to Palestine had closed.

In April 1940, Selma, Lippmann and Emma were forced to leave their apartment and move into Jewish Houses. Selma and her mother moved into a Judenhaus at Eschersheimer Landstrasse 39 in the Northern section of Frankfurt.[847] Lippmann moved to a Judenhaus at Friedberger Landstrasse 29. Jews living in a Judenhaus were in a constant state of fear, since the Gestapo would do spot checks to search for forbidden food and to make sure that the Star of David was sewn on all clothing.[848] And while the Gestapo was performing their spot checks, they would also destroy furniture, steal money and food, or beat the inhabitants.[849] Lippmann provided Selma with little support following their moves, and Selma was forced to sell furniture to survive.

By the time he moved to the Judenhaus, Lippmann had likely given up his dream to emigrate to Palestine. And he was about to face an even greater challenge, since the German government soon found out about his illegal shipment of valuables to Trieste and Lippmann was arrested on September 2, 1940.

Lippmann was charged with foreign exchange offenses (since he had sent money and goods abroad without permission) and with bribery of a government official. The charging document does not explain how Lippmann was caught, but given that the charging officials were able to identify all of the items contained in Lippmann's luggage, it seems likely that the Trieste officials notified German officials about the existence of the unclaimed luggage, and sent the items back to Germany.[850] At the time of his arrest, Lippmann also had 4 typewriters in his apartment, which he confessed he intended to send to Palestine to sell, and this violation of German law was added to his charges. Lippmann was convicted on June 4, 1941 and sentenced to 2 years and 3 months in prison.[851] A fine of 5,000 Reichsmarks was also imposed, which was collected from the sale of the objects in the luggage sent to Trieste. Lippmann was sent to Prison Diez, a prison used by the Nazis during the war to incarcerate political prisoners before they were sent to concentration camps.[852]

While we know that Selma's sister Alice was still working to emigrate from Germany in 1940, it does not appear that Selma was taking any steps to leave Germany.[853] But Selma was single-minded during this period of chaos about one thing—she wanted her divorce. She continued in her efforts following Lippmann's arrest and subsequent conviction. Selma was finally granted her divorce from Lippmann in August 1941. By this point, Lippmann was in prison and likely indifferent to the change in his marital status, if he even knew. While Selma's efforts to obtain a divorce might seem a bit crazy, it may have been an effort to control at least one aspect of her life when everything else was out of control.

Emma was living with Selma until the spring of 1941. Emma then moved to the Jewish center on Gagernstrasse 36, in the East End of Frankfurt, which included a Jewish hospital and an old age home.[854] Once one of the city's top hospitals, the Jewish hospital on Gagernstrasse was "Aryanized" on April 1, 1939 when the Jewish community was forced to sell the buildings and equipment to the city of Frankfurt for 900,000 RM, although the Jewish community was allowed to remain in the buildings.[855] The hospital on

Gagernstrasse became Frankfurt's last place for Jewish elder care.[856] Emma was 80 years old when she moved to Gagernstrasse 36, so her move may have been to the old age home.

Following the first three deportations of Frankfurt Jews in October and November of 1941 (to Lodz, Minsk, and Kaunas), there was a break in deportations. SS head Himmler had begun preparations for the mass murder of Eastern European Jews in the fall of 1941, which would include the construction of three death camps -- Belzec, Sobibor, and Treblinka.[857] On January 20, 1942, a meeting was held in Wannsee (a suburb of Berlin), chaired by Reinhard Heydrich (chief architect of the "final solution") and with the participation of 15 officials and representatives of the Reich authorities.[858] At this meeting, the Reich Security Main Office coordinated the extermination plans with the relevant ministries and authorities, and plans were made for deportations to the east of German Jews to the extermination camps.[859] Moreover, gassing was chosen as the method of choice for the extermination of Jews deported to the east.[860] In the late spring of 1942, after a break of approximately six months, the deportations resumed and the first mass deportations of Jews from the Reich directly to extermination camps began.[861] In Frankfurt, these deportations were carried out on May 8th, May 24th, and June 11th.[862]

There are no records of Selma's deportation from Frankfurt. After the Frankfurt deportations in 1941, soldiers returning from Poland reported that Jews had been taken off their transports and killed by machine guns.[863] Thus, when the new deportation orders were announced in May 1942, Frankfurt's Jews knew of the fate of the Jews deported to Kaunas, so Selma may have known that her sister Alice and her brother-in-law Alfred had been murdered. Fearing this same fate, 68 Frankfurt Jews committed suicide following the announcement of the new deportations.[864] Selma may have been among them.

Assuming Selma did not commit suicide, she was likely deported on one of the three transports to the east in May and June of 1942. While no lists of names survive for the first two transports and only an incomplete list of names survives for the third transport,[865] a number of factors suggest that Selma was on one of these transports. These three transports targeted Jews who were not married to a Christian partner and were less than 65 years old, or infirmed and less than 55 years old.[866] Further, after the last major deportations in the summer of 1942 (the only other transport from Frankfurt in the summer of 1942 was to Thereisenstadt on August 18, 1942, and the list from the transport does not contain Selma's name), the only remaining Jews were living in the Ostend (the East End) of Frankfurt.[867] Moreover, Lippmann's foreign exchange account information prepared after the war listed Selma as his wife, and noted that she had been "evacuated" (the Nazi euphemism for deported).[868] Since the three transports to Izbica are the only transports from Frankfurt that are missing the passenger names, since Selma does not appear on any of the transport lists, since Selma was living in the North End of Frankfurt and was 42 years old, and since Selma is listed in the Yad Vashem website as having perished in the Holocaust, it seems likely that she was on one of those trains, which were all bound for Izbica, Poland.[869]

Selma would have been notified prior to her transport that she would be leaving Frankfurt, but no one was told the destination.[870] Selma was limited in what she could take—50 Reichmarks to pay for the deportation costs, a suitcase or backpack weighing up to 50 kilograms, and food supplies for two weeks.[871] On the day of her departure, Selma was met by the Gestapo at her apartment, where she turned over her valuables and her keys, and was then escorted to the city's Grossmarkthalle for processing. The train left in the middle of the night, stopping at the Lublin train station in Poland to let off the younger men, who were taken to the Majdanek camp for forced labor.[872] At Lublin, all belongings—even food—were taken from those remaining on the train.[873] The women, children, and elderly men were then taken to Izbica on the trains that left on May 8th and May 24th, with the Sobibor death camp as the likely final destination.[874] For the train that left on June 11th, that train went directly to Sobibor.[875]

For the Jews arriving in Izbica, they arrived with nothing to eat (since their food had already been taken) and saw a ghetto that was extremely overcrowded.[876] The Jews arriving from Frankfurt were housed in a few wooden barracks that could accommodate about half of the prisoners; the remainder were forced to sleep outdoors.[877] The Jews remained in Izbica for no more than four days, with almost nothing to eat, and many succumbed to typhus due to the poor sanitary conditions in the ghetto.[878] While Jews from Izbica were sent to both the Belzec and Sobibor death camps at this time,[879] it is more likely that Selma was deported to Sobibor.[880] At least 10,000 Jews from Germany and Austria died at Sobibor in the months of April, May and June 1942.[881]

The Sobibor death camp was divided into three parts: an administration area, a reception area, and a killing area.[882] The killing area included gas chambers, mass graves, and barracks for prisoners assigned to forced labor.[883] Twenty cars at a time entered the reception area, where the camp guards ordered victims out of the trains and onto the platform. They were told that they had arrived at a transit camp. The deportees were to hand over any valuables and to enter the barracks, where they undressed. The deportees were then led directly into gas chambers (deceptively labeled as showers), the gas chamber doors were sealed, and in an adjacent room guards started an engine which piped carbon monoxide into the gas chambers, killing all those inside. Jewish prisoners then removed the bodies and buried the victims in mass graves.[884] Selma likely died in the gas chamber in Sobibor in May or June 1942. Selma was 42 years old.

On August 18, 1942, a transport left Frankfurt for Theresienstadt, carrying mostly older Jews who were inhabitants of several Jewish retirement homes and residents of the Jewish hospital and retirement home at Gagernstrasse.[885] Emma Heppenheimer, a resident at Gagernstrasse, was on that transport.[886] A total of 1023 Jews were transported that day.[887] Here is Emma's name on the transport list:

285) Heppenheimer   4.8.61   Biebrich   Dr. Gagernstr.36
     geb.Baer   (81)
     Emma S.

Source: http://www.statistik-des-holocaust.de/TT420818-21.jpg

Theresienstadt, located about 35 miles north of Prague in the town of Terezin, was created in 1941 for the more prominent Jews being watched by the rest of the world, as well as to peaceably deport elderly Jews.[888] Theresienstadt was intended to be a "showcase ghetto" designed to delude international organizations, but also later served as a transit camp for the death transports to Auschwitz.[889] It was considered an "old-age ghetto" for German Jews, since 70 percent of those transported to Theresienstadt were over the age of sixty.[890]

When Emma arrived at Bohusovice, the nearest train station to Theresienstadt, she was forced to walk approximately 2 kilometers, carrying all of her belongings.[891] Once she reached Theresienstadt, she was checked in and searched for items not permitted in the camp, such as jewelry or money.[892] She was then assigned housing, which was significantly over-crowded. Food was also a problem—ghetto inhabitants who worked at hard labor received the most food, while the elderly received the least.[893] Even before Emma arrived at Theresienstadt, its residents were suffering from overcrowding, unsanitary conditions, and malnutrition,[894] and these horrors awaited Emma when she arrived in August of 1942.

We do not know whether 80 year-old Emma died in Theresienstadt or was deported to a death camp.[895] In September 1942, the Germans ordered the deportation of elderly Jews to reduce the average age of the population and to re-balance the number who were working.[896] The first transport was announced on September 27th, and the deportees were told that they would be going to another ghetto and needed to pack their belongings.[897]

The second transport, leaving on September 29th, contained the Jews from Hesse-Nassau (Frankfurt is in the German state of Hesse), so Emma may have been on this transport; the average age of the 2,000 inmates on this transport was 72.[898] In total, there were eight transports in September and October, all of which went to Treblinka.[899] Assuming Emma was on the second transport, she arrived in Treblinka on October 1st or 2nd, was taken off the train, and killed almost immediately upon her arrival.[900] In these two months of transports, 17,780 older prisoners were transported from the Theresienstadt ghetto, and by the end of the year, the percentage of ghetto residents aged sixty-five years and older in the Theresienstadt ghetto had fallen from 45 to 33 per cent.[901]

Lippmann was in prison while virtually all of Frankfurt's Jews were deported, including Selma and Emma. During his time in prison, Lippmann remained in contact with his siblings through letters, but had no contact with Selma and never mentioned her in any of the letters. Lippmann's contact with his siblings ended when they were all deported.[902]

On November 18, 1942, Lippmann had completed his sentence and was released from Prison Diez. He was placed on a train just outside the prison, but instead of returning home, he was sent to Preungesheim Prison in Frankfurt. It is not surprising that Lippmann was sent to Preungesheim Prison to await deportation rather than to be released in Frankfurt as a free man. In the year since the transports had begun in Frankfurt, the Jewish population in Frankfurt had fallen from 10,592 to 817.[903] The only Jews still in Frankfurt were the Jews who either had non-Jewish spouses or worked for the Reichsvereinigung.[904]

On December 30, 1942, Lippmann was turned over to the transport department of the police for transfer to Auschwitz.[905] No transports to Auschwitz left Frankfurt in December 1942 or January 1943, but there was a transport that left Berlin on January 12, 1943 and arrived at Auschwitz the next day,[906] and it is possible that Lippmann was on that train.

Approximately 1,100 deportees from that train arrived in Auschwitz; 127 were selected for work, and the remaining deportees were sent directly to the gas chambers.[907]

Auschwitz, the most notorious of all the Nazi concentration and death camps,[908] had originally been an army barracks for the Polish army.[909] The Auschwitz concentration camp, known as Auschwitz I, first opened in the former Polish army barracks in June 1940.[910] Auschwitz II, also known as Birkenau, was built in March 1942, as an extermination camp.[911] Auschwitz II contained the gas chambers and crematoria.[912] Birkenau's function was clear—extermination of Jews.[913] Birkenau also served as a prison labor camp, and could house up to 100,000 inmates.[914] Auschwitz III, also known as Monowitz, was opened in late October 1942, and its main function was the production of synthetic fuel and rubber.[915] By the time Lippmann arrived at Auschwitz, the prisoner population at Auschwitz I, Birkenau, and Monowitz was over 80,000: 18,437 in Auschwitz I, 49,114 in Birkenau, and 13,288 at Monowitz.[916]

Selections began on a railroad unloading platform, which was located between the Auschwitz and Birkenau camps.[917] The SS doctors made most of the decisions about who were qualified for labor, and who were to be killed immediately.[918] Men and women were divided into two columns, and these columns were led to the camp doctors and other camp functionaries conducting selection.[919] For the most part, the people were judged on sight, with about 20 percent of the people in transports chosen for labor.[920] The rest were killed in the gas chambers.[921]

When Lippman arrived at Auschwitz, he was selected for slave labor. His hair was shaved, he was given a striped prison uniform, and he was registered as a prisoner.[922] Lippmann was assigned a number, and the number "3162" was tattooed on his left arm.[923] All newly arrived prisoners were then sent to quarantine.[924] The quarantine block in Birkenau contained an average of

4,000 to 6,000 prisoners.[925] Hundreds were crowded into each of the barracks, and during the day the quarantined prisoners were subjected to brutal work such as ditch-digging or draining swamps, or being forced to stand for long periods of time in the freezing cold.[926] The prisoners could be in quarantine for weeks, and only the strong among the prisoners were transferred to the working camp from quarantine. [927]

Like all prisoners at Auschwitz, Lippmann's day began at 5:30 am, since this was the winter; the day would begin at 4:30 am had this been the summer.[928] He got up to the sound of a gong, attempted to wash at one of the overcrowded latrines, was given watery coffee or tea, and forced to line up in rows at the sound of the second gong.[929] After roll call, those prisoners who had been assigned work outside the camp would walk out in their working groups, accompanied by music performed by the camp orchestra.[930] The noon meal consisted of a watery soup.[931] After a more than 11-hour work day, the prisoners would return to the camp under SS escort, carrying the corpses of those that had died while working.[932] Evening roll call began at 7 pm, followed by an evening meal of brown bread with a small amount of sausage or cheese, and then bed by 9 pm.[933]

The majority of those selected for work at Auschwitz died within a few weeks or months of their arrival at the camp as a result of overwork, mistreatment, disease or lack of food.[934] Lippmann had been in prison before being deported to Auschwitz, and was likely already in compromised health by the time he arrived at the concentration camp. Lippmann died on January 21, 1943, less than a month after he arrived at Auschwitz. Lippmann's death was recorded in the Auschwitz Death Books,[935] which is how we know that he had been selected for the slave labor pool—only slave labor deaths were recorded in the Death Books, which did not record the deaths of the 900,000 Jews murdered in the gas chambers.[936] Lippmann's cause of death was listed as "herzwassersucht," or heart failure.[937] Lippmann was 43 years old.

PART II:
Maier Heppenheimer's Family

Maier had five sons—Jacob, Leopold, Ludwig, Adolph, and Sally—and a daughter, Berta Schwarz. Jacob, his oldest, emigrated to the United States in the nineteenth century and so was safe from the Holocaust. Adolph was killed in World War I and Ludwig died in Worms, Germany in 1921. But as of the start of the war, Leopold, Sally and Berta were still in Germany.

Leopold Heppenheimer

As previously discussed, in June of 1937, Leopold was convicted of copper theft and sentenced to a little more than a year in prison. It is likely that he was released around the time of Kristallnacht. We can assume that, after his release from prison, he immediately began the process of obtaining a visa to emigrate to America.

One of the conditions for emigrating to America was obtaining a good conduct certificate from the local police department verifying that the applicant had no criminal record. For Leopold, having just been released from prison, obtaining such a good conduct certificate would have presented a significant challenge. But around the time of Kristallnacht, some elements of the German government were still focused on getting rid of the remaining Jews in Germany. In fact, based on American consular reports at the time, German police officials were issuing good conduct certificates to some visa applicants who had been convicted of crimes in order to promote the emigration of Jews from Germany.[938]

When Leopold applied for his immigration visa, he included in his application a good conduct certificate from the Mannheim Police Department verifying that Leopold had never been convicted of a crime or offense.[939] Obviously, this was a lie. Leopold was either able to take advantage of this desire to get rid of German Jew, or he may have bribed an official to issue the good conduct certificate. But because of the good conduct certificate, Leopold and his wife Helene obtained their U.S. visas on January 18, 1940. They then arranged for passage on the Italian ship Conte di Savoia and left from Genoa, Italy on February 20, 1940. Leopold and his wife arrived in New York on February 29, 1940.

Leopold repeated this same lie when he completed the Alien Registration form after arriving in America, certifying that he had never been "arrested or indicted for, or convicted of any offense (or offenses)."[940] There is no evidence that the U.S. immigration officials ever knew about Leopold's conviction for copper theft or his prison record. Had this information been known by U.S. officials, it might have prevented Leopold from emigrating to the U.S. Instead, Leopold was able to enjoy life in America as a father and grandfather.[941]

Sally Heppenheimer

Sally Heppenheimer had been living in Worms since the end of the nineteenth century, but as life there became intolerable for Jews (as was the case in many smaller cities and towns), Sally and his wife Bertha moved at the end of 1938 to Mannheim.[942] They moved to Prinz-Wilhelm Strasse 21, just outside the inner city and not far from where Max Heppenheimer and his family had lived. Sally had been forced to sell his scrap metal business, and was likely not employed after he moved to Mannheim, given that he was nearly 60 years old.

On the morning of October 22, 1940, teams of police pounded on the doors of every Jewish home in the southwestern Germans states bordering France, having secretly been compiling the list of names since July of 1940.[943] The authorities in Mannheim rounded up all the Jews in the city, including Sally and his wife Bertha.[944] Sally and Bertha were allowed about an hour to pack and could take no more than 50 kilograms of luggage and 100 Reichsmark in cash.[945] This was nearly a year before the transports began in Frankfurt.[946] Here are their names on the transport list:

3370	Henle, geb. Schneebernum		29. 9. 1883	Pr.-Wilhelm-Str. 21
3371	Heppenheimer, geb. Mayer	Berta Sara	21. 7. 1851	B 7, 3
3372	Heppenheimer	Jette Sara	11. 3. 1880	Pr.-Wilhelm-Str. 21
3373	Heppenheimer	Sally Israel	25. 7. 1864	B 7, 9

Source: http://www.statistik-des-holocaust.de/FR401022-76.jpg.[947]

Approximately 7,500 Jews were taken that day to collection points at railroad stations, and loaded onto seven special trains for the two-day trip to Camp de Gurs, an internment camp for Jews in the south of France .[948] Gurs had been hastily built in 1939 as an internment camp for refugees from the Spanish civil war, but became a camp for German Jewish refugees in October 1940.[949] Conditions at Gurs were terrible, with internees crammed into dark filthy barracks with sealed windows, rats, lice and fleas.[950] During that first winter, hundreds died from malnutrition and exposure, as well as from typhoid and dysentery.[951]

Sally's son Willy, who had already emigrated to America, was working feverishly to get his parents a visa to emigrate. Willy was successful in convincing officials that approval of his parents' visa applications was imminent, and on February 17, 1941, Sally was moved to the Camp des Milles, another internment camp near Marseille, France.[952] Between 1941 and 1942, Camp des Milles was used as a transit camp for Jews waiting for visas and, in fact, was the only transit camp in France from which emigration could be legally arranged.[953] On May 1, 1941, Sally and Bertha received their visas to the United States, and on May 12, 1941, Sally was released from Camp de Milles.[954]

After the fall of France to Germany in June of 1940, Portugal was the only neutral transatlantic harbor left in Western Europe. But an escape route had been established between Marseille and Fort-de-France in Martinique (which was under Vichy control) as a way of getting refugees to America.[955] Sally and Bertha decided to take advantage of this route and obtained passage on the Wyoming, which was scheduled to leave Marseille on May 15th.[956] Sally had just a few days to secure an exit visa from France and a transit visa to the French West Indies.[957] Sally was successful in securing the necessary visas, and he and Bertha left Marseille for Martinique, where they hoped to then find passage to New York.

Another French ship had left Marseille nine days before the Wyoming, and had been intercepted under British orders, since it was believed that French spies were onboard.[958] Fearing seizure of the Wyoming by British officials if it continued on its journey to Martinique, the French authorities ordered that the ship remain in Casablanca when it stopped to refuel.[959] The ship remained at the dock for five days, and the passengers were then removed from the ship and given a choice: they could return to France or they could be interned in a camp.[960] All the passengers chose the camp.[961] The passengers then boarded a train, and travelled approximately 180 miles through the desert to an old Foreign Legion camp, the Oued Zem.[962] The escape route to Martinique was now closed, since French ships were no longer able to cross the Atlantic.[963] Sally and Bertha thus needed to find another way to get to America, this time from Morocco.

The Oued Zem camp was composed of six run-down barracks with tin roofing and concrete floors, which made for very hot accommodations in the desert sun.[964] The men and women lived in separate barracks.[965] Sally and Bertha were fortunate in that they were able to obtain some financial support from their cousin Jacob Heppenheimer, Joseph's son who had successfully emigrated to America. But as was the case in Gurs, the conditions in Oued Zem were horrible, with people dying from malaria, diphtheria and dysentery.[966] In just a few months, the number of Jewish refugees in the camp dropped from 800 to 600 due to disease.[967]

Approximately 1,500 Jews were interned in all of the Moroccan camps during this period, and the JDC was working to get all 1,500 out of Morocco.[968] In July 1941, the JDC took "block bookings" on the Portuguese ship the Nyassa, and made these accommodations available to the Jewish organizations it was cooperating with—400 spaces for passengers leaving from Lisbon and 200 spaces for passengers leaving from Casablanca.[969] Willy was able to secure two of those 200 spots for his parents, paying HIAS $1,175.

Sally and Bertha took the train from the camp to Casablanca, boarded the Nyassa on July 24th, and arrived in New York on August 9, 1941.[970]

Berta Schwarz and the Bauernfreunds

In September 1938, Maier's daughter Berta Schwarz moved from Frankenthal to Frankfurt.[971] Berta's husband Moses died in 1937 and Berta had been forced to sell her husband's scrap metal business and their six-room apartment. Berta had the financial resources to emigrate to America, having just helped her son Walter and his wife to emigrate. Instead, Berta moved in with her daughter and son-in-law, Johanna and Heinrich Bauernfreund, taking to Frankfurt the 100,000 Reichsmarks she received from the sale of her business and the apartment.

It is not clear why Berta chose to remain in Germany rather than emigrate with her son. One reason may be because Berta's daughter and family were having trouble securing the necessary documents to leave Germany, and Berta stayed behind to help them. But Berta also struggled with severe rheumatism and at 68 years old may have been reluctant to start over in a new country.

Johanna and her husband had made the decision to emigrate to America in 1937. Johanna owned J. Bauernfreund & Co., and Heinrich was responsible for the financial aspects of the company.[972] In May of 1937 and again in May of 1938, Heinrich wrote to the German tax office to request a tax clearance certificate in order to obtain the family's passports. The family had not received their tax clearance certificate by the time Heinrich was arrested and incarcerated in Buchenwald as part of the mass arrest of Jewish men after Kristallnacht.

Following Heinrich's released from Buchenwald in December 1938, he and Johanna liquidated their scrap metal business and continued to pursue the needed tax clearance certificate. While the business was still in operation, Heinrich was required to make income tax payments in advance. As Heinrich and Johanna were liquidating the business (which was officially liquidated on June 30, 1939), the Nazi tax office insisted that the company make an advanced tax payment, which Heinrich did in April 1939. The tax office continued to insist on advanced tax payments, even though the business was no longer functioning, and could not function, since all Jewish businesses had been ordered to close.[973]

Heinrich began working in an automobile factory in September 1939 (which was likely a forced labor job), but the tax office continued to insist on payments from the already liquidated business, and started to include a tax surcharge. Johanna was not working, and so could not help to reduce the tax obligations. According to Heinrich, the taxes owed the German government forced the family to move to Freiherr-vom-Stein-Strasse 53.[974]

Heinrich wrote to the tax office repeatedly, requesting that the tax obligations be removed and a tax clearance certificate be issued. But the tax charges and surcharges presented a great challenge for the family to pay, since their monthly income had dwindled following the loss of the business. And Berta, who had arrived in Frankfurt with 100,000 RM in the bank, had less than 3,000 RM left by 1940, likely because she was helping her daughter's family with their tax problems and because of Berta's own tax obligations to the Reich. At some point in 1940, Heinrich had put down a deposit of 300 RM with the Hamburg-America Line for passage for his family to America, hoping that he would be able to resolve his tax issues with the German tax office.

On September 29, 1941, Heinrich sent one last letter to the tax office seeking a tax clearance certificate, still hoping that he would be able to obtain the necessary tax clearances required to obtain the passports to emigrate. The tax clearance certificate was finally granted on October 10, 1941. In October 1941, the family secured visas to emigrate to Cuba.[975]

The family now had the necessary tax clearance certificate and visas to Cuba, but they still needed passports and transit visas to get to Portugal. But all of Heinrich's efforts to secure the tax clearance certificate, along with

Cuban visas for him and his family, came too late. In August 1941, an order had been issued banning emigration for Jewish men and women between the ages of 18 and 45;[976] that order would have applied to Johanna. Moreover, by the time they received the tax clearance certificate, they had just nine days to obtain their passports and transit visas before the German borders were closed to all Jewish emigration, a difficult task in earlier years and virtually impossible by October 1941. Getting the required papers would have normally taken months,[977] and the family only had days.[978]

Even if Heinrich had been successful in securing all the necessary documents to leave Germany in a very short period of time, getting to Cuba would have involved enormous costs. Cuba would have required that each person pay approximately $1,500, so that the refugees would not be a burden on the country.[979] In addition, the family would have needed to pay for transportation to Portugal and then to Cuba. But by October 1941, the family had no money.

Like Margot Heppenheimer, Berta and her family were awakened on the morning of October 19, 1941, and told that they had two hours to vacate their apartment.[980] They were told to draw up an inventory of assets, which was left behind, to pack no more than 100 kilograms in a single suitcase for each of them, and to make cardboard signs containing personal information, which each then wore around their necks as they were escorted to the Grossmarkthalle. They were then processed and forced to wait until the middle of the night, when they were placed on the train to the Lodz ghetto, the first transport of Jews from Frankfurt. Here are their names on the deportation lists:

Schwarz geb. Heppenheimer	Bertha A.	Frhr.v. Steinstr. 53	26.4.73	Eichtersheim
Bauernfreund	Fred I.	Fr.v.Steinstr.53	23.9.27	Ffm.
Bauernfreund	Hans I.	"	21.2.26	Ffm.
Bauernfreund	Heinrich I.	"	16.10.90	Schlüchtern
Bauernfreund	Johanna S.	"	15.6.02	Frankenthal

Source: http://www.statistik-des-holocaust.de/list_ger_hhn_411019.html.

Both Berta and Heinrich died in the Lodz ghetto five months after their arrival - Berta on March 21, 1942 and Heinrich on March 13, 1942. Heinrich's health had been undermined by his experience in Buchenwald, and his compromised health may have led to his early death in the ghetto. The German records state that the place of death for Johanna was Lodz, but does not provide a date of death.[981] Johanna's sons are recorded as having died in the Holocaust, but there is no place or date of death recorded for either son.[982]

We do not know whether Johanna was still alive when the notices of resettlement to the Western Jews were issued on April 29, 1942 (Margot Heppenheimer had received one of these notices). Assuming Johanna was still alive, she may have been one of the 3,000 employed Western Jews in Lodz who was exempt from the resettlement. Her sons may also have been working, which would have allowed the three to remain in Lodz after the May deportations. If Johanna and her sons received an exemption to deportation, they would likely have remained in the ghetto for another two years, working in one of the 93 German businesses in Lodz, since deportations essentially stopped for about two years.[983]

By the spring of 1944, the Nazis had decided to destroy the Lodz ghetto.[984] By then, Lodz was the last remaining ghetto in Poland, with a population of approximately 75,000 Jews.[985] In June and July of 1944 the Germans resumed deportations from Lodz, and about 3,000 Jews were deported to Chelmno and gassed.[986] The remaining Jews were deported to Auschwitz in August 1944.[987] At some point, Johanna died in Lodz. Assuming Fred and Hans had remained alive in Lodz until 1944, they were either deported to Chelmno when the deportations resumed in July 1944 or were deported to Auschwitz in August 1944.

PART III:
Lazarus Heppenheimer's Family

Lazarus had five sons: Jacob, Gustav Arthur (who went by his middle name Arthur), Hugo, Robert, and Berthold. By the late 1930s, two had already died: Hugo had been killed during World War I and Arthur had died on November 20, 1936. Lazarus' son Berthold, his wife Martha, and their two children Fritz and Helga had emigrated to the United States in 1937. Lazarus' other two sons—Jacob and Robert—were living outside of Germany, but were living in lands that would soon become part of the Greater German Reich. And some of Lazarus' grandchildren were still in Germany. The survival of these family members would depend on resourcefulness and a bit of luck. But for some, even resourcefulness and luck would not be enough to survive.

Jacob Heppenheimer

Following his return to Strasbourg in 1924, Jacob became a French citizen and built a very successful scrap metal business.[988] Jacob's only child Gertrude married Joseph Reich on January 1, 1932 and also lived in Strasbourg with her family. In 1939, there were 20,000 Jews in Alsace-Lorraine, and Strasbourg was the largest city of the two provinces.[989]

When World War II began in September 1939, the French government evacuated many of the people living in Alsace-Lorraine, including 14,000 Jews, south to what would later become the Free Zone.[990] Jacob's son-in-law Joseph convinced Jacob that the home would be looted upon their departure, and so the family left with many of their valuables.[991] The family moved to a house on Course Emile-Zola in Villeurbanne, a town just outside of Lyon in the Free Zone. After Germany invaded France in May 1940, another 5,000 Jews escaped Alsace-Lorraine, and the remaining Jews were deported to the Free Zone in July 1940.[992] As a result of the evacuation of the Jews from Alsace and Lorraine, Lyon saw an increase in Jewish population of 19,400.[993]

After Germany's invasion of France, Germany and France signed a ceasefire agreement which divided France into five zones, including the Free Zone.[994] The Free Zone was controlled by the Nazi-collaborative Vichy government (as opposed to the German government, which directly controlled occupied France), and while Jews were subject to anti-Semitic actions in the Free Zone, there were no mass deportations of Jews while the Vichy government controlled the region.[995] The only deportations that occurred in the Free Zone in the early years of the war were focused on foreign (non-French) Jews.[996] When German forces took control of the Free Zone in November 1942, deportation began to slowly increase.[997] Deportations intensified in the spring of 1944, and included both foreign and French Jews, so that many Jews fled the region or went underground.[998]

The Heppenheimer family found it necessary to leave their house in Villeurbanne in 1944 following the increases in deportations that now included French Jews like the Heppenheimers. Jacob was suffering from diabetes at the time, and so he and his wife went into hiding close to their home, first in a doctor's clinic in Lyon and then in the countryside near Lyon, in Saint-Romain-au-Mont-d'Or. Jacob's daughter and her family, however, decided to escape to Switzerland. Throughout the war, Switzerland had turned away Jews attempting to flee from France, but that policy changed in the spring of 1944, and by July 1944, Jews were admitted without restriction.[999] Gertrude, pregnant at the time, was able to cross into Switzerland with her family on May 30, 1944. [1000]

Lyon was liberated by U.S. and French troops on September 3, 1944,[1001] and the Heppenheimer family was able to return to the house in Villeurbanne by mid-1945. The war, however, had been hard on Jacob's health. His diabetes had worsened, and he was almost blind by the end of the war. Jacob lived long enough to be reunited with his family, but died in 1945 of diabetes at the age of 64 or 65. Jacob had survived the German occupation of France, but not the effects of that occupation.

While Jacob's family struggled throughout the war and were ultimately forced to flee their home in the middle of 1944, they all survived the war. Jacob and his family had two things going for them at the start of the war that helped their survival. First, the Jews from Alsace-Lorraine fared better than French Jews as a whole. Approximately 25 percent of all Jews living in France were deported, while just 15 percent of the Jews from Alsace-Lorraine were deported (likely because they had been expelled to the Free Zone in 1940, rather than to occupied France).[1002] And French Jews (those with citizenship) fared better still—the survival rate for French Jews as a whole was between 87 and 88 percent.[1003]

Arthur's Widow Jettchen (Henny) Heppenheimer and their Daughter Bettina

Lazarus' son Arthur was married to Jettchen (Henny) and they had a daughter Bettina, who was born in 1911.[1004] Bettina married Hans Schnitzler on May 11, 1933.[1005] The young couple moved into Bettina's parent's apartment after their marriage. Hans was not Jewish, but the marriage was permissible at the time since the Nuremberg Laws of 1935, which made it illegal for a Jew to marry a non-Jew, had not yet been enacted.

Arthur died on November 20, 1936 at the age of 51, and the following year Henny, Bettina, and Hans moved to Munich.[1006] Henny had been working for Arthur's scrap metal company since 1932 (perhaps because Arthur was already ill), and continued to trade metals until forced to sell the company on September 30, 1937.[1007] It seems strange that Henny, her daughter and her son-in-law would move to Munich, given that it was considered the "capital of the Nazi movement."[1008] Hans became a businessman in Munich. On February 23, 1938, Bettina gave birth to a son, Gregor.

It does not appear that either Henny or Bettina were trying to emigrate to America. Instead, they settled into their life in Munich, moving into a house they shared with another family at Grunwalder Strasse 238. But

Henny's fate began to diverge from her daughter's in 1940 because Bettina was married to a non-Jew. On June 1, 1940, Henny was forced to move into a Jewish House at Herzogstrasse 65.[1009] And then, the following year, Henny was deported.

On November 7, 1941, Henny was informed by the Jewish Community in Munich that she would be on the first transport to Riga in Lithuania.[1010] Henny and the other deportees were brought to the Milbertshofen barracks camp, just north of Munich, where they slept on straw awaiting deportation.[1011] At 4:00 am on November 20, 1941, Henny and approximately 1,000 other Jews from Munich and Augsburg were marched in the pouring rain to the Milbertshofen freight station and put on a train.[1012] Here is her name on the transport list:

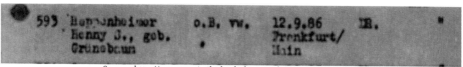

Source: http://www.statistik-des-holocaust.de/OT411120-33.jpg.

While the train was scheduled to go to Riga, it was rerouted to Kaunas, Lithuania.[1013] Upon her arrival, Henny and the rest of the Jews on the train were forced to climb a hill to the Ninth Fort and placed in the fort's cellars.[1014] There they languished for three days.[1015] On November 25, 1941, the prisoners were taken in groups of 50 to a pit in the area of the Fort and shot.[1016] Henny died on the same day and at the same place as Alice and Alfred Falkenstein, Joseph Heppenheimer's daughter and son-in-law.

Henny's daughter Bettina enjoyed "privileged" mixed marriage status,[1017] because she was married to a German non-Jew.[1018] This status prevented Bettina and her son from being deported in the early years of the war, since deportation lists excluded Jews married to non-Jews.[1019] Instead, Bettina became a *"Zwangsarbeit,"* or forced laborer, beginning in 1941. She was working at Firma Brettschneider, a hat factory, earning 75 Reichmarks a week.[1020] Bettina was fortunate in that she was able to continue living in her apartment in Munich, rather than in a forced labor camp.[1021] Still, Bettina was likely subjected to harassment at work, since her identity card, which contained a prominent "J" for Jew, meant that all her co-workers knew that she was Jewish. Bettina continued to work as a forced laborer for Firma Brettschneider until 1944.[1022]

During this time period, Bettina's husband Hans was still living at home with the family. German men up to the age of 45 were subject to the draft,[1023] but Hans, who was born in 1906, somehow avoided the draft and continued to work as a businessman. But Germany began to suffer heavy losses in Russia beginning in 1943, so that by 1944, Germany began drafting all males, regardless of health issues, up to the age of 60. Whatever Han's issues were that prevented him from serving earlier in the war no longer prevented him from being drafted into the Wehrmacht in 1944.[1024]

While Bettina and her son were protected from deportation, they were not protected from the bombs that destroyed much of Munich. Between 1942 and 1945, Munich was hit by 74 flight attacks, and about 50 percent of Munich was destroyed, including about 90 percent of the downtown area.[1025] We know that Bettina's apartment building was not hit, since she was able to remain in the apartment through the war.

While intermarried couples and their children were protected from deportations in the early years of the war, as the war continued, Nazi tolerance of mixed marriages waned. Beginning in 1943, Jews whose mixed marriages ended through divorce or the death of the non-Jewish spouse were deported.[1026] In parts of Germany, beginning in 1944, intermarried Jews were deported to concentration camps or ghettos.[1027] Finally, in February 1945, even as it was clear that Germany was losing the war, the Reich Security Main Office lifted its protection for intermarried Jews and ordered all remaining Jews deported.[1028]

Jewish spouses in Munich were ordered to be deported to Thereisenstadt in February 1945, but some ignored the deportation orders and fled their apartments.[1029] 160 Munich Jews managed to avoid this final deportation; all had been in mixed marriages.[1030] Bettina and her son were among those that avoided the deportation, likely fleeing their apartment when Bettina became aware of the February 1945 deportation order. On April 1, 1945, U.S. troops liberated Munich,[1031] and Bettina and her son returned to their apartment.[1032] A total of 4,500 Jews had been deported from Munich during the war, with just 300 returning from Thereisenstadt after it had been liberated by the Soviet army to join the 160 still living in Munich.[1033]

Bettina decided in 1946 to emigrate to America with her son Gregor.[1034] On December 2,1949, Bettina applied to the International Refugee Organization for financial support. In her application, she noted that her husband was missing from the war, although she listed herself as a widow. On November 5, 1951, Bettina and her son filed a Resettlement Registration Form to emigrate to America. By the time she filed the form, Bettina had located and divorced her husband. On September 30, 1952, Bettina and her son (now 14 years old) sailed to New York on the Groota Beer.[1035] Her passage was paid by her cousin Martin Knobloch (who had emigrated to America from Germany in 1939), and she moved to his house in Mount Holly, New Jersey.[1036]

Robert Heppenheimer and his Daughter Gertrud

Robert had returned from Strasbourg and was living in Frankfurt when he was forced to leave Germany in 1935, likely because of his involvement with the Socialist Workers Party of Germany.[1037] Robert moved to Prague, Czechoslovakia, and sought permission to stay.[1038] Robert's application included the following photo:

Source: https://www.holocaust.cz/en/database-of-digitised-documents/
document/421078-heppenheimer-robert-nezpracovano/.

While Robert was in the scrap metal business in Frankfurt, and likely worked for his brother Jacob in the scrap metal business while in Strausbourg, Robert could only find work in Prague selling newspapers in a restaurant.

German refugees like Robert had been arriving in Prague since 1933.[1039] For Jews seeking a safe haven from Germany, Prague seemed a sensible choice. German was widely spoken among many members of the Prague Jewish community and Jews remained a part of Czech society through the 1930s.[1040] However, in January 1939, the Prague government ordered the expulsion of Jews who had immigrated since 1914.[1041] Robert was not expelled, although we do not know how he was able to remain in Prague, since he was a recent immigrant.

On March 15, 1939, Germany invaded and occupied the Czech provinces of Bohemia and Moravia, including the city of Prague, creating the Protectorate of Bohemia and Moravia.[1042] According to Adolf Simon, a childhood friend of Robert's from Frankfurt, the night before the German invasion of Bohemia and Moravia, about 1,500 Jewish Zionists left Prague by train in an attempt to escape the Nazis. Simon believed that Robert was among those on the train. The Jewish community had been told that this train would represent an easy way to escape Czechoslovakia, and were also told that they would receive help along the way. While it was not entirely clear where they would ultimately end up, the promise of escaping Czechoslovakia ahead of a German invasion caused the 1,500 Jews to board that night.

Unfortunately, the train was stopped by the Gestapo on the Czech/Austrian border.[1043] All the Jews on the train were forced off the train and inspections were carried out by a large number of uniformed officers. Some on the train were immediately arrested and jailed, and the remainder were taken back to Prague. Assuming Robert had been on this train, he would have been among the Jews sent back to Prague, since he continued to submit requests to remain in Prague in 1940 and 1941.[1044]

Following the German invasion of Bohemia and Moravia, Robert's life changed very quickly. The Nazis had instituted restrictions on Jews in Germany over a period of years. The new restrictions on Czech Jews were instituted over a much shorter period. On June 21, 1939, a decree was issued to apply the race criteria of the Nuremberg Laws to define Jewishness.[1045] On that same day, Jews were excluded from economic life and were forced to register their assets.[1046] In August 1939, Jews were segregated in Prague restaurants and prohibited from using public baths and swimming pools.[1047] A curfew of 8 pm was imposed on Jews beginning in September 1939.[1048] In January 1941, Jews were forced from their nicer apartments and directed to live in old tenements.[1049] On September 1, 1941, Jews were directed to wear the Yellow Star of David.[1050]

At the same time that the Nazis were imposing limitations on Jewish life, the Nazis were also supporting Jewish emigration while simultaneously erecting greater barriers to emigration.[1051] Robert sought permission to emigrate and submitted a form to the police on May 22, 1940 for purposes of emigration.[1052] But with no money, the challenges to emigrate were likely too much for Robert to overcome.

The October 4, 1941 order for the deportation of Jews from the cities of the Reich and the Protectorate to Lodz (which began the deportations of Jews in Frankfurt) included an order to deport the first 5,000 Jews from Prague, out of a total Jewish population of 40,000.[1053] These Jews were deported to Lodz, beginning on October 16, 1941.[1054] Robert was deported on the first of these transports.[1055] He was on Transport A, No. 675.[1056] Upon his arrival, Robert received his housing assignment—Muhl Gasse 13, Flat 42.[1057]

While we can only guess that Margot Heppenheimer and the Bauernfreunds received notices of resettlement in Lodz, we know that Robert was issued the notice on April 29, 1942 and that he was scheduled to be on the May 12, 1942 transport to Chelmno. We know this because Robert was quarantined in the infirmary at the time and found out that the notice had been delivered to his home. A letter written by nine people in the Lodz infirmary, including Robert, to the Lodz Office of Resettlement requested that they receive a deportation exemption, since they had not received their notice (since it had been delivered to their home addresses) and "are dying, sick, and also very lice-infested and not at all able to be transported."[1058] They were also asking for their food rations, which they had tried to collect on May 13th and which had been halted since the nine had been on the deportation list for May 12th.[1059] While 4,500 Jews had their resettlement notices rescinded after applications had been submitted for exemption, there is no confirmation that Robert had actually received an exemption. Still, because the last transport to leave Lodz for Chelmno left on May 15th, and because the records note that only one of the patients in the infirmary had been deported on the last train to Chelmo, Robert likely avoided the transports to Chelmno that left in May.

Deportations from Lodz occurred in September of 1942, when more than 15,000 sick, elderly or crippled Jews and children under the age of 10 were deported to Chelmno.[1060] After this transport, the deportations stopped until May 1944.[1061] Given that Robert was already sick in April 1942, he may have died of that illness, although there is no death certificate for Robert in the archives.[1062] He may have been transported to Chelmno in that September transport of the sick if he had not recovered from his illness.[1063] If he had recovered from his illness, he may have remained in Lodz until the deportations began again in 1944, at which point he would have been deported to Chelmno or Auschwitz. All we know is that Robert died in the Holocaust.

Robert had a daughter Gertrud, who was born out of wedlock on November 3, 1920. Robert then married her mother, Margarete Auelmann, who was not Jewish, on October 6, 1921. Robert and Margarete lived together in the Altstadt district of Frankfurt until 1927, at which point Robert and Margarete divorced and Margarete moved to the Westend. Margarete then married a non-Jew. Although she had a Jewish father, Gertrud was raised as a Protestant.

When the Nuremberg Laws were passed in 1935, Gertrud was just 15 years old and her life was likely turned upside down. The Nuremberg Laws defined a "full Jew" as having three or four grandparents and a "half-Jew" as having two grandparents.[1064] While Gerturd was raised as a Protestant, she was now a half-Jew under the Nuremberg Laws. And half-Jews were treated like "full Jews" in almost every respect; for example, "half-Jews" could only marry other Jews or half-Jews.[1065] Half-Jews also were given an official designation: Mischlinge of the 1st degree.[1066]

Gertrud had remained in contact with Robert after her parents' divorce. She last saw him in February 1937, and continued to have written contact with Robert until February 1939. Thus, Gertrud knew that her father was Jewish and that her birth name was Heppenheimer. But rather than be classified as half-Jewish, Gertrud (likely with help from her mother) made the decision to pass as an Aryan.

The first act Gertrud took to pass as an Aryan probably came when she obtained a passport to visit her father in Prague in 1937, since Robert could not travel to Germany.[1067] Rather than use her birth name on her passport, which would have revealed her Jewish background (since it tied her to her

Jewish father), Gertrud used her mother's maiden name (Auelmann) as her last name.[1068] In order to obtain this passport, Gertrud needed a forged birth certificate, since she could not use her own birth certificate. As it turns out, that act of deception kept her safe throughout the war.

Gertrud continued the pretense that she was an Aryan when she married Franz Fokuhl, a non-Jew, in September 1940, and identified herself as Protestant.[1069] And Gertrud continued to pose as a non-Jew in 1941 when she gave birth to a baby boy who died the following day.[1070] Gertrud's mother filled out the death certificate and used Gertrud's passport for identification, which identified Gertrud as "Gertrud Adelheid Fokuhl, born Auelmann."[1071]

By using the surname "Auelmann" for both her marriage license and her passport, Gertrude was able to avoid detection as a half-Jew. She would have been required to explain the absence of her father's birth certificate when applying for both the passport and the marriage certificate.[1072] Because Gertrud was born out of wedlock, she might have been able to claim that her mother did not know who the father was. And if she had a baptismal certificate that included the last name of "Heppenheimer," she would have needed to obtain a forged certificate for the baptismal certificate, as well. Jews were able to obtain both forged birth certificates and forged baptismal certificates during this period.[1073] Gertrud's efforts were clearly a success, since she was able to marry as a Protestant and her deceptions were never discovered.

Simply living in Frankfurt during the war presented a risk to Gertrud and her daughter, who was born in 1942, since at any moment her true identity could have been discovered. Jews who chose to go underground during the war avoided the neighborhoods in which they were raised, for fear of recognition, and moved to other neighborhoods using false identifies.[1074] These underground Jews also relied on underground groups to provide them with shelter, false identity cards and rationing books.[1075] Gertrud moved with her mother and step-father to Wolfsgangstrasse 98 in the Westend section of Frankfurt in 1939 or 1940. It is likely that none of Gertrud's neighbors knew that her father was Jewish. Gertrud and her husband moved in with Gertrud's parents after their marriage, and remained in this residence throughout the war. And because Gertrud lived with her mother and step-father, and because her husband was a soldier and drawing pay, Gertrud did not have to work and run the risk of being discovered as being half-Jewish by her co-workers. During the war, the Nazis used Jews as "catchers" to discover Jews posing as Aryans,[1076] but Gertrud was able to avoid this potential trap.

During the war, half-Jews found themselves in forced labor camps or deported to Theresienstadt.[1077] Because Gertrud successfully passed as an Aryan, she avoided both. Had her lie been discovered, she likely would have been imprisoned or sent to a concentration camp.[1078] And her mixed marriage status (since she was married to a non-Jew) would have allowed her to avoid deportation only in the early years of the war. That status would not have saved her, since nearly all Jews in mixed marriages in Frankfurt were ultimately deported to Thereisenstadt.[1079]

Deportation would likely have meant death for Gertrud and her daughter, but living in Frankfurt was still not easy for any German. Food rationing had begun in September 1939 for all Germans, but "Aryans" ate relatively well until the middle of 1943, when Frankfurt became the target of air raids for the first time.[1080] The air raids of March 18 and 22, 1944 were the heaviest attacks on the city, transforming large parts of the city into a smoking rubble.[1081] The air raids claimed more than four thousand lives, and by the fall of 1944, only 70,000 of the existing 160,000 apartments in Frankfurt were habitable.[1082] The city also suffered from fuel and food shortages in the last two years of the war, in addition to the housing shortages.[1083] Fortunately for Gertrud, she was able to remain in her apartment throughout the war, but she likely struggled for food and fuel during the last years of the war, as did most Germans living in Frankfurt.

At the end of the war, a list of 160 Jews and half-Jews living in Frankfurt was published in the Aufbau, a German language newspaper in the U.S.[1084]

Gertrud was not among the list of survivors, likely because she had never registered with the Frankfurt authorities. Approximately 600 Jews returned to Frankfurt when the war ended.[1085] About half of those who returned had been married to Aryan spouses and the other half were those classified as Jewish because of the Nuremberg racial laws.[1086] In total, it is estimated that 3,000 Germans Jews survived the Holocaust by living underground, passing as Aryans or being married to gentiles.[1087] But we may never know the true number, since there were likely people like Gertrud who had passed as non-Jews during the war and never alerted the German authorities.

Gertrud was among the lucky few who were deemed to be Jews by the Nuremberg Laws and who managed to avoid deportation and death. By successfully living as a non-Jew throughout the war, Robert Heppenheimer's only child survived.[1088]

Hugo's Widow Pessa Zejdel and Hugo's Son Gustav Heppenheimer

Lazarus's son Hugo had been killed in World War I, but his widow Pessa and son Gustav (born in 1914) were still in Germany when World War II began. After Hugo's death, Pessa married David Zejdel (also spelled Seidel or Saidel) in 1923 and they had a son Alfred, who was born in 1929. David was a tailor and owned a men's tailor shop in Frankfurt with Pessa—David Seidel u. Frau (David Seidel and Wife).[1089] Notwithstanding the various anti-Jewish laws and actions, David's shop was able to remain open until the end of 1938. Gustav was living with his parents at Bronnerstrasse 24 in the Innenstadt section of Frankfurt and was working in their shop as a tailor.[1090]

By 1938, David and Pessa made the decision to leave Germany. On August 3, 1938, Pessa filed a request for a tax clearance certificate in order to obtain her passport.[1091] David filed his request for a tax clearance certificate on September 21, 1938. At the same time, David was attempting to sell a building he owned at Klostergasse in Frankfurt's Alstadt, intending to use the proceeds to purchase steamship tickets for the family to sail to America.[1092] In the early years of the Third Reich, David had been forced by the city to renovate the building, spending 3,000 RM on improvements. By 1935, the building was valued at 14,300 RM. In 1938, the city of Frankfurt, interested in purchasing the building, discouraged others from purchasing the property and forced David to accept its offer of 6,500 RM. Believing he had no choice, David accepted the city's offer in October of 1938.

As David and Pessa were working to leave Germany, they were mindful of the precariousness of their positions not just as Jews but also as Polish citizens.[1093] Both had residency permits that allowed them to live in Germany. On March 25, 1938, in an attempt to prevent impoverished Polish nationals from returning to Poland, the Polish government had revoked the Polish citizenship of those Polish nationals living in Germany.[1094] On October 26, 1938, the German government revoked the residence permits for Polish Jews living in Germany and ordered their expulsion.[1095] The next day, 17,000 Jews were forcibly deported, among them David Zeydel. Pessa and Alfred left for Poland on October 29th. Because Poland had previously suspended their Polish passports, these refugees were forced to remain at the border.[1096] Poland ultimately allowed some of the Jews at the border to enter Poland, but approximately two thousand Jews from Frankfurt were able to return to their homes in Frankfurt,[1097] including David and Pessa.

Back in Frankfurt, the family knew they needed to leave Germany since they no longer had valid residency permits. David immediately inquired about the status of the money from the sale of his building and was told by the Frankfurt authorities that the money was not in his account because they had not expected him to return from Poland. He was then told that he needed to obtain approval from the local court for the sale before he would receive any of the money. Speaking with an assessor from the court, David was told that the contract price was too low, since the property was valued at 14,300 RM, and that any approval would need to be delayed.

Meanwhile, feeling the pressure to leave, David borrowed the equivalent of $559 from a friend and purchased four steamship tickets for the family at the end of 1938. By early 1939, the court approved the sale of the building. On February 15, 1939, David asked in a letter to the tax office for accelerated consideration of his clearance request since he was being pressured to leave Germany. On June 12, 1939, David was sent a letter from the Frankfurt Chief of Police, directing that he, Pessa and their son Alfred leave Germany by July 10, 1939.

On June 28, 1939, David, Pessa, and their son Alfred received a tax clearance certificate, which allowed them to obtain German passports to leave Germany. Pessa obtained her passport on August 26, 1939.[1098] Presumably, both David and Alfred obtained passports on the same day. Gustav, however, did not obtain a German passport, although we do not know why. Instead, Gustav was issued an identity card on August 1, 1939.[1099]

While the family had intended to emigrate to America, it was becoming more difficult to obtain US visas. But after Kristallnacht, England eased its immigration regulations for Jewish refugees,[1100] and David took advantage of this opportunity, likely just after he obtained his passport at the end of August. David emigrated to England with just 8.50 RM, intending to have the rest of the family soon join him. However, England declared war on Germany on September 3, 1939, likely just days after David arrived in England. The window was now closed for any emigration to England.

Soon after David left Germany, Pessa, Gustav and Alfred were forced to move into a Jewish House, sharing two rooms in an attic. After the move, Gustav was forced to work as a coal worker, earning 35 Reichsmarks a week.[1101] We do not know whether Pessa also had a forced labor job.

While Pessa was likely working hard to try to leave Germany, by October of 1941, the window for any emigration was permanently closed. On November 9th, Pessa received a notice that she and her sons were to report to the Grossmarkthalle on November 12th, where they would be deported to Minsk. This was to be the second deportation of Jews from Frankfurt (the first deportation having occurred on October 19th), and Pessa must have realized that transport to a ghetto would be bad for her and her sons. So she made a decision that she knew would still put her family in jeopardy—she decided that she and her sons would try to escape from Germany. Thus, instead of reporting to the Grossmarkthalle, the family went into hiding with Christian friends, leaving their apartment in the middle of the night.[1102]

The family was now wanted by the Gestapo. Pessa decided to try to escape across the French/German border, likely to live with her brother-in-law Jacob Heppenheimer, who was now living outside of Lyon.[1103] Pessa thought that they would be able to cross the German/French border in the city of Metz, and so all three went to Metz.[1104] But after the family arrived, they realized that they would need to cross one of the bridges over the Moselle River to get into France. The bridges were all too well guarded, and so the family reluctantly returned to Frankfurt.

Still, the Gestapo was looking for Pessa, Gustav, and Alfred and they could not remain in hiding for long. So they decided to try to escape again, this time to Belgium. Gustav was able to borrow a car and drove to Cologne to try to locate a smuggler who could help them cross the border.[1105] Jews had been forced in 1938 to forfeit their drivers licenses,[1106] so the fact that Gustav was driving illegally likely only added to the stress of his journey. Gustav located a smuggler and returned to Frankfurt. The family then left Frankfurt and went to Cologne to attempt their escape.

The family crossed the Belgium/German border near the Belgium town of Malmedy in the middle of the night in early December 1941. During their journey, they were forced to cross a river in their clothes. They remained in those wet clothes in freezing temperatures until they reached Brussels on December 11, 1941.[1107]

Before Germany invaded Belgium on May 10, 1940, many Germans Jews escaped to Belgium.[1108] In fact, after Kristallnacht, Germany became the main source of refugees entering Belgium.[1109] And while the Belgium border policy for Jews was very restrictive, those who managed to cross the border could count on clemency.[1110] At the time, only 6% of the 70,000 Jews living in Belgium had Belgian nationality, and about 12,000 Jewish refugees had come from Germany.[1111] After Germany invaded Belgium, thousands of Jews fled Belgium, many going to France, with the number of Jews in Belgium falling to between 50,000 and 60,000.[1112] Still, after concluding that they could not cross the German/French border, Gustav and his family must have thought they had no better options than to cross into Belgium.

Belgium required all foreigners to register with the Police des Etranger,[1113] so the day after their arrival, the family went to the Foreign Office in Brussels to register. Strangely, both Pessa and Gustav stated in their registration that they had come to Belgium by way of Luxembourg, having been in Luxembourg just three days before crossing the Belgium/Luxembourg border. This seems a rather odd tale, given that Luxembourg was a hostile place for Jews at the time,[1114] and crossing the border into Luxembourg would have required crossing a bridge over a significant river, which would have made sneaking across the border nearly impossible. It may be that, fearing expulsion if they told the Belgian authorities that they had directly crossed into Belgium from Germany, they thought they stood a better chance if they claimed that they had crossed, instead, from Luxembourg.

When Pessa registered with the Brussels authorities on December 12th, she stated that she was living in "Mr. Rohr's" residence on Boulevard de Waterloo,[1115] was stateless,[1116] was a political refugee, and had a German foreign passport issued on August 26, 1939 that was valid until August 1, 1942.[1117] In his registration, Gustav also noted that he was stateless, was a political refugee, and had a German identity card.[1118] Pessa and Gustav's registrations were valid until June 12, 1942, at which point they would need to be renewed.[1119]

In addition to the requirement that they register with the Police, the family was also required to enroll in the Jewish Register,[1120] which they also did on December 12th. Below is a copy of Gustav's registration in the Jewish register:

Source: Jewish Museum Belgium—Brussels

The above register identifies Gustav with the middle name "Israel" and his mother with the middle name "Sara," as had been required by the Nazi authorities.[1121] Pessa registered on behalf of herself and her son Alfred, since children under the age of 15 were required to be included on the parent's form.

On January 13, 1942, Pessa, Gustav and Alfred submitted a notice to the Brussels police that the family had moved from Boulevard de Waterloo to Rue De Docteur Meersman in the Bussels neighborhood of Anderlecht.[1122] This was approximately a month after their arrival in Brussels, so they presumably left Mr. Rohr's residence and found an apartment of their own. At the time, Anderlecht was a Jewish quarter within Brussels.[1123]

Unlike other Jews who hid in Belgium during the war, Gustav, his mother and his brother registered with the municipal authorities, and renewed such registrations when required. Gustav's registration card contains the renewals on the right side:

Source: Directorate General War Victims, Brussels, Belgium.

We do not know if Gustav or Pessa had jobs while living in Brussels, although thousands of Jews worked for the Germans in Belgium in various jobs.[1124] Still, Brussels was a more hospitable place for Jews than Frankfurt. For example, on May 27, 1942, Germany issued an order requiring that all Jews wear yellow Stars of David, and required that they be distributed by the municipalities around Brussels.[1125] The mayors of these municipalities refused to cooperate in the distribution of the yellow badges, and the German authorities in Brussels were required to distribute them themselves.[1126] Many of the city's residents expressed their solidarity with the Jews by wearing similar yellow badges.[1127]

While Belgium was at first a safer country for Pessa and her sons than Germany, that did not last. Deportations of Belgian Jews began in mid-1942, with Jews first being taken to the Dossin Barracks in Mechelen, Belgium.[1128] The first transport to Auschwitz left from the Dossin Barracks on August 4, 1942.[1129] In July 1942, German police directed that notices be issued for Jews to report to the Dossin Barracks.[1130] Belgian Jews were not voluntarily showing up at the Barracks, so 4 major raids were conducted in August and September of 1942, with 4,000 Jews arrested.[1131] Pessa left the apartment she was sharing with her sons around noon on September 28, 1942, and was arrested in one of these raids. She was taken to the Dossin Barracks and was deported to Auschwitz on October 10, 1942. She was immediately sent to the gas chambers upon her arrival.

After the deportations began, German Jews in Belgium went into hiding en masse.[1132] In response, beginning in October 1942 and continuing until the end of the war, German police paid a bounty for information on Jews, which resulted in 8,000 Jews being captured in Belgium.[1133] Gustav continued to check-in with Belgium authorities, so no bounty was necessary to find him. While Gustav avoided deportation for nearly two years, he was ultimately arrested on October 5, 1943.

Gustav's younger half-brother Alfred avoided deportation to the Dossin Barracks and survived the war.[1134] In fact, more than half the Jewish population in Belgium survived the war, but mostly because they had gone underground.[1135] Being so visible to authorities by registering every six months made it almost inevitable that Gustav would be arrested.

Gustav's registration card was the only item he had on him at the time of his arrest, and it was confiscated and catalogued in the Dossin Barracks archives. Gustav was registered as person 214 on the Deportation List of transport XXII. Transport XXII left the Dossin Barracks with 659 Jews on January 15, 1944, bound for Auschwitz. Here is Gustav's name on the transport page:

Source: *Directorate General War Victims, Brussels, Belgium.*

During the two-day journey, five people managed to jump off the train.[1136] When the train arrived at Auschwitz on January 17th, the selection process began.

In Gustav's transport, 416 Jews were immediately taken to the gas chamber and 238 were selected for slave labor, including Gustav. Gustav's head was shaved, he was given a striped prison uniform, and he was given his prison number, 172331, which was tattooed on his left arm.[1137] Gustav was assigned to Auschwitz III, also known as Monowitz, which was a labor camp for the I.G. Farben rubber factory.[1138] By the time Gustav was selected for Auschwitz III, the camp had 60 barracks and housed almost 11,000 prisoners.[1139]

The barracks at Monowitz were as overcrowded as those in Birkenau, but at least were heated in the winter.[1140] In addition to the standard Auschwitz meals, an additional portion of watery soup—the so-called "Buna-Suppe" (Monowitz was also referred to as Buna)—was served as a supplement to the food rations.[1141] I.G. Farben officials utilized a "rudimentary piecework system," with a motivational scheme for increased performance, including the right to wear watches and the payment of scrip that could be used in the camp canteen (which offered cigarettes and other low-value trifles for sale).[1142] Still, life at Monowitz was a horror for the prisoners, who were subjected to constant beatings, chronic hunger, and untreated illnesses.[1143]

On February 16, 1944, about a month after he had arrived at Monowitz, Gustav was hospitalized in the prison infirmary with diarrhea.[1144] The most difficult patients to treat were those suffering from diarrhea, since the causes were difficult to diagnose with limited laboratory facilities available, and these patients were the most likely to be chosen for selection.[1145] In addition, I.G. Farben had specific rules regarding hospitalization. First, only those whose recovery would take no more than 2 weeks were supposed to be admitted to the hospital; those whose recovery would take longer than 2 weeks were sent immediately to the gas chamber at Birkenau.[1146] Moreover, no more than five percent of the inmates could be sick at any time, so that any excess would be disposed of by shipment to the gas chambers.[1147] Notwithstanding the rules regarding hospitalization, Gustav managed to survive this hospitalization, and subsequent hospitalizations, in part because of the efforts of some medical personnel to bring some level of humanity to an otherwise inhumane existence.

The infirmary in Monowitz had essentially been built by prisoner physicians, and by the time Gustav arrived at Auschwitz, the hospital consisted of nine barracks.[1148] Stefan Budziaszek, a Polish doctor who had been arrested for anti-Nazi activity in 1941, was put in charge of the hospital, with SS oversight.[1149] Sympathetic staff within the infirmary (who were also prisoners) were able to manipulate the "2 week" regulations by returning prisoners to their barracks as "healthy" or moving the patient to a recovery ward, and then re-admitting them to the infirmary.[1150] And Gustav was clearly the beneficiary of these efforts by the prisoner doctors and staff.

Gustav was hospitalized for nearly two months beginning on February 16th and we do not know how he avoided the gas chamber during this period—we can only guess that he was moved to a recovery ward or "discharged" and then readmitted to the infirmary. Gustav even had a medical test ordered on March 20th to determine the cause of his diarrhea, which was unusual for the infirmary. Gustav was discharged from the infirmary on April

11th and then readmitted on April 13th. Gustav remained in the infirmary until April 26th, within the two-week framework. Gustav appears one final time in the infirmary records, staying from June 12th until July 1st, at which point he was discharged.

For prisoners like Gustav, the greater risk for death in Auschwitz was not in the infirmary, but the actual work in the factory. For those selected for Auschwitz III, their life expectancy usually was a few months.[1151] When their performance declined or they became unable to work because of prolonged illness or disability, the prisoners—at the instigation of I.G. Farben employees— were sent to the gas chambers at Birkenau in regularly held selections.[1152] Selections took place at the camp gate when the prisoners marched out in the morning, in the prisoner infirmary, and in the roll-call square.[1153]

As the Soviet Red Army approached Auschwitz in January 1945, the SS decided to evacuate the Auschwitz camp complex, including the Monowitz concentration camp.[1154] In the last roll call before evacuation on January 17, 1945, there were 10,030 in Auschwitz I, 11,576 in Birkenau, 10,244 in Monowitz, and about 20,000 in the remaining Auschwitz sub-camps, with an overall population of 54,651.[1155] Thousands were killed in the camps in the days before the evacuations.[1156] The remaining prisoners were marched west (the so-called "Death Marches"), and the SS shot anyone who fell behind.[1157] Prisoners also suffered from starvation and exposure and as many as 15,000 prisoners died during the evacuation marches from Auschwitz.[1158] Before they left Auschwitz, the SS blew up the gas chambers and crematoria in Birkenau.[1159]

There are no other records in the Auschwitz archives for Gustav after his release from the infirmary on July 1, 1944. In the final days of the war, the SS and I.G. Farben destroyed the camp's records in an attempt to conceal their crimes, so the prisoner card index and the "death books" of Monowitz only survive in fragmentary form.[1160] The list prepared by the German Federal

Archives for victims of the Holocaust lists Gustav as having been murdered, but we do not know when he died.[1161] He may have died soon after his last release from the infirmary, given the average life expectancy of prisoners in Monowitz and given how ill Gustav had been. Or he may have died on the death march, unaware of how close was to surviving the Holocaust.[1162]

Gustav Heppenheimer, the son of a fallen German World War I soldier, had eluded Gestapo capture in Frankfurt and had escaped Germany after the borders had been closed for Jewish emigration, thus avoiding the transports that took his relatives away to their deaths in 1941 and 1942. He avoided arrest in Belgium for almost two years. And when he was finally arrested and deported to Auschwitz, he avoided the gas chambers, having been selected for work instead. Unfortunately, at some point, Gustav's luck ran out. When Gustav died, he was 31 or 32 years old.

Epilogue:
The Family After the War

The war in Europe ended in May 1945 with the defeat of Germany. Many members of the Heppenheimer family were able to escape from Germany, even those who waited until the last minute to leave. Joseph Heppenheimer's four living children with his first wife—Bertha, Johanna, Jacob and Benny—escaped Germany with their children, as did Max's widow and children, although Benny's wife was unable to secure her visa in time and perished in the Holocaust. Maier's sons Leopold and Sally were able to escape, but only after the war began. Lazarus Heppenheimer's son Berthold was also able to emigrate from Germany with his wife and children.

The Heppenheimers who were able to escape from Germany did not rest once they arrived safely in America. Throughout the war, family members continued to work to locate those left behind and to secure passage for them out of Germany. As of November 1944, Benny was working with HIAS to locate his wife, Margot. And even after the war, Heppenheimer family members did not give up their efforts to find those left behind. Herb Harvey (Benny's son), having arranged to be assigned to a military unit in Germany, sought information about his mother after the war.[1163]

Unfortunately, by the fall of 1941, no one could have saved those who ultimately perished in the Holocaust. Most German Jews were able to escape Nazi Germany. In January 1933, approximately 522,000 Jews lived in Germany, and by the eve of World War II, 214,000 Jews remained in

Germany.[1164] By May of 1941, approximately 170,000 Jews were still living in Germany, and almost all perished.[1165]

Most of the Heppenheimers who died in the Holocaust died in the early years of the war, following their initial deportation. But Gustav nearly survived to the end of the war and liberation. In addition, the Heppenheimer family members were not deported to a single destination, but were deported to nearly every region controlled by Germany and to the most notorious of German concentration camps and ghettos.

The family members who died in the Holocaust, other than Margot Heppenheimer, were unknown to my husband's generation. And as improbable as it may seem, given the circumstances at the time, some Heppenheimer family members did survive the Holocaust, and those family members were also unknown to my husband's generation. During my initial research, I only found (and only expected to find) family members who had died in the Holocaust, so it was a happy surprise to discover these survivors. There were elements of serendipity in their survival, as was likely the case for most Holocaust survivors. Had Bettina Schnitzler (Lazarus Heppenheimer's granddaughter) not moved to Munich and remained instead in Frankfurt, she and her son would likely have been deported to Thereisenstadt, since virtually all Frankfurt Jews in mixed marriages had been deported by the end of 1944. Or had Robert Heppenheimer's daughter Gertrud not obtained a passport in her teens using her mother's maiden name, she might not have been able to pass as an Aryan after the war began. And had Lazarus' son Jacob remained in Frankfurt rather than return to Strasbourg in the 1920s and had he not then emigrated to America, he and his family would have been deported as well.

While the stories of the Heppenheimer family who perished during the Holocaust reflect the experiences of many of the German Jews who perished during the Holocaust, the stories of the Heppenheimer family members that emigrated to America likely also reflect the experiences of those who escaped, particularly the older members of the family. While it must have been a great relief for those who managed to leave Germany, it was especially hard for the older family members, who lived their entire lives in Germany, spoke only German and were accustomed to affluent lives.

The four family members who had been in the Gebruder Heppenheimer OHG scrap metal company and were still alive after the suicide of Max—Jacob, Benny and Adolph Heppenheimer and Isidor Wolfsheimer—left Germany in the late 1930s and early 1940s without the financial resources they had in Germany. Jacob was 59 years old when he arrived in America on November 24, 1938, and by the time of the 1940 U.S. census, Jacob was working part-time as a clerk in a painting company. By the time Jacob submitted his World War II Draft Registration Card in 1942, he was unemployed, and it is not clear that he ever worked again.[1166] Jacob died on September 16, 1950 at the age of 71. Jacob's cousin Adolph also emigrated to America in 1938, but he was 65 years old when he emigrated and never worked following his immigration. Adolph died on August 22, 1944. When Benny arrived in America in 1941, he was 58 years old and found work in a warehouse in 1942. According to his son Herb, Benny was never the same after he left his wife behind in Germany.[1167] He worked in the warehouse until arthritis forced him to stop working completely in 1946. Benny died on November 9, 1953 at the age of 71. And Isidor Wolfsheimer, who arrived in America in 1941, died on June 19, 1944 at the age of 70, likely never working in America following his immigration.

After the establishment of the Federal Republic of Germany (FRG) in 1949, the FRG began negotiating with the State of Israel for financial reparations. [1168] While some in Israel had mixed feelings about the acceptance of "blood money" from the Germans, Israel and the FRG signed the Luxembourg Agreements in 1952, which provided for direct payments to Israel.[1169] In 1953, the FRG enacted legislation for individual compensation, which included pensions, one-time payments, and medical treatment.[1170]

After enactment of the compensation legislation, Heppenheimer family members submitted applications for reparations for their lost businesses. Interestingly, Sally Heppenheimer also sought to void the sale of Ludwig Heppenheimer OHG to Mauthe & Merz, arguing that Franz Mauthe and Daniel Merz had pressured him to sell the business for substantially below its value.[1171] Mauthe & Merz settled the claim by paying Sally 10,000 DM in 1951.[1172] The Heppenheimer family also sought reparations for those lost in the Holocaust. Benny's sons filed a reparation request for their mother, Margot. Maier's daughter Berta Schwarz died in the Holocaust, and her son Walter sought reparations for his mother. Robert Heppenheimer's daughter Gertrud sought reparations for the loss of her father.

Conclusion

As I researched my husband's family and German Jewish history in general, I came to understand that the Heppenheimer family history is essentially the history of the Jewish people in Germany. Hearing about opportunities in the German lands, the Heppenheimer ancestors likely left Poland and settled in Eichtersheim. Jewish occupations and residency were severely restricted in the German lands, but the Heppenheimer family ancestors were still able to operate grain trading businesses and to actually own property. When German Jews were given rights as German citizens following emancipation, Jakob Heppenheimer's sons took full advantage of the opportunities now afforded Jews by establishing successful scrap metal businesses. The Heppenheimer family remained strongly committed German citizens (even losing sons in World War I), and had assumed that the commitment would always be honored.

Without the contributions from Jews in metals trading (as well as in other sectors of German industry and commerce), Germany might not have grown to be the industrial and commercial power it was when the Nazis took control in 1933. Through the 1930s, German Jews saw their rights slowly eliminated. The restrictions imposed on the Jews began to look a lot like the restrictions imposed on Jews before emancipation. But unlike the earlier period, when Jews were an economically marginal group, Jews were financially successful by the 1930s and these new restrictions posed an existential threat.

Many of Jakob and Babette Heppenheimer's progeny who lived in Germany were able to escape Germany before the Holocaust. Except for the few family members that left during the early Nazi years, most Heppenheimers waited until after Kristallnacht to leave Germany, thinking that the Nazi actions were just another pogrom and that they would ultimately resume their lives as German citizens. But they also remained because they were strongly connected to Germany, with successful businesses and strong ties to the community. They were both German Jews and Jewish Germans. Such strong ties caused some of the family to wait until it was almost too late to leave, and, unfortunately for others, until it was too late.

The Heppenheimers who could not leave Germany found themselves in the most notorious of ghettos (Lodz and Theresienstadt) and the most notorious of Nazi death camps (Auschwitz, Chelmo, Sobibor, and Treblinka). The Heppenheimers suffered during Kristallnacht and were among those Jews deported to Buchenwald and Gurs. Even those Heppenheimers who emigrated to America still experienced the depravations imposed on Jews by the Nazis before they left. And when they could leave, they left Germany with nothing. Those who did not or could not leave often perished in the most horrific of ways. But three who remained in Europe did survive. The two Heppenheimer family members who were able to survive the Holocaust in Germany did so in the only ways Jews could survive: by either marrying a non-Jew or by passing as an Aryan. And Lazarus' son Jacob was able to survive because he had returned to Strasbourg from Frankfurt and become a French citizen.

In justifying the actions taken against Jews, the Nazis had maintained that Jews dominated much of the German economy, to the detriment of the average German. The Nazis may have been correct that Jews were overrepresented in many important sectors of the German economy, but the Nazis were wrong about the Jewish intentions. German Jews were overachievers and such overachievement came from a profound wish to win respect and acceptance.[1173] Recognizing the challenges of systemic German anti-Semitism, Jews overcompensated to prove their value to Germany.[1174] As one author noted, "the nineteenth and twentieth centuries demonstrate a degree of attainment by so small a group of the population as has rarely been equaled in any civilization."[1175] Henry and Joseph Heppenheimer moved to Frankfurt, likely poor but also very ambitious. For the first time, the Heppenheimer brothers were full citizens and could accomplish what they could not dream of accomplishing in Eichtersheim. When Joseph died in 1923, Gebruder Heppenheimer was a thriving business. But it was also a business that helped to grow the German economy. Joseph Heppenheimer was not interested in Jewish world domination; Joseph was interested in being a successful and productive member of German society, and likely worked day and night (and even on the Jewish Sabbath) to achieve that goal. The Nazis showed their "appreciation" to the Jews that helped Germany develop into a world power by plundering their assets and by either expelling them from Germany or by murdering them.

The Heppenheimers who emigrated to America during the Nazis' rise to power abandoned the scrap metal businesses that had allowed the family to prosper for more than 60 years. But the family would experience one last benefit from the scrap metal business. Adolph Keller, who sponsored the visa applications of so many of the Heppenheimers who emigrated to America in the 1930s and early 1940s, made his fortune in the scrap metal business, having started in the business when he went to work for his father-in-law, Henry Heppenheimer. It is likely that this fortune enabled him to sponsor so many family members.

After Germany surrendered and the world discovered the extent of what had been done to European Jewry, many Germans initially claimed ignorance, maintaining that they had been led to believe that the Jews were being resettled in the East to be put to work.[1176] We now know that was not the case, and that many Germans either knew or had very good reason to suspect that the Jews were being exterminated.[1177] Reparations were an initial way for Germany to admit its guilt and seek atonement.[1178] Beginning in the 1980s, German leaders began to publicly take responsibility for the Holocaust, and in 2018, German Foreign Minister Sigmar Gabriel acknowledged that Germany was solely responsible for the attempted extermination of all Jews.[1179] While visiting Auschwitz in 2019, German Chancellor Angela Merkel emphasized that the "crimes are and will remain part of German history and this history must be told over and over again."[1180]

Germans have coined the term "Erinnerungskultur," or "culture of remembrance," to refer to the policy of confronting Nazi-era crimes by acknowledging responsibility for the Holocaust.[1181] Erinnerungskultur has resulted in large-scale government-funded memorials throughout Germany, and has also resulted in grassroots initiatives like the "Stolpersteine" or "stumbling stones" - small engraved brass paving stones commemorating victims in the streets where they used to live.[1182] A number of Heppenheimer family members who fell victim to the Holocaust are remembered in large scale memorials, such as at the Börneplatz Memorial Site in Frankfurt. And a few Heppenheimer family members have been remembered as part of the Stolpersteine project. While it is comforting to know that their names are not lost to history, one set of stumbling stones actually demonstrates why it is important to tell the family stories, and to tell them correctly.

The residents of Böhmerstrasse 60 decided to have stumbling stones placed in front of their building to remember Emma Heppenheimer and Selma and Lippmann Lewin, and the stones were laid in 2014.[1183] None of the apartment owners had any connection to Emma, Selma or Lippmann, but presumably chose to participate in the Stolpersteine project because of Erinnerungskultur. Here are their stones:

Source: https://www.frankfurt.de/sixcms/detail.
php?id=1907322&_ffmpar[_id_inhalt]=29627381

The residents of the building had assumed that Selma and Lippmann were husband and wife and died as husband and wife.[1184] Unfortunately, the Holocaust erased many of the stories, both the happy and the sad, and the sponsors of the stones had no idea that, when Selma and Lippmann left Böhmerstrasse 60, they separated as a couple and had only disdain for one another when they ultimately divorced.[1185]

For those Heppenheimers who could not escape the Nazis and were murdered in the Holocaust, like Selma, their stories had mostly been lost. As I learned more about the Heppenheimers' family history and the Heppenheimers who were murdered, it became clear to me that their stories needed to be told, to bear witness to those murdered and to preserve their memory. We must celebrate the lives they lived and never forget the contributions they made to a country that rejected them in the most horrible of ways. But we must also not forget how easy it was for the Nazis to effectively demonize and ultimately eliminate a people from its borders. We must tell the stories of the Heppenheimers who perished in the Holocaust as we remember the words of the great writer and Holocaust survivor Primo Levi: "It happened, therefore it can happen again."

The challenge for me in researching the Heppenheimer family was the absence of many historical records. The extensive bombings during World War II resulted in the destruction of an enormous number of government records. For example, most of the historical records of the city of Mannheim, where Max Heppenheimer and several of his cousins lived, were destroyed during the war.[1186] In addition, as it became clear to the Germans that they were losing the war, they began to destroy the evidence of their many crimes. Thus, there are limits on the amount of information available regarding the Heppenheimer family members who perished in the Holocaust. And I wish I had more information about the personal side of these family members. I know what they did for a living and where they lived, but much of who they were as individuals is lost to history. Still, there are enough records available to provide a general picture of the family, and based on this information, we can see a family both patriotic and driven to succeed. The Heppenheimer family believed the promises made when the German government provided Jews with the same rights enjoyed by other German citizens, and were likely devastated when, one by one, those promises were broken.

Unfortunately, there is one final piece to the family puzzle that will likely remain unsolved—why my father-in-law never mentioned (even to his beloved wife) that he had lost a grandmother and two aunts in the Holocaust. This question is what drove my initial interest in researching the Heppenheimer family history, and remained in the back of my mind as I continued to uncover the many layers of the family's history. The two postcards sent to Max Heppenheimer from his step-mother Emma and his half-sister Alice (discussed in Chapter 6) suggest a close relationship with both, at least as of 1923. So what happened? We know that Max experienced multiple business failures, culminating in his suicide in 1935. Did his son Curtis blame the family for Max's suicide? Or was the loss of his grandmother and aunts simply too much for him to share after he emigrated to America? We will never know the answers to these questions, but on some level, it really does not matter. My father-in-law believed in family and I am sure he would say now, if he were still alive, that telling their stories is the most important thing. And if there had been problems within the family, I am sure Curtis would now say that all is forgiven.

Index

Notes

1.   Eichtersheim was located about 22 miles southeast of Mannheim. The town no
        longer exists, having been merged with the neighboring town of Michelfeld to
        form Angelbachtal. *See* https://www.angelbachtal.de/freizeit-kultur/geschichte/
        ortsgeschichte.html.

2.   Germany as a country did not exist until 1871, when the German states were
        unified into the German Empire. Hagen Schulze, *Germany: A New History,*
        (Cambridge: Harvard University Press, 1998), 144-45.

3.   The Thirty Years War was a series of conflicts between Protestants and Catholics
        in the German lands. *See* "The Thirty Years War as Foil for the War in Syria," at
        https://sites.utexas.edu/culturescontexts/tag/thirty-years-war/. The war started as
        a conflict between the Catholic Holy Roman Emperor and his Protestant subjects,
        but grew into a continent-wide political conflict over the balance of power in
        Europe. *See* "The Thirty Years' War and its Effect on Sacred Baroque Music," at
        https://www.ukessays.com/essays/music/the-thirty-years-war-and-its-effect-on-
        sacred-baroque-music.php.

4.   "Jewish Life in Kriachgau before 1933," at https://www.jlk-ev.de/page10/page36/
        page36.html. While Jews were present in the German-speaking parts of Europe
        since Roman times, the numbers of Jews in the German lands remained relatively
        small. *See* Ruth Gay, *The Jews of Germany,* (New Haven: Yale University Press,
        1992), 4-8. The plague epidemic in 1348 and 1349 resulted in the death of a
        quarter of the Christian population, but led to the deaths of three-quarters of the
        Jewish population in pogroms, since they were blamed for the plague. *See* "Jewish
        Life in Kriachgau before 1933," at https://www.jlk-ev.de/page10/page36/page36.
        html. Virtually all remaining Jews were then forced to leave the German lands.
        The Jews from the German lands fled to Poland, which saw its Jewish population
        grow from 15,000 to 150,000 during this period. *See* David Levinson, *Jewish Ger-
        many: An Enduring Presence from the Fourth to the Twenty-First Century,* (Elstree:
        Vallentine Mitchell, 2018), 28.

5.   H.I. Bach, *The German Jew: A Synthesis of Judaism and Western Civilization,
        1730-1930*, (New York: Oxford University Press, 1984), 36-37.

6.   B.W. DeVries, *Of Mettle and Metal: From Court Jews to World-Wide Industrial-
        ists,* (Amsterdam: NEHA Amsterdam, 2000), 36. The German lands in the seven-
        teenth century were divided into hundreds of tiny duchies, church territories and
        city-states, and only some of the towns permitted Jewish residency. *See* R. Po-chia
        Hsia and Hartmut Lehmann (Eds.), *In and Out of the Ghetto: Jewish-Gentile Re-
        lations in Late Medieval and Early Modern Germany,* (Washington, D.C.: German
        Historical Institute, 1995), 95. Eichtersheim was one of the towns that permitted

Jewish residency. *See* Leonhard Dorfer, *Judisches Leben in Eichtersheim*, (Ubstadt Weiher: Verlag Regionalkultur, 2011), 10.

7.   DeVries, *Of Mettle and Metal: From Court Jews to World-Wide Industrialists*, 36. In fact, Court Jews enabled their rulers to revive their stagnant economies to prepare for 19th century modernization. *Ibid*, 27; Shulvass, *From East to West: The Westward Migration of Jews from Eastern Europe During the Seventeenth and Eighteenth Centuries*, 15.

8.   *See* "Eichtersheim" at http://www.alemannia-judaica.de/eichtersheim_synagoge. htm; https://www.jlk-ev.de/page24/page4/files/Expo_S.PDF.

9.   Sabine Ullmann, *"Poor Jewish Families in Early Modern Rural Swabia,"* (International Review of Social History 45, 2000), 93.

10.   Jill Storm, *Culture and Exchange: The Jews of Konigsberg*, (St. Louis: Washington University, 2010), 36 at https://openscholarship.wustl.edu/cgi/viewcontent. cgi?referer=&httpsredir=1&article=1334&context=etd.

11.   Ullmann, *Poor Jewish Families in Early Modern Rural Swabia*, 94. The Jews who could not obtain permission to settle became part of a permanent wandering class. *See* Marion Kaplan, *Jewish Daily Life in Germany, 1618-1945*, (Oxford: Oxford University Press, 2005), 12; Gay, *The Jews of Germany*, 229; Mark Haberlein and Michaela Schmolz-Haberlein, "Competition and Cooperation: The Ambivalent Relationship between Jews and Christians in Early Modern Germany and Pennsylvania," in *The Pennsylvania Magazine of History and Biography*, Vol. CXXVI, No. 3 (July 2002), 424.

12.   Ullmann, *Poor Jewish Families in Early Modern Rural Swabia*, 37. The rights and duties of the schutzjuden were strictly regulated and could be quite onerous. Under the terms of the schutzbrief, the Jew had to, for example, pay his taxes on time, be quiet on Sundays and Christian holidays, accommodate foreign Jews (those who did not live in the town) only up to three days, and lend money at a fixed rate. *See* Museum of the History of Jews in the Ostalb Region in the Former Synagogue in Bopfingen-Oberdorf, 11, quoting from "Reminders of the Taxes on the Jewish Community in Oberdorf," at https://www.ostalbkreis.de/sixcms/ media.php/26/EhemaligeSynagogeOberdorf-Katalog-englisch-2013.pdf. The schutzjuden could not be expelled from the community for the duration of the contract. *See* Emily C. Rose, *Portrait of our Past: Jews of the German Countryside*, (Philadelphia: The Jewish Publication Society, 2001), 28.

13.   There is some reference to Jews in Eichtersheim in the late seventeenth century, although their stays were temporary. "Eichtersheim" at http://www.alemannia-judaica.de/eichtersheim_synagoge.htm; https://www.jlk-ev.de/page24/page4/files/ Expo_S.PDF

14.   The records for Jews in Eichtersheim from this period, including the annual tax register and requests for schutzbriefs, can be found in the archives of the Lords of Venningen for Eichtersheim at Generallandesarchiv Bestand 69 von Venningen at https://www2.landesarchiv-bw.de/ofs21/olf/struktur.php?bestand=14445&klassi=003.002&anzeigeKlassi=003.002.001. All information relating to the Jews living in Eichtersheim in this section of the chapter is derived from these records unless otherwise noted.

15.   The 1705 tax register included two Josefs. Based on a review of the tax records, and other records of the period, it is likely that one of these Josefs was Josef

Moses. Josef Moses was likely 26 years old at the time, based on a review of other records.

16. https://www.jlk-ev.de/page24/page4/files/Expo_S.PDF; Gustav Schleckmann, *Das Barockdorf im Eichtersheim,* (Angelbachtal: Eigenverlag der Gemeinde, 1989), 24. These Jews identified in the Beetbuch were Aron, Leser, Gromelle, and Michal. Dorfer, *Judisches Leben in Eichtersheim,* 10. While Jews generally were forbidden from owning any property in the German lands, that was not the case in Eichtersheim. *See* David S. Landes ,"The Jewish Merchant: Typology and Stereotypology in Germany," in *Year Book XIX of the Leo Baeck Institute,* (London: Secker & Warburg, 1974), 12.

17. Josef Moses' father's Hebrew name was Jechiel. *See* http://www.landesarchiv-bw. de/plink/?f=2-2412909. The name Jechiel was not in the Eichtersheim tax register and we do not know the German name he might have used had he been in the tax register. Josef Moses' youngest son was Michel Joseph and his Hebrew name was Jechiel. Assuming Michel Joseph was named after his grandfather, it is possible that Joseph Moses also gave his son the grandfather's German name, Michel. If this is the case, it is possible that the "Michal" identified in the Beetbuch as a Jewish homeowner was Joseph Moses' father.

18. In the 1723 Electoral Palatinate census, there is a "Josef" who is 44 years old and a widower. *See* Dorfer, *Judisches Leben in Eichtersheim,* 11. This person was likely Josef Moses, based on a review of the tax registers and other records. I was able to determine who Josef Moses' sons were, as well as determine the relationships of most of Eichtersheim's Jewish residents during this period, based, in part, on the Waibstadt cemetery records, where the Jews in this region were buried. *See* Eichtersheim Jewish Cemetery," at http://www.alemannia-judaica.de/eichtersheim_friedhof.htm; http://www.landesddarchiv-bw.de/plink/?f=2-1896204-39; and http://www.landesarchiv-bw.de/plink/?f=1-446830-27. Jews from Eichtersheim continued to be buried in the Waibstadt cemetery until the 1840s, when Eichtersheim opened a Jewish cemetery. To further establish connections among the Eichtersheim Jews, I also relied on the Eichtersheim Standesbuch (discussed later), the 1809 Eichtersheim names list (discussed later), the findagrave.com website, and other genealogical websites.

19. It was common in the German lands for Jews to use their first name and their father's first name as their second name. *See* "Germany Names, Personal," at https://www.familysearch.org/wiki/en/Germany_Names,_Personal#:~:text=-Jews%20in%20Germany%20followed%20the,state%20to%20require%20fixed%20 surnames. In addition, Jews in the Eichtersheim records distinguished between those with the same first names by referring to the older as "alt" (or old) and the younger as "yung" (or young).

20. Maier Lazarus's birth date is derived from the 1809 names list, which listed his age as 39.

21. When he first applied for a schutzbrief, Maier Lazarus used the name "Mayer Leser." Leser is the familiar of Elieser, which was Leser Joseph's Hebrew name. "Given Names, Judiasm, and Jewish History," at https://www.jewishgen.org/databases/GivenNames/nature.htm. When he adopted his surname, Maier Lazarus used the name "Maier Lazarus." German Jews often used the Latin version "Lazarus" for Elieser. *See* Joachim Mugdan, "The Names of Jews," Institute of General Linguistics, University of Munster, Germany, at https://www.jewishgen.

org/InfoFiles/namfaq0.htm; "Lazar," The Museum of the Jewish People at Beit Hatfutsot, at https://dbs.bh.org.il/familyname/lazar.

22. Monika Richardz, "Emancipation and Continuity: German Jews in the Rural Economy," in *Revolution and Evolution: 1848 in German-Jewish History*, ed. W.E. Mosse, et al. (Turbingen: Mohr 1981), 96 (1981). The Jews in Eichtersheim could not easily move to other places within Germany until emancipation later in the nineteenth century (which is discussed later).

23. Dorfer, *Judisches Leben in Eichtersheim*, 11.

24. Leser Joseph and Michel Joseph's oldest brother Benedict had died in 1751, but their brother Seligmann was also among those assessed the smaller fine. Seligmann died the following year.

25. For a description of Mühlfrucht, *see* D.M. Sering, *Die Vererbung des ländlichen Grundbesitzes im Königreich Preussen* (Berlin: Verlagsbuchhandlung Paul Parey, 1899), 99, at https://books.google.com/books?id=VV8uAAAAMAA-J&newbks=0&printsec=frontcover&dq=%22M%C3%BChlfrucht%22&hl=en&source=newbks_fb#v=onepage&q=M%C3%BChlfrucht&f=false.

26. Four Jews owned property in 1710 and four Jews owned property in 1790, so it is possible that the Venningen family allowed just these properties to be owned by the town's Jews.

27. Leser Joseph's house became the site of the town's new synagogue in the 1830s. *See* Dorfer, *Judisches Leben in Eichtersheim*, 80-81. As discussed below, it is possible that Leser Joseph's house was also used as the town's synagogue.

28. For example, *see* "Hachenburger Judenvorsteher," at https://www.regionalgeschichte.net/westerwald/hachenburg/einzelaspekte/infos-zur-stadtgeschichte/buergerliches-leben-191/themenbereiche/juedische-mitbuerger-221/judenvorsteher-223.html.

29. Several years after assuming the role of Judenvorsteher, Joseph Michel's title changed to Judenschutz, which has been translated as "Jewish mayor." *See* Alex Huettner, "The Jewish Congregation of Kirchen," Leo Baeck Institute, 27, at https://archive.org/stream/thejewishcongreg1439unse/thejewishcongreg1439unse_djvu.txt. Joseph Michel retained this title until the Jewish Edict, which is discussed later in this chapter, was issued in 1809.

30. A florin is another name for a gulden, which was the currency during the period. *See* J. Rowbotham, *A New Guide to German and English Conversion,* (London: Dulau and Co., 1849). 198.

31. As discussed later, French forces under Napoleon had invaded the German lands in 1796.

32. While Protestants were long discouraged from marriage even between second cousins, marriages between cousins (even first cousins) was common among Jews in the German lands during this period. *See* David Warren Sabean, "Kinship and Prohibited Marriages in Baroque Germany: Divergent Strategies among Jewish and Christian Populations," *Leo Baeck Institute Yearbook, 47* (2002), 91-92, 102, at https://escholarship.org/uc/item/4x337501.

33. We can conclude that Maier Lazarus likely married Rebecka by working backwards starting from records from the early nineteenth century. Based on the records from the Eichtersheim Standesbuch after 1809, we know that Maier Heppenheimer had married Rebekka Wertheimer (based on her death record)

and had a daughter Rebecka (based on her death record). Jews do not name children after a living relative, particularly a mother, so Rebekka was very likely not Rebecka's mother. The Waibstadt cemetery records note that Michel Joseph's daughter Rivka (the Hebrew name for Rebecka) died, although it does not provide a date for her death. The gravestones for the women who were buried in the Waibstadt cemetery at this time identified the women as "wife of," but for some reason, Michel's daughters (Rivka, Elisabetha, and Zerle) were buried as "the daughter of Jechiel" (Michel Joseph's Hebrew name), even though all three were married. Because Michel Joseph was a man of importance in Eichtersheim, the family may have decided to honor him by including his name on his daughters' gravestones. While Jews do not name children after a living parent, if the mother dies in childbirth, the child is often named for the mother. *See* "Naming Traditions," at https://www.jewishgen.org/InfoFiles/GivenNames/slide7.html. There were no other Rivkas from Eichtersheim who died around 1803—in fact, every woman from Eichtersheim who died around this time period and who was married had been married to a person other than Maier Lazarus. Assuming Maier had married Michel Joseph's daughter Rebecka, and Rebecka died in childbirth, this would explain why Maier had an older daughter named Rebecka.

34.   *See* previous footnote.

35.   To distinguish between Maier's two wives, the elder's name is spelled "Rebecka" (which was the way her daughter's name was spelled) and the younger is spelled "Rebekka" (which is how it is spelled in the Eichtersheim records). We know that Rebekka, who was Maier's second wife, was the daughter of a Wertheimer based on her death record, but we can conclude that she was the daughter of Joseph Michel, rather than Joseph Michel's father (Michel Joseph) from his second marriage, because Michel Joseph already had a daughter named Rebecka. Further, Rebekka could not have been the daughter of any of Michel Joseph's other sons, since they all married after Rebekka was born.

36.   Michel Joseph had at least two sons with his first wife—Joseph Michel and Hirsch Michel. Joseph Michel, the eldest son, was born in 1747. We know this because Joseph Michel's age was included in the 1809 names list, discussed later in this chapter. Joseph Michel obtained his schutzbrief in 1772. Joseph Michel likely married around this time, and he married Dorothea (Hebrew name Dobritsch). *See* http://www.landesarchiv-bw.de/plink/?f=4-1224085-201. Michel Joseph remarried around 1763, since his oldest son from his second marriage (Marx) was born in 1763. Michel Joseph had at least four children with his second wife, including Maier Lazarus' first wife Rebecka.

37.   We know that Rebekka was the mother of Jakob, since Jakob's marriage record notes that his parents were Maier Heppenheimer and Rebekka, born Wertheimer. *See* www.landesarchiv-bw.de/plink/?f=4-1224101-26. We know that Zerle was born around 1810, since her birth was noted in the Eichtersheim Standesbuch. *See* http://www.landesarchiv-bw.de/plink/?f=4-1224100-58. It is possible that Maier and Rebekka had other children who died in infancy, and that Maier had other children with his first wife. This is particularly likely, since Maier's son Jakob (Hebrew name Yaakov Jehuda) was not named for Maier's father Leser, and Maier would likely have named his first-born son after his father. None of those deaths were recorded in the Eichtersheim records.

38.   Dorfer, *Judisches Leben in Eichtersheim*, 12.

39.   David Sorkin, *The Transformation of German Jewry, 1780-1840*, (Detroit: Wayne State University Press, 1989), p.28; Gay, *The Jews of Germany*, 125.

40.   The London Encyclopedia, Volume III, (London, 1829), 366; *See* https://www.leo-bw.de/detail-gis/-/Detail/details/ORT/labw_ortslexikon/6649/ort. While Baden grew five-fold in territory and population, and its Jewish population increased from 2,265 to 14,200, Jews were still clustered in the towns that permitted Jewish residency before 1805, so that Jews lived in only 173 out of 1550 settlements in Baden. *See* Sorkin, *The Transformation of German Jewry, 1780-1840*, 29; Hasia R. Diner, *A Time for Gathering—The Second Migration 1820-1880*, (Baltimore: The Johns Hopkins University Press, 1992), 9.

41.   Sorkin, *The Transformation of German Jewry, 1780-1840*, 28. Christian Wilhelm von Dohm, a councillor in the Prussian War Ministry, wrote a book in 1781 promoting Jewish emancipation, and this was followed the next year by the Edict of Toleration issued by Emperor Joseph II in Austria, calling for the toleration of Jews. *Ibid*, 23.

42.   David Sorkin, *Jewish Emancipation: A History Across Five Centuries*, Princeton: Princeton University Press, 2019), 112.

43.   Ibid.

44.   Adolf Lewin, "Zur Judenemanzipation in Baden," *Monatsschrift für Geschichte und Wissenschaft des Judentums*, Jahrg. 49 (N. F. 13), H. 9/10 (September/Oktober 1905), 606, at https://www.jstor.org/stable/23079610; Loyd E. Lee, The Politics of Harmony: Civil Service, Liberalism, and Social Reform in Baden, 1800-1850, (Newark: University of Delaware Press, 1980), 28.

45.   Lee, *The Politics of Harmony*, 28.

46.   Lewin, "Zur Judenemanzipation in Baden," 606-07; Lee, *The Politics of Harmony*, 144.

47.   Lewin, "Zur Judenemanzipation in Baden," 610.

48.   Dr. Erwin Manuel Dreifuss, *Die Familiennamen der Juden unter besonderer Beruecksichtigung der Verhaeltnisse in Baden zu Anfang des 19. Jahrhunderts*, (Frankfurt/Main: J. Kauffmann Verlag,1927), 24-26.

49.   Larry L. Ping, *Gustav Freytag and the Prussian Gospel: Novels, Liberalism, and History*, (Oxford, Peter Lang, 2006), 126.

50.   Leo Spitzer, *Lives in Between Assimilation and Marginality in Austria, Brazil, and West Africa, 1780-1945*, (Cambridge: Cambridge University Press, 1989), 27.

51.   Dorfer, *Judisches Leben in Eichtersheim*,15. The Standesbuchs are digitized and are available on the Landesarchiv Baden-Wurttemberg website at http://www.landesarchiv-bw.de/plink/?f=4-1224100. In addition, a guide to the residents of Eichtersheim (including the Jewish residents) was created from the Standesbuchs by Josef Seitz in the book *Eichtersheim und Seine Einwohner 1699-1903*, (Lahr-Dinglingen : Interessengemeinschaft Badischer Ortssippenbücher, 2014). The first recording of events for Jews in the Eichtersheim Standesbuch was in 1810, the year after the Edict was issued.

52.   I was able to conclude that this person was very likely Maier Lazarus Heppenheimer based on the information contained in the names list and a comparison of that information to other relevant documents. The 1809 names list contains the following columns: the person's original name, the new surname, the age of

the person, the spouse (represented by the number 1), the number of sons, the number of daughters, and the total number in the family. We know that Maier Lazarus Heppenheimer had three children at the time of his death (Rebecka, Jakob and Zerle) and that his daughter Rebecka was born in 1803 and his son Jakob was born in 1806. *See* https://www.findagrave.com/memorial/170986257/rebecka-heppenheimer. Zerle was born around 1810, so she would not have been recorded on the names list. The names list shows that Maier Lazarus "Maier" had a wife and one son and one daughter, just like Maier Lazarus Heppenheimer. In the tax registers for 1810 and 1811, the Eichtersheim Jews continued to use only their first name and the name of their father as a second name (rather than their new surnames), and "Maier Lazarus" is in both registers. For the taxes owed for 1811, he is represented on the tax register by his widow. (Since the tax register is for taxes for all of a particular year, it seems likely that the 1811 tax register was prepared sometime in 1812.) Since Maier Lazarus Heppenheimer died in 1812, as explained below, the Maier Lazarus in the 1811 tax register is likely Maier Lazarus Heppenheimer. Finally, there is no record of another "Maier Lazarus" in Eichtersheim before 1812 or of a "Maier Lazarus Maier" in any of the Eichtersheim records before or after 1809.

53. Four brothers adopted the first name of their father, Meir, as their surname and became Joseph Maier, Wolf Maier, Michel Maier, and Jakob Maier in the 1809 Eichtersheim names list.

54. The Eichtersheim names list contains a total of 25 new surnames, and these surnames reflect the types of surnames chosen by German Jews following the directive that Jews adopt surnames, mainly choosing names based on places or professions. In terms of place names, in addition to Heppenheimer and Wertheimer, the Eichtersheim Jews chose the surnames Eichtersheimer, Edesheimer, and Jöhlinger. In terms of professions, Eichtersheim's Jews chose the names Zimmern (carpenter), Metzger (butcher), and Kaufmann (businessman).

55. Heppenheim is about 40 miles north of Eichtersheim. Surnames based on a place do not always mean that the person came from that place. Instead, the person may have had ancestors that came from the place or that person may have conducted trade in the place. *See* "Wertheim," at https://dbs.bh.org.il/familyname/wertheim.

56. Wertheim is located in the northern part of Baden, more than 60 miles from Eichtersheim, and we do not know why this family looked there to choose a surname. Rabbi Samson Wertheimer, whose family originally came from Wertheim, was one of the most famous Jews in the eighteenth century, and families with any connection to Rabbi Wertheimer (even through a mother) adopted this name when required to take a surname. This may have been the case for Michel Joseph's sons in choosing the surname Wertheimer. *See* "Wertheimer Family Tree DNA," at https://www.familytreedna.com/groups/wertheim/about.

57. In Maier's wife Rebekka's death record in the Eichtersheim Standesbuch, Maier is described as having been a "handelsmann" and a "schutzburger." GLA Karlsruhe 390 Nr. 4736, 250, at www.landesarchiv-bw.de/plink/?f=4-1224100-250.

58. *See* Eichtersheim Standesbuch, GLA Karlsruhe 390 Nr. 4736, p. 250, at www.landesarchiv-bw.de/plink/?f=4-1224100-250. *See* Robert Wideen, *The Jewish Presence in Soufflenheim,, Soufflenheim Genealogy Research and History (2018), 14, at https://nebula.wsimg.com/d079a6dca69a1360ebdcda60f0c8a855?AccessKey-Id=B148577D7422636F7E01&disposition=0&alloworigin=1.*

59. Dorfer, *Judisches Leben in Eichtersheim*, 39.

60. Alex Huettner, "The Jewish congregation of Kirchen (Efringen-Kirchen, Kreis Loerrach), 1736-1940 : 200 years Jewish history in the Markgraeferland," (translated by Justin J. Mueller, 1993), 27, at https://archive.org/stream/thejewish-congreg1439unse/thejewishcongreg1439unse_djvu.txt; "Ulrich Baumann, "The Object's Memory: Remebering Rural Jews in Southern Germany," Restitution and Memory: Material Restoration in Europe, Dan Diner and Gotthart Wunberg (Eds.), (New York: Berghahn Books, 2007), 132.

61. Ibid, 119.

62. Other Eichtersheim Jews also improved their status in the first years of the Jewish Edict. Eichtersheim's Jews submitted a supplement names list around 1815 that also included occupations. The 1815 list was compiled by Berthold Rosenthal, a German historian and genealogist, and can be found at http://www.archive.org/stream/lbi_brc_mf484_reel02#page/n323/mode/1up. *See also* "Name Adoption List of Eichtersheim, 1815(?)," at https://www.a-h-b.de/en/projects/genealogy/name-adoption-lists/eichtersheim (which transcribes the list prepared by Berthold Rosenthal). In 1809, approximately half of Eichtersheim's Jews (12) were nothandels. By 1815, a number of the nothandels in the 1809 list had moved to "regular" trades.

63. Axel Huettner, The Jewish Congregation of Kirchen," Leo Baeck Institute, 27.

64. Maier's death was not recorded in the Eichtersheim Standesbuch, even though Jews had begun recording births, marriages and deaths in 1810. However, there are other records that indicate that Maier died in 1812. As previously discussed, during this period, all Jews living in Eichtersheim were buried in the Waibstadt Cemetery. A review of the burial records during this period reveals that there were five Meirs (the Hebrew spelling for Maier) from Eichtersheim who were buried in the Waibstadt Cemetery. Three of the Meirs died in the 1700s, and the fourth Meir, who died in 1843, was Maier Lazarus Heppenheimer's second wife's brother Maier Wertheimer. The fifth Maier was "Meir son of Eliezer," who was buried in the cemetery on May 31, 1812. As explained earlier, for taxes owed for 1811, Maier Lazarus was being represented for the first time by his widow. Further, when Maier's daughter Rebecka died in 1814, the Eichtersheim Standesbuch noted that Rebecka's father "Mayer Heppenheimer" was deceased and had been a resident of Eichtersheim. Since Maier Lazarus Heppenheimer died between 1809 and 1814, and the only Meir that was buried in the Waibstadt Cemetery during this period was Meir son of Elieser, this person was very likely Maier Lazarus Heppenheimer. In reviewing both the Waibstadt cemetery records and the Standesbuch for Eichtersheim, there were other Eichtersheim residents who died in 1812, were buried in the Waibstadt cemetery and were also not included in the Standesbuch, so it may be that, in the early stages of recording deaths, errors were made. In fact, Maier's father-in-law Joseph Michel Wertheimer, the mayor of the Eichtersheim Jews until 1809, died after the 1809 names list was submitted and before the 1815 supplemental names list was submitted, but his death was not recorded in the Eichtersheim Standesbuch. His death is noted in the Waibstadt cemetery records, but his death date is recorded as sometime in the 1810s.

65. Gustav Schleckmann, *Das Barockdorf im Eichtersheim*, (Angelbachtal: Eigenverlag der Gemeinde, 1989), 86. (1989). 1816 was known as the "Year without Summer" because of the cold weather and snow. Levinson, *Jewish Germany: An Enduring Presence from the Fourth to the Twenty-First Century*, 95.

66. As was the case for Meir, Rebekka's gravestone does not include her surname. Her gravestone simply reads "Rivka wife of Meir." *See* http://www.landesar-chiv-bw.de/plink/?f=2-2791543.

67. Zerle later left Eichtersheim to marry Chaim Wolfsbruck. Zerle died childless in 1870. *See* https://www.findagrave.com/memorial/170225664/zerla-wolfsbruck.

68. Sorkin, *The Transformation of German Jewry, 1780-1840*, 34.

69. Ibid., at 35.

70. Stefi Jersch-Wenzel, "Legal Status and Emancipation," *Germany-Jewish History in Modern Times, Volume 2 Emancipation and Acculturation 1780-1871,* Michael A. Meyer (Ed.), (New York: Columbia University Press, 1997), 24 and 29.

71. Franz Hundsnurscher and Gerhard Taddey, The Jewish Communities in Baden, (Stuttgart: W. Kohlhammer Verlag 1968), 12. As of 1824, a total of 25 different Jewish taxes were still being levied in the Baden lands, although those special taxes were finally abolished in 1828. *Ibid.*

72. Gotz Aly, *Why the Germans, Why the Jews*, (New York: Metropolitan Books, 2011), 33.

73. https://kehilalinks.jewishgen.org/berlin/Jews_in_Germany.html.

74. https://jewish-history-online.net/article/zimmermann-ludwig-holst.

75. Dorfer, *Judisches Leben in Eichtersheim*, 25.

76. Dorfer, *Judisches Leben in Eichtersheim*,12; Dagmar Herzog, *Intimacy and Exclusion: Religious Politics in Pre-Revolutionary Baden,* (Princeton: Princeton University Press, 1996), 8.

77. Gay, *The Jews of Germany*, 32; Dorfer, *Judisches Leben in Eichtersheim*, 56.

78. Ibid.

79. Dorfer, *Judisches Leben in Eichtersheim,* 49.

80. The new synagogue was built at the site of the house Maier Lazarus Heppen-heimer inherited from his father. The plaque states that the synagogue dates back to 1790, and so likely includes the old synagogue. Before his death in 1793, Joseph Leser owned a house that included a "schul." The word "schul" is German for school, but it is also the Yiddish word for synagogue. Thus, it is possible that Leser Joseph's house had been used by the town for religious services. Presum-ably, Maier Lazarus sold that house (or it was sold after his death), and the house was used as the town's synagogue until it was replaced with the new synagogue. Just before Kristallnacht in 1938, the synagogue was sold to a private individual, and so was not destroyed in the pogrom.

81. Hundsnurscher, *The Jewish Communities in Baden*, 11.

82. Dorfer, *Judisches Leben in Eichtersheim*, p. 61.

83. Dorfer, *Judisches Leben in Eichtersheim*, 62. In 1809, Baden allowed Jews to estab-lish their own primary schools. Jean-Paul Carvalho & Mark Koyama & Michael Sacks, "Education, identity, and community: lessons from Jewish Emancipation," *Public Choice,* Springer, vol. 171(1) (2017), 16.

84. Ibid., 62.

85. Ibid., 62-64. The first Jewish schools in Baden were founded around 1820 in the larger communities of Mannheim and Karlsruhe. Hundsnurscher, *The Jewish Communities in Baden*, 14. These early schools established by the Jewish communities did not survive more than a generation, since Jewish parents tended to send their children to Christian schools later in the century. Michael A. Meyer, "Jewish Communities in Transition," in *Germany-Jewish History in Modern Times, Volume 2 Emancipation and Acculturation: 1780-1871, 116*. That was the case for the Eichtersheim Jewish school, which closed its doors in 1868 as a result of rising costs and falling student enrollment. Dorfer, *Judisches Leben in Eichtersheim*, 65-67.

86. Dorfer, *Judisches Leben in Eichtersheim*, 56-57. The order also directed that the person reading from the Torah must have received permission from the Synagogue Council, that the congregation is prohibited from leaving the synagogue until the service is over, that children under 5 years old are prohibited from attending services, and that any errors in the reading of the Torah are to be immediately corrected. The Jewish community was expected to comply with all of the directives in the order. *Ibid.*

87. Kaplan, *Jewish Daily Life in Germany, 1618-1945*, 128.

88. Ibid.,129.

89. Jakob's daughter Johanna noted that her parents had been native German speakers in the 1920 U.S. Federal Census.

90. Aly, *Why the Germans, Why the Jews*, 29.

91. Seitz, *Eichtersheim und Seine Einwohner 1699-1903*, 132. Babette's father Hirsch Joseph Michel was a son of Joseph Michel, Jakob's grandfather, and the brother of Jakob's mother Rebekka. See http://www.landesarchiv-bw.de/ plink/?f=4-1224085-201. Hirsch Joseph left Eichtersheim for the adjacent town of Duhren around 1805. Unlike his father and brothers, who were traders, Hirsch Michel was a master butcher, and may have left Eichtersheim to apprentice with a master butcher in Duhren. See http://www.landesarchiv-bw. de/plink/?f=2-2421006. And unlike his father and brothers, who chose the surname "Wertheimer" when required to do so in 1809, Hirsch Joseph chose the surname "Michel." Interestingly, Hirsch's youngest son Abraham changed his surname to Wertheimer. See https://www.findagrave.com/memorial/174382483/hirsch-joseph-michel. Moreover, when Hirsch Michel's wife died, her death record referred to her as Johanna Wertheimer. See http://www. landesarchiv-bw.de/plink/?f=4-1224092-542. Still, when Hirsch Michel died, the record referred to him as Hirsch Michel. See http://www.landesarchiv-bw.de/ plink/?f=4-1224085-201.

92. Jakob's marriage record in the Standesbuch notes that he was schutzburger. GLA Karsruhe 390 Nr. 4737,. 26. www.landesarchiv-bw.de/plink/?f=4-1224101-26. The birth record for his son Joseph in 1851 notes that Jakob was both a schutzburger and a handelsmann. GLA Karlsruhe 390 Nr. 4737, 208. http://www.landesarchiv-bw.de/plink/?f=4-1224101-208.

93. Seitz, *Eichtersheim und Seine Einwohner 1699-1903*,132. Jews name their children after deceased relatives, and it is relatively easy to guess for whom each of Jakob's children was named: Maier after Maier Lazarus Heppenheimer; Johanna after Babette's mother, who died in 1837; Hirsch after Babette's father Hirsch, who died in 1846; Rebecka after Jakob's mother; Joseph after Jakob's grandfather

Joseph Michel Wertheimer; and Lazarus after Maier Lazarus Heppenheimer's father Leser Joseph.

94.   Dorfer, *Judisches Leben in Eichtersheim*, 39.

95.   Helmut Castritius, et. al., *Forschungen Zur Geschichte Der Juden, Band 3,* Hannover: Verlag Hahnsche Buchhandlung Hannover, 1996), 126. Peasants had been emancipated in Baden in 1783, so that they could buy their way out of medieval serfdom and hold land as private family property. Jerome Blum, *The End of the Old Order in Rural Europe,* (Princeton: Princeton University Press, 1978), 228; Dr. Titus Bahner, et al., *Releasing the True Value of Land: The Land Market and new Forms of Ownership for Organic Agriculture, Hitzacker/Germany,* (Oct. 2012), 8, *https://www.ibda.ch/wp-content/uploads/2014/12/Releasing-True-Value-of-Land-20141218.pdf.* The payments involved, however, burdened the peasant families for two or three generations, which explains their reliance on Jewish dealers. *Ibid.*

96.   Landes, David "The Jewish Merchant: Typology and Stereotypology in Germany," in *Publication of the Leo Baeck Institute, Year Book XIX,* (London: Secker & Warburg, 1974), 12.

97.   Hasia R. Diner, *A Time for Gathering: The Second Migration, 1820-1880,* 11.

98.   Monika Richardz, "Emancipation and Continuity: German Jews in the Rural Economy," in *Revolution and Evolution: 1848 in German-Jewish History*, W.E. Mosse, et al. (Eds.) (Turbingen: Mohr 1981), 98 (1981). Non-Jewish traders tended not to extend credit, so that peasants who could only pay in installments could only buy from Jews. *Ibid.*

99.   Gay, *The Jews of Germany*, 223; Monika Richarz, "Cattle trade and Country Jews in the 19th century: A Symbiotic Economic Relationship in Southwest Germany," *Menora: Jahrbuch fur Deutsch-Judische 1990*, (R. Piper GmbH & Co. 1990), 77.

100.   Dorfer, *Judisches Leben in Eichtersheim*, p. 39. The life of the trader was very hard. For example, the typical cattle trader would be away from home most of the week. He left home on Sunday, with a week's supply of kosher meat, bread, and fruit. At night, the trader would stay at a Jewish inn, a German inn that catered to Jewish travelers, or with a Jewish family. At the end of the week, he would have brought his cattle to a nearby cattle market to sell. The Jewish presence was so great at these markets that many of them provided kosher eating houses. After he was finished at the market, the trader would then return to his home on Friday for the Sabbath meal with his family. The trader would attend services in the synagogue and rest on the Sabbath, and would begin the work week again on Sunday. *See* Richardz, "Emancipation and Continuity: German Jews in the Rural Economy," 97; 110-11; Levinson, *Jewish Germany: An Enduring Presence from the Fourth to the Twenty-First Century*, 70; Werner, J. Cahnman, "Village and Small-Town Jews in Germany," in in *Publication of the Leo Baeck Institute, Year Book XIX,* (London: Secker & Warburg, 1974), 121.

101.   Ibid.

102.   "Richarz, *Cattle trade and Country Jews in the 19th century: A Symbiotic Economic Relationship in Southwest Germany,* 85.

103.   Michael Anthony Riff, "The Anti-Jewish Aspect of the Revolutionary Unrest of 1848 in Baden and its Impact on Emancipation," in *Year Book XXI of the Leo Baeck Institute*, (London: Secker & Warburg 1976), 28.

104.   Israel Smith Clare, *Illustrated Universal History*, (Philadelphia: P.W. Ziegler & Co., 1885), 374.

105.   Reinhard Rurup, "The European Revolutions of 1848 and Jewish Emancipation," in *Revolution and Evolution: 1848 in German-Jewish History*, 4.

106.   Richardz, *Emancipation and Continuity: German Jews in the Rural Economy*, 103.

107.   Riff, "The Anti-Jewish Aspect of the Revolutionary Unrest of 1848 in Baden and its Impact on Emancipation," 27.

108.   Ibid.

109.   Dorfer, *Judisches Leben in Eichtersheim*, 45-47.

110.   Ibid.

111.   https://www.ohio.edu/chastain/dh/frktele.htm.; Michael Brenner, "Between Revolution and Legal Equality," in *Germany-Jewish History in Modern Times, Volume 2 Emancipation and Acculturation: 1780-1871*, 291.

112.   Jonathan Richard Hill, *The Revolutions of 1848 in Germany, Italy, and France*, (Eastern Michigan University 2005), 13 https://commons.emich.edu/cgi/viewcontent.cgi?referer=https://www.google.com/&httpsredir=1&article=1044&context=honors.

113.   Monika Richardz, "Viehhandel und Landjuden im 19. Jahrhundert. Eine symbiotische Wirtschaftsbeziehung in Südwestdeutschland," *Menora. Jahrbuch für deutsch-jüdische Geschichte*, J. H. Schoeps (Ed.) (München: Piper, 1990), 83.

114.   Richardz, *Emancipation and Continuity: German Jews in the Rural Economy*, 103.

115.   Martyn Lyons, *Post-Revolutionary Europe: 1815-1856*, (Houndsmill: Palgrave Macmillian 2006), 148; "The Anti-Jewish Aspect of the Revolutionary Unrest of 1848 in Baden and its Impact on Emancipation," *Year Book XXI Publications of the Leo Baeck Institute*, (London: Secker & Warburg, 1976), 40.

116.   Unless otherwise noted, all of the information contained in this paragraph is derived from the Regional Church Archive Karlsruhe, Landeskirchliches Archiv Karlsruhe, 003.00, SpA 1886.

117.   "Sinsheim Historischer," at https://www.sinsheim.de/pb/site/Sinsheim/get/documents/sinsheim/PB5Documents/pdf/HistorischerStadtrundgang08_neu1.pdf.

118.   J.R. McCulloch, *McCulloch's Universal Gazetteer: A Dictionary, Geographical, Statistical, and Historical, of the Various Countries, Places, and Principal Natural Objects in the World*, (New York: Harper & Brothers, 1855), 253. Spelt remained a dominant grain until more productive strains of wheat replaced it in the early twentieth century. Thomas Robisheaux, *Rural Society and the Search for Order in Early Modern Germany*, (Cambridge: Cambridge University Press, 2002), 25.

119.   John MacGregor, *Germany: Her Resources, Government, Union of Customs, and Power*, (London: Whittaker and Co., 1848) 107.

120.   From the Owner Card Index in the Angelbachtel archives. There is no record in the archives of the house owned by Jakob Heppenheimer in the 1840s.

121.   Ibid.

122.   Kaplan, *Jewish Daily Life in Germany, 1618-1945*, 14 and 17.

123. From the Owner Card Index in the Angelbachtel archives; Seitz, *Eichtersheim und Seine Einwohner 1699-1903.*

124. Schleckmann, *Das Barockdorf im Eichtersheim*, 70. While Rebecka and Maier are buried in the cemetery in Waibstadt, the next generation are either buried in the cemetery in Eichtersheim or in the towns or cities to which they had emigrated. Five Heppenheimers are buried in the Eichtersheim cemetery: Rebecka and Maier's son Jakob and his wife Babette, their son Maier, and Babettte's nieces Hanchen and Jette (they were the daughters of Babette's brother Liebmann). Maier married Hanchen and then Jette. Their marriages are discussed in Chapter 2.

125. Dorfer, *Judisches Leben in Eichtersheim*, 13.

126. Seitz, *Eichtersheim und Seine Einwohner 1699-1903*, 132.

127. Ibid.

128. Ibid.

129. Ibid. While German law had only recently allowed marriage to a deceased wife's sister, previously believing it constituted incest, such a practice had long been common among Jews in Germany. *See* David Warren Sabean, "Kinship and Prohibited Marriages in Baroque Germany: Divergent Strategies among Jewish and Christian Populations," 102.

130. When Jakob's wife Babette died in 1862, the two younger sons (Joseph and Lazarus) were 11 and 8. Jakob and Babette's two daughters Johanna and Rebecka (who were 17 years old and 15 years old, respectively, at the time of their mother's death) likely assumed responsibility for the care of their brothers.

131. According to the town records, the house was transferred to Heinrich Wagenblass, although the date of the transfer was not recorded. *See* Owner Card Index in the Angelbachtel, Germany archives, Heidelbergerstrasse 11. Heinrich Wagenblass was born in Eichtersheim in 1842 and moved to Mannheim in 1869, so it seems likely that the house was sold to Wagenblass around the time of Babette's death in 1862. After the sale of the house, no Heppenheimer would ever again own a house in Eichtersheim.

132. Rudolf Glanz, *The German Jewish Mass Emigration*, American Jewish Archives, (April 1970), 57. These early Jewish immigrants wrote letters home about the great opportunities in America, propelling still more young Jews to emigrate. *See* Diner, *A Time for Gathering—The Second Migration 1820-1880*, 39. 200,000 German Jews arrived in America between 1820 and 1880, accounting for about 4 percent of total German emigration. *Ibid.*; Avraham Barkai, *Branching Out: German-Jewish Immigration to the United States, 1820-1914*, (New York: Holmes & Meier 1994), 9; *See also* Sanford Pinsker, *Is the Jewish-American Experience Over*, VQR (1993), https://www.vqronline.org/jewish-american-experience-over. The Jews of Eichtersheim were part of this migration; between 1843 and 1890, at least 55 Jews from Eichtersheim emigrated to America. *See* http://www.alemannia-judaica.de/eichtersheim_synagoge.htm.

133. Diner, *A Time for Gathering—The Second Migration 1820-1880*, 46-47.

134. Alice Goldstein, *Determinants of Change and Response Among Jews and Catholics in a Nineteenth Century German Village*, (New York: Columbia University Press, 1984), 19.

135. Johanna (later changed to Hanna) married Louis Rosenblatt, a widower from Cleveland, Ohio, on August 20, 1876 in New York, and moved to Cleveland with

Louis to care for Louis' 10 children from his first wife. Hannah and Louis had four additional children. They moved to New York City in the 1880s, before the birth of their last child. Johanna died on March 22, 1925, at the age of 79. Around the time that Johanna married, Rebecca (later changed to Regina) married Frederich Von Stein. Fritz was Protestant, which made Rebecka the first Heppenheimer to marry a non-Jew. The Steins moved to California, had three children, and then moved back to New York City, where their last two children were born. Regina moved back to New York around the time her sister Johanna moved back to New York. Regina died on December 25, 1906, at the age of 56.

136.   Seitz, *Eichtersheim und Seine Einwohner, 1699-1903,* 132. Sara was from Steinbach, a town just outside of Frankfurt. *See* https://www.myheritage.com/research/record-10817-594295-SF/hirsch-heppenheimer-and-sara-hammel-in-germany-hesse-marriage-index?s=573925011. Hirsch and Sara had nine children: Jacob (born March 4, 1871); Adolph (born June 23, 1873); Bertha (born Nov.7, 1874); Selma (born May 8, 1876); Max (born July 25, 1877); Helene (born May 30, 1879); Hedwig (born April 10, 1881); Leo (born November 13, 1883); and Elsa (born May 16, 1890).

137.   https://dbs.bh.org.il/place/frankfurt-am-main. By the time Hirsch moved to Frankfurt, the city was a welcoming town for Jews, but that was not always the case. *See* Helga Krohn, "Ein "Gruss aus Frankfurts Schonstem Stadtteil"—Blick in die Frankfurter Stadtentwicklung," in *Ostend: Blick in Ein Judisches Viertel,* (Frankfurt am Main: Judisches Museum Frankfurt am Main, 2000), 23. In 1424, Jews were declared enemies of the people and were locked behind a walled ghetto. *See* Amos Elon, *The Pity of It All,* (London: Penguin Books, 2002), 26. By 1743, three thousand Jews (about 10 percent of the population) were crowded into a space intended for three hundred. *Ibid.* Those three thousand Jews lived in two hundred houses, averaging 15 people to a house. Kaplan, *Jewish Daily Life in Germany, 1618-1945,* 13. The Judengasse (or Jew's Alley), where these 3,000 Jews lived, was closed off by high walls and the three heavy gates were locked at night and on Sundays and Christian holidays. *Ibid.* During the Napoleonic occupation, Jews were emancipated and the gates of the ghetto were removed. *Ibid.,* 133. Even after Jewish rights were once again restricted, Jews were allowed to live outside the Judengasse, and only the poorest Jews continued to live on the Judengasse. *Ibid.* By 1864, Jews were finally given freedom of trade and freedom of residency in Frankfurt. *See* A. Freimann and F. Kracauer, *Frankfort,* (Philadelphia: The Jewish Publication Society of America,1929), 221.

138.   Levinson, *Jewish Germany: An Enduring Presence from the Fourth to the Twenty-First Century,* 114.

139.   *See* https://www.jewishvirtuallibrary.org/frankfurt-on-the-main.

140.   Elon, *The Pity of It All,* 133.

141.   Jonathan C. Friedman, *The Lion and the Star: Gentile-Jewish Relations in Three Hessian Communities, 1919-1945,* Lexington, Kentucky: The University Press of Kentucky, 1998), 32. The Judengasse was razed in two phases: in 1874, the dilapidated buildings on the west side of the street were razed, and in 1884, most of the buildings on the east side of the street were demolished. *See* http://www.judengasse.de/ehtml/page812.htm. When Hirsch first moved to Frankfurt, he lived at Rechneigrabenstrasse 17, in the Altstadt and near the end of the old Judengasse.

142. Solveig Eggerz, *The German-Jewish Epoch of 1743-1933: Tragedy or Success Story,* The American Council for Judiasm, http://www.acjna.org/acjna/articles_detail. aspx?id=457, (2007).

143. Ibid.; David Welch, *Modern European History 1871-200: A Documentary Reader,* (London: Routledge Taylor & Francis Group 1994), 1. While this new country had a Parliament, it was largely powerless—Bismarck essentially ruled Germany (holding the key positions of Chancellor and Prime Minister), and was responsible only to the Kaiser. *Ibid.*

144. Aly, *Why the Germans, Why the Jews,* 15. The two key sentences in the law read as follows: "All still-existing restrictions on civic and citizenship rights based on differences of religious creed are hereby revoked. In particular, eligibility for participating in local and national political representation and holding public office is declared to be independent of religious creed." *Ibid.*

145. Seitz, *Eichtersheim und Seine Einwohner 1699-1903,* 132. Mina was born in Tairnbach, a town near Eichtersheim, on June 13, 1854. Mina's parents were Isaac and Regina Flegenheimer (or Flehenheimer). *See* Mulhausen Kathlolische und Israelitische Gemeinde Standesbuch 1851-1860, 390 Nr. 6068, 1 Band, 106, at http://www.landesarchiv-bw.de/plink/?f=4-1227189-106. Isaac's grandfather Israel Moses lived in Tairnbach and adopted the surname "Flahenheimer" in 1809. *See* http://www.archive.org/stream/lbi_brc_mf484_reel02#page/n831/mode/1up. Isaac was born "Jesaias" to Israel's son Gerson Aron in Tairnbach in 1821. *See* Seitz, *Eichtersheim und Seine Einwohner 1699-1903,* 349; https://www.findagrave.com/memorial/179547411/gerson-aron-flegenheimer. Mina's mother Regina was born in Eichtersheim and was Jakob Heppenheimer's first cousin (her father was Benedikt Wertheimer, Rebekka Heppenheimer's brother), which is likely how Joseph knew Mina. Thus, Joseph Heppenheimer and Mina were second cousins.

146. Aly, *Why the Germans, Why the Jews,* 70; W.E. Mosse, *Jews in the German Economy: The German-Jewish Economic Elite 1820-1935,* (Oxford: Oxford University Press, 1989), 396. For example, between 1871 and 1873, German entrepreneurs built as many blast furnaces and established as many ironworks and machine plants as in the previous seventy years. *See* Rudolf Glanz, *The German Jewish Mass Emigration,* American Jewish Archives, (April 1970), 71.

147. Mosse, *Jews in the German Economy: The German-Jewish Economic Elite 1820-1935,* 397-98.

148. Ibid., 399-400.

149. Fritz Stern, *Gold and Iron: Bismark, Bleichroder and the Building of the German Empire,* (New York: Vintage Books, 1979), 471.

150. Eggerz, *The German-Jewish Epoch of 1743-1933: Tragedy or Success Story.*

151. The larger cities in Germany had annual address books, which listed heads of households, their addresses, and, often, their occupations. The relevant address books for Frankfurt are available on both the Ancestry.com website and the website of Goethe University's digital collections, http://sammlungen.ub.uni-frankfurt.de/. Unless otherwise noted, the information about where the Heppenheimer family members lived and their occupations was derived from these address books.

152. Detlev Claussen, *Theodor Adorno: One Last Genius,* (Cambridge, MA: Belknap Press of Harvard University Press, 2008), 21.

153. Dieter Bartetzko, et. al., *Frankfurt in Fruhen Photographien 1850-1914*, (Munchen: Schirmer/Mosel, 1977), 46.

154. Ibid.

155. Bartetzko, *Frankfurt in Fruhen Photographien 1850-1914*, 47.

156. Franz Adickes became mayor of Frankfurt in 1891 and instituted an approach in the Ostend that allowed for separate residential and industrial development. *See* John Mullin, "American Perceptions of German City Planning at the Turn of the Century" (1976). Urbanism Past and Present, 9, at https://scholarworks.umass.edu/larp_faculty_pubs/35.

157. Krohn, Ein "Gruss aus Frankfurts Schonstem Stadtteil"—Blick in die Frankfurter Stadtentwicklung, 17.

158. Ayako Sakurai, *Science and Societies in Frankfurt am Main*, (London: Routledge, 2013), 89.

159. Hirsch and Joseph both moved to Louisenstrasse 15. The next year, Joseph moved across the street to Louisenstrasse 18. In 1882, both families moved to Bergerstrasse in the Ostend, Hirsch to Bergerstrasse 20 and Joseph across the street to Bergerstrasse 18.

160. Seligmann published, among other works, a prayer book (siddur) that became the definitive prayer book for Central European Jewish communities, "Siddur Avodas Yisrael." *See* "Destroyed German Synagogues and Communities: Biebrich," at http://germansynagogues.com/index.php/synagogues-and-communities?pid=66&sid=242:biebrich. Even today, many Jewish prayer books rely on the Hebrew text contained in Seligmann's siddur. *See* "A New Siddur," http://hirhurim.blogspot.com/2007/06/new-siddur.html. While Seligmann had attended religious schools early in his life, he was mostly self-taught. Still, he was able to use his body of work to obtain a PhD from the University of Leipzig in 1876. Robert Sheinberg, "Seligmann Baer's *Seder Avodat Yisrael* (1868): Liturgy, Ideology, and the Standardization of Nusah Ashkenaz," 25 (2014) at http://anyflip.com/vstw/amjc/basic.

161. Emma's older sister Mina married Kaufmann Bing in Biebrich and then moved to Frankfurt, where Kaufmann worked for a textile goods manufacturer. It may be that Kaufmann and Mina Bing knew Joseph Heppenheimer and introduced Emma to Joseph following Joseph's wife's death.

162. Rachel Heuberger/Helga Krohn, *Hinaus aus dem Ghetto—Juden in Frankfurt am Main 1800-1950*, (Frankfurt am Main: S. Fischer Verlag, 1988), 95.

163. Hans-Otto Schembs, *Der Borneplatz in Frankfurt am Main*, (Frankfurt am Main: Verlag Waldemar Kramer 1987), 96.

164. Heuberger, *Hinaus aus dem Ghetto—Juden in Frankfurt am Main 1800-1950*, 93-94.

165. https://frische-zentrum-frankfurt.de/frischezentrum/historie/. As discussed later, the Grossmarkthalle took on a more sinister role during the Holocaust.

166. When Lazarus moved to the Judengasse neighborhood, he was living at Allerheiligenstrasse 44. Lazarus and his family moved north of the Judengasse neighborhood in 1896 to Vilbelerstrasse 29, but then returned to the Judengasse neighborhood in the Altstadt in 1900. The family then moved back to the Northeast section of the city in 1902, moving to Bornheimer Landstrasse 64.

167.   A Jewish community had been founded in Frankenthal near the end of the eighteenth century, and the first synagogue was built around 1790. *See* http://juden-in-frankenthal.de/geschichte-der-juden/17-bis-19-jahrhundert/.

168.   http://germansynagogues.com/index.php/synagogues-and-communities?pid=67&sid=462:frankenthal; http://juden-in-frankenthal.de/geschichte-der-juden/17-bis-19-jahrhundert/.

169.   It is not clear why Maier remained in Eichtersheim when all of his siblings had left Eichtersheim years earlier. It may be that his wives, as sisters, had a close relationship with their mother Sara and were reluctant to leave her. And it may be that Sara was reluctant to leave the region she knew. Sara likely lived with her daughters (and Maier) until her death in 1880. Maier may also have had a successful trading business and was happy living in Eichtersheim. But what drove Maier out of Eichtersheim may not have been just the death of his second wife Jette, but also the death of his daughter Selma. Selma was born on May 17, 1885. Jette died in 1886, but Maier still remained in Eichtersheim. Selma died on May 19, 1887, having just turned two years old. *See* Seitz, *Eichtersheim und Seine Einwohner 1699-1903*, 132. Maier moved to Frankenthal later that year, perhaps trying to put the past few years of death, including the death of his youngest child, behind him. When Maier died in Mannheim in 1913, he chose to be buried in Eichtersheim, the only one of his siblings to do so, perhaps because both of his wives were buried there.

170.   Eggerz, *The German-Jewish Epoch of 1743-1933: Tragedy or Success Story,* 1.

171.   *See* https://www.jewishvirtuallibrary.org/wilhelm-marr; *see also* https://www.ushmm.org/wlc/en/article.php?ModuleId=10005175 .

172.   Peter Pulzer, *Jews and the German State,* (Detroit: Wayne State University Press, 2003), 105.

173.   Dorfer, *Judisches Leben in Eichtersheim,* 13.

174.   Ivan Berend, *An Economic History of Nineteenth Century Europe,* (Cambridge: Cambridge University Press, 2013), 220; DeVries, *Of Mettle and Metal,* 98.

175.   Joseph A. Biesinger, *Germany: A Reference Guide from the Renaissance to the Present*, New York: Facts on File, 2006), 84; DeVries, *Of Mettle and Metal,* 98. In 1871, Germany had approximately 21,000 kilometers of railroad track, but by 1890, the German railroad network had more than doubled to 43,000 kilometers. *See* Colleen A. Dunlavy and Thomas Welskopp, *Myths and Peculiarities: Comparing U.S. and German Capitalism,* GHI Bulletin No. 41(Fall 2007), 47, https://www.ghi-dc.org/fileadmin/user_upload/GHI_Washington/Publications/Bulletin41/033.pdf. As befits a relatively late industrializer, the German economy transformed rapidly between 1870 and 1913, enjoying an increase of 100 percent in real gross domestic product per capita. *Ibid.*

176.   In the 1860s, the open hearth process was invented, which allowed for the use of scrap metal in the production of steel. *See* Frederick J. Schottman, "Iron and Steel," *Mineral Facts and Problems,* (Washington, D.C.: Department of the Interior, 1985), 406.

177.   "History of the Steel Industry (1850—1970), Part 3, http://www.sabachem.com/Index.aspx?Page_=dorsaetoolssabachemnews&PageID=24&Page-IDF=0&lang=2&tempname=sabachemeng&sub=3&printpage=true&-BlockName=tool_dorsaetoolssabachemnews_sample_sabachemeng_block472&order=printskin&isPopUp=false. The world's steel production

increased from a half-million tons in 1870 to 28 million tons in 1900. *See* Richard W. Bulliet, et. al. (Eds.), *The Earth and its People, A Global History, Volume 2,* (Stanford: Cengage Learning, 2012), 577.

178. Dunlavy, *Myths and Peculiarities: Comparing U.S. and German Capitalism,* 36. In fact, by 1913, Germany's iron, steel and metal industries became its strongest industry, with some 2 million workers producing a sixth of the country's industrial output. *See* Berend, *An Economic History of Nineteenth Century Europe,* 221.

179. W.O. Henderson, *The Rise of German Industrial Power 1834-1914,* (Berkeley: University of California Press, 1975), 237.

180. A. Marcus, "Jews as Entrepreneurs in Weimar Germany," *Yivo Annual of Jewish Social Science,* (New York: Yiddish Scientific Institute, 1953), 176.

181. "Buying Combinations in the Metal Market," The U.S. Federal Trade Commission, Mining and Scientific Press, Volume 116, (January 19, 1918), 85.

182. S.M. Auerbach, "Jews in the German Metal Trade," in *The Leo Baeck Institute Year Book,* Volume 10, Issue 1, (January 1965), 188. The owners of Metallgesellschaft converted to Christianity, likely to enhance their business prospects. The German Jewish metal traders were active internationally, as Europe became increasingly dependent on foreign ores and metals. *See* Susan Becker, "The German Metal Traders Before 1914," in *The Multinational Traders,* ed. Geoffrey Jones, (London: Routledge, 1998), 70.

183. Geoffrey Gareth Jones and Andrew Spadafora, *Waste, Recycling and Entrepreneurship in Central and Northern Europe, 1870-1940,* Harvard Business School General Management Unit Working Paper No. 14-084 (March 4, 2014).

184. Geoffrey Jones, *Varieties of Green Business: Industries, Nations and Time,* (Cheltenham: Edward Elgar Publishing Limited, 2018), 39.

185. Ibid, 40.

186. The scrap metal market was very important to German manufacturing, particularly for the smaller companies that were able to compete with the larger companies because of the availability of scrap metals at relatively cheap prices. *See* Artur Adey, *Die Organisation und die Funktionen des deutschen Metallhandels,* dissertation for doctorate at the University of Cologne (1930), 96. And because of the lack of mineral resources, Germany relied for much of its metal supply on scrap and metallic residues. *See* Article on Meno Lissauer, at https://ia600300. us.archive.org/2/items/metallgesellscha01wasz/metallgesellscha01wasz.pdf, 470. While Jews played an insignificant role in new iron trading, in terms of scrap iron, Jewish traders represented 43.9 percent of all traders. Moreover, by 1913, 70 percent of all German companies that dealt in metals (both virgin and scrap) were Jewish-owned. *See* Marcus, *Jews as Entrepreneurs in Weimar Germany,* 177-78.

187. Richardz, "Viehhandel und Landjuden im 19. Jahrhundert. Eine symbiotische Wirtschaftsbeziehung in Südwestdeutschland," 81.

188. Gay, *The Jews of Germany,* 224.

189. An advertisement in the 1934 Frankfurt Address Book states that Gebruder Heppenheimer was established in 1877.

190. Hirsch and Joseph's families were still living together in the same apartment when they opened their first facility. Clearly, the focus on both brothers was on business over comfort.

191. Artur Adey, *Die Organisation und die Funktionen des deutschen Metallhandels,* dissertation for doctorate at the University of Cologne (1930), 81-82.

192. Ibid.

193. Ibid.

194. Felix Prager, *Hauser-Verzeichniss von Frankfurt-Sachsenhausen und Bornheim,* (Hansebooks: 1890), 25.

195. The Waste Trade Journal, Volume 4, Atlas Publishing Company, (January 11, 1908), 15.

196. *Handels-Adressbuch von Frankfurt am Main,* (Frankfurt: Druck und Verlag von Mahlau & Waldschmidt, 1900), 42. Both sons married in Germany after their parents emigrated to America. Jacob married Helene Michel on October 19, 1899. Unfortunately, Jacob died on February 3, 1900, leaving behind a pregnant widow. Adolph married Mathilde Schott on January 17, 1902.

197. Adolph would remain connected to Gebruder Heppenheimer until he emigrated to America in 1938.

198. At the time of Hirsch's emigration to America, Metallgesellschaft, headquartered in Frankfurt and started by Jews, was one of the largest metal trading companies in the world. Metallgesellscaft opened a New York affiliate in 1887. Becker, *The German Metal Traders Before 1914*, 70.

199. Henderson, *The Rise of German Industrial Power 1834-1914*, 173.

200. Ibid., 179.

201. https://www.immigrantentrepreneurship.org/entry.php?rec=167.

202. Ibid.; Becker, *The German Metal Traders Before 1914*, 80-81.

203. Smelting is the process of separating the desired metal from other materials. Pekka Roto, "Smelting and Refining," *Encyclopedia of Occupational Safety and Health,* Jeanne Mager Stellman (Ed.), Geneva: International Labour Office, 82.2, at https://www.google.com/books/edition/Encyclopaedia_of_Occupational_Health_and/nDhpLa1rl44C?hl=en&gbpv=1&bsq=smelting.

204. The facility was located on approximately 3 to 4 acres, and also included a scrap yard. Adolph lived at the house connected to the facility when it was first purchased, and then Joseph's son Benny lived there with his family. Both of Benny's sons were born there. Between 20 and 50 workers worked at the facility. *Recollections of Herb Harvey, as told to his nephew Steve Harvey in 1994 and 1995 ("Recollections of Herb Harvey").*

205. Other metal traders were also purchasing smelter facilities at the time, perceiving that vertical integration would be beneficial. *See* Becker, *The German Metal Traders Before 1914*, 75.

206. In German law, a Prokurist is a person that is "authorized to execute every kind of judicial or extrajudicial transaction and to perform every legal act associated with the operation of a commercial business." A Prokurist may not, however, sell real property unless authorized to do so by the company. *See* https://www.hk24.de/en/fairplay/business-law/authorizations-germany/1159414.

207. Being both in the iron and metals scrap business increased the complexity of the business for Gebruder Heppenheimer. The scrap iron business involved a smaller assortment of materials and was a simpler business to run. The metals business, on the other hand, required that the Heppenheimers have a comprehensive knowledge of metals and alloys and their market prices. *See* Marcus, *Jews as Entrepreneurs in Weimar Germany,* 181.

208. The Waste Trade Journal, Volume 4, Atlas Publishing Company, 15. The National Copper Company was incorporated in New Jersey in August 1905, with a capital stock of $7,000, which was increased to $50,000 in December 1906. *See https:// timesmachine.nytimes.com/timesmachine/1908/01/10/105001840.pdf.*

209. The Waste Trade Journal, Volume 4, Atlas Publishing Company, 14.

210. Ibid., 14-15. H. Heppenheimer & Sons, the scrap metal business, was incorporated on August 14, 1906, with a capital stock of $50,000. *See https://timesmachine. nytimes.com/timesmachine/1908/01/10/105001840.pdf.*

211. Adolph Keller proved to be extremely important to the future of a number of members of the Heppenheimer family in Germany. Even though he was not a blood relative (having married into the family), Keller provided letters of support to a number of Heppenheimers trying to leave Nazi Germany in the 1930s, including Curtis Heppen. Such letters of support enabled many Heppenheimers to escape Nazi Germany. While we do not know why Adolph was so generous to people he likely had never met, he may have felt that he owed his later success in the scrap metal business to his father-in-law, Henry Heppenheimer.

212. The Waste Trade Journal, (October 24, 1914), 11.

213. The Waste Trade Journal, Volume 4, Atlas Publishing Company, 14. Henry and his sons Leo and Max were, respectively, President, Treasurer, and Secretary of each corporation. *See https://timesmachine.nytimes.com/timesmachine/1908/01/10/105001840.pdf.*

214. The Waste Trade Journal, Volume 4, Atlas Publishing Company, (December 14, 1907), 15.

215. The Waste Trade Journal, Volume 4, Atlas Publishing Company, (February 22, 1908), 4; *see also* The Brass World and Platers Guide, Volume 4, Bridgeport, Conn., (January 1908), 34. At the time, it was reported that the two companies had liabilities in the aggregate of approximately $200,000. *See https://timesmachine.nytimes.com/timesmachine/1908/01/10/105001840.pdf.*

216. Henry was back in the scrap metal business by 1913, opening Williamsburg Smelting and Refining Works in New York. *See* The Waste Trade Journal, (July 5, 1913), 11. His son Leo managed the business. *Ibid.* Henry died the following year. Leo died a few years later in 1917 at the age of 34, having been ill for several years. *See* The Waste Trade Journal, (June 23, 1917), 16. Henry's son Max remained in the metals business, stating in the New York State census of 1925 that he was a metal dealer and in the 1930 Federal census that he was the manager of a metal factory. But Henry's family in America never achieved its earlier success in the scrap metal business.

217. *See* https://hetarchief.be/en/zoeken/heppenheimer.

218. Viktor Slotosch was a metalworking factory. *See* https://www.frankfurt.de/six-cms/detail.php?id=2345174&_ffmpar_az[_stadtteil_name]=Bergen-Enkheim.

219. Glückauf Berg- und Hüttenmännische Zeitschrift, (November 8, 1913), 1880, at http://delibra.bg.polsl.pl/Content/11438/Vol49_No45.pdf.

220. L. Bennett, "Assets Under Attack: Metal Theft, the Built Environment and the Dark Side of the Global Recycling Market," Environmental law and management, 2008, 20, 180, at https://pdfs.semanticscholar.org/654a/765086661e09b07fad-915caa1ca77a6b20f1.pdf.

221. The Torch, December 14, 1907, 3 at http://sammlungen.ub.uni-frankfurt.de/periodika/periodical/zoom/7613411?query=heppenheimer. The newspaper reporting the theft noted that Gebruder Heppenheimer was one of the largest scrap metal companies in Frankfurt. *Ibid.*

222. Ibid.

223. Alsace, which had originally been part of France, became part of Germany following France's defeat in the Franco-Prussian War in 1871. Allison Carrol, *The Return of Alsace to France 1918-1939,* (Oxford: Oxford University Press, 2018), 1. Following German annexation, Alsace citizens opting to retain their French citizenship left Alsace, and were replaced by German citizens. *See* Janet and Joe Robinson, *Handbook of Imperial Germany,* (Author House, 2009), 122. By 1910, the year Jacob moved to Strasbourg, twelve percent of the Alsace and Lorraine populations were German immigrants, and in the larger cities, such as Strasbourg, the population of immigrant Germans was between 30 and 40 percent. *Ibid*

224. An OHG, or an open trading company, was a partnership in which all of the partners are fully liable and fully liable to third party creditors. *See* https://www.frankfurt-main.ihk.de/existenzgruendung/rechtsfragen/idem/ohg/. As discussed later, Gebruder Heppenheimer was also registered as an OHG.

225. Paul Theobald, *Sie Waren Unsere Nachbarn Die Einzelschicksale der in der Stadt Frankenthal (Pfalz) Zwischen 1933 und 1945 Lebenden Juden,* (Radeberg: Verlag DeBehr, 2019) Kindle Edition.

226. Ibid.

227. Theobald, *Sie Waren Unsere Nachbarn Die Einzelschicksale der in der Stadt Frankenthal (Pfalz) Zwischen 1933 und 1945 Lebenden Juden.*

228. *See* Reparations Request of Walter Schwarz, Hessisches Landesarchiv Hauptstaatsarchiv Wiesbaden, 518-50789.

229. Berta's daughter Johanna was also in the scrap metal business, owning J. Bauernfreund & Co. with another partner in Frankfurt, but that business did not begin until the mid-1930s. As discussed later, it appears that Johanna started her business only after her husband could no longer continue to operate his metals business following bankruptcy and imprisonment.

230. As will be discussed later, Adolph moved back to Germany around the start of World War I.

231. http://www.wormserjuden.de.

232. Landesarchiv Baden-Württemberg- Generallandesarchiv Karlsruhe, File No. 480-8086.

233. Ibid.

234. Marion A. Kaplan, *The Making of the Jewish Middle Class: Women, Family, and Identity in Imperial Germany,* (New York: Oxford University Press, 1991), 7. The increase in Jewish population resulted, in part, from a large increase in the number of Eastern Europeans entering Germany. By 1910, Jews from eastern Europe accounted for 12.8% of the German-Jewish population. Keith Pinckus, *Constructing Modern Identities: Jewish University Students in Germany, 1815-1914,* (Detroit: Wayne State University Press 1999), 82.

235. *See* Mordechai Breuer, "Frankfurt on the Main," https://www.jewishvirtuallibrary.org/frankfurt-on-the-main. While the absolute number increased, the Jewish percentage of the population in Frankfurt decreased, from 11% of the total population in 1871 to 7.6% of the population in 1900. Ibid.; Steven M. Lowenstein, "Was Urbanization Harmful to Jewish Tradition and Identity in Germany?" *People of the City: Jews and the Urban Challenge,* Ezra Mendelsohn (Ed.) (New York: Oxford University Press, 1999), 87.

236. Ibid., 241. Until about 1860, Germany had been a borrower rather than a lender nation. Henderson, *The Rise of German Industrial Power 1834-1914,* 240.

237. Mordechai Breuer, Frankfurt on the Main," https://www.jewishvirtuallibrary.org/frankfurt-on-the-main.

238. Aly, *Why the Germans, Why the Jews,* 31.

239. *See* http://sammlungen.ub.uni-frankfurt.de/cm/periodical/pageview/3521735?query=joseph%20heppenheimer. The hospital, Shaare Zedek Medical Center, is still in existence and is considered the largest multi-disciplinary medical center in Jerusalem. *See* www.szmc.org.il.

240. Lazarus had died in 1903 and Henry's son Jacob had died in 1900.

241. *Memorial at the Frankfurt Grossmarkt—Two phase competition,* 27, https://www.competitionline.com/upload/downloads/12xx/1209_3016174_Auslobung-competition%20brief_.pdf

242. By contrast, in 1913, 87 percent of Frankfurt's residents were considered low-income. Bartetzko, *Frankfurt in Fruhen Photographien 1850-1914,* 47.

243. The boarding school—Madchen-Pensionat Ettlinger—offered instructions in household, cooking, handicrafts and scientific and social education to young women from small towns. *See* Klara Erlanger, "Ein halbes Jah rim Madchen-Pensionat Ettlinger, Roderbergweg 30," in *Osten: Blick in Ein Judisches Viertal,* 78.

244. Takahito Mori, *From Luxury to Necessity: Frankfurt am Main as the Pioneer of Urban Electrification,* Discussion Paper Series No. 2016-12, 6.

245. Bartetzko, *Frankfurt in Fruhen Photographien 1850-1914,* 60.

246. Helmut Nordmeyer, *Gastronomie in Alt-Frankfurt,* (Erfurt: Sutton Verlag, 2013), 123.

247. Paul Arnsberg, *Bilder aus dem Judischen Leben im Alten Frankfurt,* (Frankfurt am Main: Waldemar Kramer, 1970), 166; 175. Coffee and tea consumption in these coffee houses likely hindered alcohol abuse in Frankfurt among Jews. *Ibid.,* 166.

248. Ibid., 176-77.

249. Ibid., 175-76.

250. Ibid., 176.

251. Ibid., 177.

252. Ibid., 175. The Heppenheimer family may have dined at Café Goldschmidt or may have visited Kursaal Milani, a café in the Ostend, where concerts occurred in the evenings and where Jews in the Ostend often met on the Sabbath. *Ibid.*, 171.

253. Café Goldschmidt remained open until the middle 1920s. The last owner of the Café died in a concentration camp during the Holocaust. *Ibid.*, 178.

254. http://www.trampage.de/zeittafel_p215.html

255. Helga Krohn, "Ein 'Gruss aus Frankfurts schonstem Stadtteil'—Blick in die Frankfurter Stadtentwicklung," 19.

256. Ibid., 24.

257. Friedman, *The Lion and the Star,* 15. *See also* "Jewish Communities of Prewar Germany," at https://encyclopedia.ushmm.org/content/en/article/jewish-communities-of-prewar-germany. The government would collect taxes from the Jewish community and forward those amounts to the Gemeinde. *See* Giora Lotan, "The Functionary in Jewish Communal Life," in *Year Book XIX of the Leo Baeck Institute,* (London: Secker & Warburg, 1976), 212.

258. "The Succession From the Frankfurt Jewish Community Under Samson Raphael Hirsch," *Historia Judaica,* 106 (October 1948)

259. Friedman, *The Lion and the Star,* 47. While most of the Orthodox Jews in Frankfurt went to the Boerneplatz synagogue, there was a split among Orthodox Jews. *See* http://www.juedisches-frankfurt.de/orte/erinnerungsstaette-synagoge-friedberger-anlage. In 1873, a bill was passed in Germany that allowed members of a church to leave that church while still remaining Christians. *The Succession From the Frankfurt Jewish Community Under Samson Raphael Hirsch,* Historia Judaica, p. 108. Orthodox Jews bristling against liberal Judaism pushed for their own secessionist bill, which passed in 1876. *Ibid.* at 109. Led by Samson Raphael Hirsch, some of Frankfurt's Orthodox Jews left the Gemeinde and established a separate Orthodox community. Friedman, *The Lion and the Star,* 18. The separatist Israelitische Religionsgesellschaft (IRG) built a synagogue on Friedberger Anlage in 1907 to replace an earlier synagogue. http://www.juedisches-frankfurt.de/orte/erinnerungsstaette-synagoge-friedberger-anlage. The synagogue was the largest in Frankfurt with 1,600 seats. *Ibid.*

260. Diner, *A Time for Gathering—The Second Migration 1820-1880,* 22. The Reform movement added an organ, German sermons and hymns, and shortened prayers. Ibid., 23.

261. Freimann, *Frankfurt,* 263.

262. Michael A. Meyer, "Jewish Identity in the Decades After 1848," in *Germany-Jewish History in Modern Times, Volume 2 Emancipation and Acculturation: 1780-1871,* 323.

263. *See* http://germansynagogues.com/index.php/synagogues-and-communities?pid=54&sid=468:frankfurt-am-main-boernestrasse-the-main-synagogue.

264. Rachel Heuberger (Ed.), *100 Years Western Synagogue Frankfurt am Main 1910-2010,* 20-21, at https://jg-ffm.de/mandanten/1/images/religioeses_leben/synagogen/100_Jahre_Westend_Synagoge_100_ani.pdf.

265. http://www.juedisches-frankfurt.de/orte/erinnerungsstaette-synagoge-friedberger-anlage.

266. http://germansynagogues.com/index.php/synagogues-and-communities?pid=66&sid=260:bockenheim-1.

267. Benno Nietzel, *Handeln und Uberleben: Judische Unternehmer aus Frankfurt am Main 1924-1964*, (Gottingen: Vandenhoeck & Ruprecht, 2012), 31.

268. Ibid.

269. As discussed later, we know that Joseph's sons conducted business on Saturday.

270. Rachel Heuberger, *100 Years Western Synagogue Frankfurt am Main 1910-2010*, 11-12.

271. Ibid., 14.

272. Ibid., 14.

273. Ibid., 15. Bat mitzvah ceremonies were first performed in Germany in the mid-nineteenth century. Scott-Martin Kosofsky, *The Book of Custom: A Complete Handbook for the Jewish Year*, (San Francisco: Harper San Francisco, 2004), 5.

274. Susanne Wiborg, "Why is there no comprehensive education in Germany? A historical explanation," *History of Education*, Vol. 39, No. 4, (July 2010), 541.

275. Ibid.

276. Ibid.

277. Jennifer Hart, "Tracking German Education: An Examination of Three Postwar Periods," Loyola University Chicago, Master's Theses, 3134, 26, at https://ecommons.luc.edu/luc_theses/3134.

278. Given the fact that Joseph sent his children to the Philanthropin, the Jewish school of the Reform movement, he likely embraced the Reform movement. Still, Joseph maintained ties with the Orthodox community. Rabbi Nehemiah Nobel, one of the Frankfurt Gemeinde's Orthodox rabbis, had been a well-known and influential Orthodox Rabbi in Frankfurt and a leader of the centrist wing of German Orthodoxy (as opposed to the separatist wing let by Rabbi Samson Raphael Hirsch). *Philosophical and Theological Writings*, Franz Rosenzweig, Hackett Publishing Company, Inc. p. 146-147 n. 3 (2000). When Rabbi Nobel died in 1922, Gebruder Heppenheimer donated 24 trees in memory of the rabbi. *See* http://sammlungen.ub.uni-frankfurt.de/cm/periodical/pageview/2707295?query=heppenheimer. This gesture may have been a recognition of the importance of maintaining good relationships with all members of the Jewish community as a Jewish business. This would not be that dissimilar from the advertisements placed by the Gebruder Heppenheimer in their early years of business in the Orthodox Jewish paper. But it also may have been reflective of Rabbi Nobel's important place in the Frankfurt community. Rabbi Nobel had promoted women's suffrage in Jewish community elections. Because of his and other's efforts, Jewish women were granted the right to vote and hold office in the Frankfurt community council in 1920, so that by 1924, four women sat on the Frankfurt community council and one on its executive committee. Donald L. Niewyk, *The Jews in Weimar Germany*, (Baton Rouge: Louisiana State University, 1980), 121. Rabbi Nobel was also at the center of a revival of interest in classical Judaism among young people from assimilated liberal homes post-World War I, who were enthralled by his sermons and their accessibility, and Gebruder Heppenheimer may have supported such outreach to Frankfurt's Jewish youth. Paul Mendes-Flohr, "Jewish Cultural and Spiritual Life," *German-Jewish History in Modern Times: Renewal and Destruction, 1918-1945, 139.*

279. Programm der Realschule der Israelitischen Gemeinde (Philanthropin) zu Frankfurt a. M. Ostern 1896, 67, https://books.google.com/books?id=OLk-sAAAAYAAJ&pg=PA67&dq=heppenheimer+frankfurt&hl=en&sa=X&ved=2a-hUKEwiI-6nx7N_kAhUomeAKHVniDF84MhDoATAJegQICBAC#v=onep-age&q=heppenheimer&f=false. Although I could find no evidence that Henry's children attended the Philanthropin, given his support of the school through fundraisers, his children also likely attended.

280. Reparations Request of Bertha Marx, Hessisches Landesarchiv Hauptstaatsarchiv Wiesbaden, HHStAW 518-30144.

281. Carvalho, "Education, Identity, and Community: Lessons from Jewish Emancipation," 18.

282. Shulamit Volkov, *Germans, Jews, and Antisemites—Trials in Emancipation,* (Cambridge: Cambridge University Press, 2006), 283. At the beginning of the nineteenth century, approximately 2 percent of Germany's doctors were Jewish. By the end of the nineteenth century, Jews made up 16 percent of all German doctors, and nearly half of all Jews attending universities in 1900 were there to study medicine. John Efron, *Medicine and the German Jews: A History*, (New Haven: Yale University, 2001), 234.

283. Volkov, *Germans, Jews, and Antisemites—Trials in Emancipation*, 283.

284. In his recollections, Herb Harvey, a grandson of Joseph Heppenheimer, noted that the family's focus was on making money and that university education was not valued by the family. *See Recollections of Herb Harvey.* One can imagine that, growing up with economic challenges in Eichtersheim, being financially successful was the goal for the sons of Jakob Heppenheimer.

285. Kaplan, *The Making of the Jewish Middle Class: Women, Family, and Identity in Imperial Germany*, 154. Jewish middle-class families had considered employment outside the home (other than in the family business) unladylike and improper for their daughters. *Ibid.*, 169.

286. Ibid., 171.

287. Ibid. For example, Joseph's daughter Bertha was 22 years old when she married in 1898 (after having left school at 14) and Johanna was 25 years old when she married in 1902.

288. Ibid., 137.

289. Ibid.

290. As discussed later, Alice opened an applied arts studio in Nuremberg in the late 1920s and became a member of the dressmakers guild in Frankfurt in 1933 when she opened her dressmaking shop, which would have required an apprenticeship. Alice would have received such training for both fields in an arts and crafts school.

291. Wolf-Dietrich Greinert, *Mass Vocational Education and Training in Europe,* (Cedefop Panaorama Series, 2005), 65.

292. Jeremy Aynsley, *Designing Modern Germany,* (London: Reaktion Books, 2009), 9. These arts and crafts schools were incorporating the arts and crafts movement into their curriculum, which included the revival of handcrafted objects, integration of art into everyday life, and an aesthetic incorporating indigenous materials

and native traditions. *See* http://artdaily.com/news/12042/The-Arts-and-Crafts-Movement-in-Europe-and-America#.W6peRxNKj64.

293. Arthur Henry Chamberlain, *The Condition and Tendencies of Technical Education in Germany,* (Syracuse: C.W. Barden Publisher, 1908), https://www.gutenberg.org/files/26595/26595-0.txt.

294. Ibid.

295. Michael Cowan, "The Ambivalence of Ornament: Silhouette Advertisements in Print and Film in Early Twentieth-Century Germany," 787, https://pdfs.semanticscholar.org/5863/3c6493fb45f59f232fcb34beefdac990a8ef.pdf.

296. https://www.adbk-nuernberg.de/en/academy/history/. The school has since become a school of fine arts, and is the oldest art college in the German-speaking world. *Ibid. See also* Anne-Kathrin Herber, "Frauen an deutschen Kunstakademien im 20. Jahrhundert. Ausbildungsmöglichkeiten für Künstlerinnen ab 1919 unter besonderer Berücksichtigung der süddeutschen Kunstakademien," Dissertation for a Doctorate in Philosophy at the University of Heidelberg, p. 94, http://archiv.ub.uni-heidelberg.de/volltextserver/11048/1/Dissertation_Teil_I_Anne_Kathrin_Herber.pdf. There was an arts and crafts school in Frankfurt -- the Die Frankfurter Kunstgewerbeschule or the Frankfurt School of Applied Arts -- but it does not appear that it accepted women students at the time Alice would have attended. *See* http://www.frankfurt-live.com/die-frankfurter-kunstgewerbeschule-und-ihre-akteure-vortrag-im-institut-f-uumlr-stadtgeschichte-99900.html.

297. In the first academic year women were accepted by the Nuremberg School of Applied Arts—1906/1907—14 women attended out of a total of 171 students. *Ibid.*; Anne-Kathrin Herber, "Frauen an deutschen Kunstakademien im 20. Jahrhundert. Ausbildungsmöglichkeiten für Künstlerinnen ab 1919 unter besonderer Berücksichtigung der süddeutschen Kunstakademien," 95. Most of the students attending were from Bavaria, but there were others attending from elsewhere in Germany. *Ibid.*, 96.

298. Kara L. Ritzheimer, "Trash, Censorship, and National Identity," (Cambridge: Cambridge University Press, 2016) 136.

299. http://sammlungen.ub.uni-frankfurt.de/periodika/periodical/search/7338480?query=heppenheimer.

300. *See* http://sammlungen.ub.uni-frankfurt.de/periodika/periodical/pageview/9589278?query=%22josef%20heppenheimer%22.

301. Worms is one of the oldest German cities, and its Jewish community dates back to Roman times. *See* https://www.jewishgen.org/yizkor/pinkas_germany/ger3_00191.html. By the time Ludwig and Sally moved to Worms, the Jewish community numbered about 1,300, representing approximately 3 percent of the population. *Ibid.* By the turn of the twentieth century, the members of the Worms Jewish community owned a variety of stores and manufacturing establishments, including 5 metal manufacturing facilities. *Ibid.* Most of the Jews of Worms were non-observant and their shops remained open on Saturdays. *Ibid.*

302. Mannheim was significantly larger than Frankenthal, with 6,402 Jews living there by 1913. *See* https://dbs.bh.org.il/place/mannheim. Jews had first settled in Mannheim in the seventeenth century, and there was an active and vibrant Jewish community by the time Leopold moved to the city. *Ibid.* The Reform movement was strong in Mannheim by the turn of the twentieth century. *See* Isaac Landman

et al., *The Universal Jewish Encyclopedia, Volume 7,* (New York: Universal Jewish Encyclopedia, Inc. 1942), 330.

303.   Friedman, *The Lion and the Star,* 28.

304.   Ibid.

305.   After a few years with Gebruder Heppenheimer, Marcus became responsible for the financial management of the company. Bertha and Marcus had two daughters. Their daughter Bettina was born on March 19, 1901, and their daughter Erna was born on January 16, 1906. When Marcus Marx died in 1925, the company provided Bertha with a pension of 200 RM a month. *See* Hessisches Landesarchiv Hauptstaatsarchiv Wiesbaden, HHStAW 518-30144.

306.   Johanna and Isidor had a daughter Martha, who was born on August 4, 1903.

307.   They had a daughter Melanie, born on October 20, 1909 and a son, Ernst (later Ernest Harvey), born on March 7, 1914. Joseph's other two children from his first marriage—Benny and Max—would marry Jewish women after the war. Those marriages are discussed in Chapter 6.

308.   Maier's oldest son Jacob had emigrated to America and his wife was likely Jewish and Maier's son Adolph never married.

309.   Seitz, *Eichtersheim und Seine Einwohner 1699-1903,* 132. Helene was born in Eichtersheim and she likely knew Leopold before he moved to Frankenthal with his family.

310.   http://www.wormserjuden.de/.

311.   Ibid.

312.   *See* https://www.geni.com/people/Jacob-Heppenheimer/6000000040124840016 ?through=6000000040123242589#/tab/overview. Jacob's engagement to Rosalie was announced in Das Judische Blatt, the Jewish paper of the Alsace and Lorraine region, on July 11, 1913. *See* http://sammlungen.ub.uni-frankfurt.de/cm/periodical/pageview/9052561?query=heppenheimer; http://judaisme.sdv.fr/histoire/document/bulletin/blatt.htm.

313.   "World War I," at https://www.history.com/topics/world-war-i/world-war-i-history; "Germany from 1871 to 1918; The German Empire, 1871-1914," Britannica, at britannica.com/place/Germany/Germany-from-1871-to-1918.

314.   *See* "Assassination of Archduke Franz Ferdinand," at https://www.ushmm.org/learn/timeline-of-events/before-1933/assassination-of-archduke-franz-ferdinand.

315.   "Outbreak of World War I," at https://www.history.com/topics/world-war-i/outbreak-of-world-war-i.

316.   Paul Mendes-Flohr, "In the Shadow of the World War," *German-Jewish History in Modern Times,* Volume 4, 8.

317.   Ibid., 8-9. The philosopher Martin Buber, prophet of the Jewish cultural renaissance, welcomed World War I as a war that would unite Germans and Jews in a joint "world historical mission" to free the Jews from tsarist Russia." *See* Eggerz, *The German-Jewish Epoch of 1743-1933: Tragedy or Success Story,* 9.

318.   Friedman, *The Lion and the Star,* 22.

319.   Donald L. Niewyk, *The Jews of Weimar Germany,* 9.

320.   Pulzer, *Jews and the German State,* 195.

321. "German Veterans Association Badges, Grand Duchy Hessen," at http://www. omsa.org/files/jomsa_arch/Splits/1991/4123_JOMSA_Vol42_5_10.pdf; "XVIII. Army Corps (German Empire)," at http://oer2go.org:81/wikipedia_de_all_ novid_2017-08/A/XVIII._Armee-Korps_(Deutsches_Kaiserreich).html.

322. *Histories of the Two Hundred and Fifty-one Divisions of the German Army Which Participated in the War (1914-1918),* Document No. 905, (Washington, D.C.: War Department, 1920), 315, 352. Each of Frankfurt's divisions participated in the First Battle of the Marne in 1914, which led to four years of trench warfare, and the Battle of the Somme in 1916, one of the bloodiest battles in human history. *Ibid.*

323. Ibid., 316, 353.

324. Ibid., 316; "History of the Great War of 1914 to 1918" at https://www65.statcan. gc.ca/acyb07/acyb07_2017e-eng.htm

325. Notice in the Neue Judische Press, January 4, 1918, page 4, contained in http:// sammlungen.ub.uni-frankfurt.de/cm/periodical/pageview/2705509?query=hep- penheimer. An Iron Cross 2nd Class was given for a single act of bravery in the face of the enemy, or actions above and beyond the call of duty. *See* https://www. epicmilitaria.com/1914-iron-cross-2nd-class.html.

326. "How the First World War Ended," https://www.bl.uk/world-war-one/articles/ how-the-first-world-war-ended; "Armistice of November 1918: Centenary Debate on 5 November 2018," *House of Lords Library Briefing,* 3, at http://researchbrief- ings.files.parliament.uk/documents/LLN-2018-0112/LLN-2018-0112.pdf.

327. "Armistice of November 1918: Centenary Debate on 5 November 2018," *House of Lords Library Briefing,* 3.

328. *Histories of the Two Hundred and Fifty-one Divisions of the German Army Which Participated in the War (1914-1918),* 354.

329. *See* "Rank Insignia of the German Army, 1914-1918," at http://www.worldwar1. com/sfgrank.htm.

330. "Armistice of November 1918: Centenary Debate on 5 November 2018," *House of Lords Library Briefing,* 5. One of the last battles of the war took place in Le Ques- noy on November 4. *See* "1918: Spring Offensive and Advance," https://nzhistory. govt.nz/war/western-front-1918.

331. Ibid.

332. City Archive Mannheim, 6/1967_00224 Jews in Court/Rassenchande II (1937), Hakenkreuzbanner, June 4, 1936. Leopold's wife Helene became a Prokurist for his company during the war, likely to keep the company functioning during her husband's absence.

333. Reparations Request of Sally Heppenheimer, Landesarchiv Baden-Württemberg- Generallandesarchiv Karlsruhe, File No. 480-8086.

334. *Die jüdischen Gefallenen des deutschen Heeres, der deutschen Marine und Schutz- truppen, 1914-1918,* (Berlin: Der Schild, 1932), 144.

335. *Histories of Two Hundred and Fifty-One Divisions of the German Army Which Participated in the War (1914-1918),* War Department Document No. 905, (Washington, D.C.: Government Printing Office, 1920), 256.

336. Ibid., 257

337. *Die jüdischen Gefallenen des deutschen Heeres, der deutschen Marine und Schutztruppen, 1914-1918,* 144.

338. *Die jüdischen Gefallenen des deutschen Heeres, der deutschen Marine und Schutztruppen, 1914-1918,* 110.

339. *Histories of Two Hundred and Fifty-One Divisions of the German Army Which Participated in the War (1914-1918),* 284; https://en.wikipedia.org/wiki/85th_Landwehr_Division_(German_Empire)

340. https://en.wikipedia.org/wiki/85th_Landwehr_Division_(German_Empire)

341. *Die jüdischen Gefallenen des deutschen Heeres, der deutschen Marine und Schutztruppen, 1914-1918,* 110.

342. Paul Mendes-Flohr, "In the Shadow of the World War," *German-Jewish History in Modern Times,* Volume 4, 8-9. The total Jewish population of Germany was 539,000 in 1910, with about half being women and a little more than 20 percent being children under the age of 18. *See* Erich Rosenthal, "Trends of the Jewish Population in Germany, 1910-39," *Jewish Studies,* Vol. 6, No. 3, (Indiana University Press, 1944), 236-247. Thus, as many as one-half of all Jewish men in Germany fought in the war.

343. Eggerz, *The German-Jewish Epoch of 1743-1933: Tragedy or Success Story,* 9.

344. Ritchie Robertson (Ed.), *The German-Jewish Dialogue: An Anthology of Literary Texts, 1749-1993,* (Oxford: Oxford University Press, 1999), xxii; Aly, *Why the Germans, Why the Jews,* 102. The Prussian War Ministry was responsible for all of Germany with the exception of Bavaria, Saxony and Wurttemberg. "The Prussian War Ministry," at https://encyclopedia.1914-1918-online.net/article/prussian_war_ministry. The actual results of this census were never published, and were likely destroyed in the Allied bombing of Berlin and Potsdam in World War II that destroyed the entire archives of the German army. *See* David J. Fine, *Jewish Integration in the German Army in the First World War,* (Berlin: de Gruyter, 2012), 16.

345. Gay, *The Jews of Germany,* 243.

346. "History of the Jews Until the End of the First World War," in http://www.frankfurt1933-1945.de/. After the war, antisemitism sparked by the Jewish census caused Jewish German war veterans to create the Reichsbund Juedischer Frontsoldaten (RJF), or the Union of German Jewish War Veterans, in February 1919. 40 Jewish soldiers who had served on the frontlines of the German army during World War I established it to disprove the popular belief that, during World War I, Jews had either only held desk jobs or had avoided serving in the army altogether. One of their proofs of Jewish service was the fact that 12,000 Jewish soldiers had died fighting for Germany. By 1933, the RJF had grown to include 30,000 members in 360 local branches. After Hitler rose to national power, the RJF tried to avoid being affected by the Nazis' anti-Jewish policies and attempted to win themselves a privileged status. They were able to maintain their unique status until the Nuremberg laws were passed in 1935, at which point they lost their preferential treatment. *See* https://www.yadvashem.org/odot_pdf/Microsoft%20Word%20-%205781.pdf.

347. Mosse, *Jews in the German Economy: The German-Jewish Economic Elite 1820-1935,* 386.

348. Ibid., 386-88.

349. "Elimination of German Resources for War," Hearings Before a Subcommittee of the Committee on Military Affairs, United States Senate, 7th Cong. 1st Sess., (June 26, 1945), 284.

350. CU 150: The History of the Copper Group, Aurubis AG, 30, https://www.aurubis.com/binaries/content/assets/aurubis-en/dateien/jubilee/cu_150.0_engl_einzelseiten.pdf.

351. Artur Adey, *"Die Organisation und die Funktionen des deutschen Metallhandels,"* 11, 81.

352. Frank Carrigan ,"The Imperial Struggle for Control of the Broken Hill Base-Metal Industry, 1914-1915," *Essays in the Political Economy of Australian Capitalism,* Volume Five, E.L.Wheelwright and Ken Buckley (Eds.), (Sydney: Australia & New Zealand Book Company, 1983), 170.

353. "Disarmament and the Metals," Engineering and Mining Journal, Vol. 112, No. 22, (Nov. 26, 1921), 878.

354. Ibid.

355. Artur Adey, *"Die Organisation und die Funktionen des deutschen Metallhandels,"* 99.

356. D.C. Williamson, "Walter Rathenau and the K.R.A. August 1914—March 1915," *Journal of Business History* 23, Jahrg., H. 2., (1978), 118-21.

357. Ibid., 123; Artur Adey, *"Die Organisation und die Funktionen des deutschen Metallhandels,"* 102.

358. Williamson, *"Walter Rathenau and the K.R.A. August 1914-March 1915,"* 124.

359. Ibid.

360. Mark D. Karau, *Germany's Defeat in the First World War: The Lost Battles and Reckless Gambles That Brought Down the Second Reich,* (Santa Barbara: Praeger, 2015), 51.

361. *"Disarmament and the Metals,"* Engineering and Mining Journal, Vol. 112, No. 22, (Nov. 26, 1921), 878.

362. *CU 150: The History of the Copper Group, Aurubis AG, 30,* https://www.aurubis.com/binaries/content/assets/aurubis-en/dateien/jubilee/cu_150.0_engl_einzelseiten.pdf

363. For example, the K.R.A. subcontracted with Norddeutsche Affinerie AG, a Jewish-owned metals company, to smelter metals to produce copper and tin. *CU 150: The History of the Copper Group, Aurubis AG,* 31, at . https://www.aurubis.com/binaries/content/assets/aurubis-en/dateien/jubilee/cu_150.0_engl_einzelseiten.pdf.

364. Frankfurter Zeitung, July 6, 1916, 6, at http://sammlungen.ub.uni-frankfurt.de/periodika/periodical/pageview/6928891?query=heppenheimer.

365. https://chroniclingamerica.loc.gov/lccn/sn83045081/1915-04-11/ed-1/seq-11.pdf.

366. "German War Bonds: The Financial Source of the War," at https://boerse.ard.de/boersenwissen/boersengeschichte-n/die-finanzquelle-des-krieges100.html.

367.   Gerd Hardach, "Financial Mobilization in Germany 1914-1918," EABH Papers, No. 1408 Septt. 2014), 11-12, at http://bankinghistory.org/wp-content/uploads/eabhpapers14_08.pdf.

368.   Ibid.

369.   Frankfurter Zeitung und Handelsblatt, Sept. 29, 1917, 3, at http://sammlungen.ub.uni-frankfurt.de/periodika/periodical/zoom/7020364?query=Kriegsanleihe%20heppenheimer.

370.   Frankfurter Zeitung und Handelsblatt, June 10, 1917, at http://sammlungen.ub.uni-frankfurt.de/periodika/periodical/zoom/6950658?query=%22joseph%20heppenheimer%22.

371.   With the massive devaluation of money, the German government was able to pay off these debts with little effort, but with the subscribers of the war bonds receiving practically no money. "Krieg—Mensch und Moral," at https://www.blb-karlsruhe.de/aktuelles/ausstellungen/virtuelle-ausstellungen/schlaglichter-100-buecher-des-jahres-1918/krieg-mensch-und-moral/.

372.   *CU 150: The History of the Copper Group, Aurubis AG,* 32.

373.   *"Disarmament and the Metals,"* Engineering and Mining Journal, Vol. 112, No. 22, (Nov. 26, 1921), 878.

374.   Gerhardt Buer, *"Die Beteiligung der Juden an der deutschen Eisen- und Metallwirtschaft,"* Der Morgen, 3 (1) (1927), 96-97.

375.   Aly, *Why the Germans, Why the Jews,* 106-07.

376.   Gay, *The Jews of Germany,* 240.

377.   Adam Fergusson, *When Money Dies: The Nightmare of Deficit Spending, Devaluation, and Hyperinflation in Weimar Germany,* (New York: Public Affairs, 2010), 127.

378.   The Expelled Germans of Alsace-Lorraine After Versailles," Institute for Research of Expelled Germans, " http://expelledgermans.org/elsassgermans.htm.

379.   Ibid.

380.   Fergusson, *When Money Dies* 127.

381.   The Expelled Germans of Alsace-Lorraine After Versailles," Institute for Research of Expelled Germans, http://expelledgermans.org/elsassgermans.htm..

382.   Ibid.

383.   Gerald D. Feldman, *Iron and Steel in the German Inflation 1916-1923,* (Princeton: Princeton University Press, 1977), 13.

384.   Ibid., 11 and 51.

385.   *CU 150: The History of the Copper Group, Aurubis AG,* 32.

386.   Feldman, *Iron and Steel in the German Inflation 1916-1923,* 475.

387.   *CU 150: The History of the Copper Group, Aurubis AG,* 32.

388.   *Germany Trades Steel for Paper,* The Iron Trade Review, (January 19, 1922), 201.

389.   Adey, *Die Organisation und die Funktionen des deutschen Metallhandels,* 134.

390.   Feldman, *Iron and Steel in the German Inflation 1916-1923,* 4.

391. Ibid., 4.

392. Benny and Max both became personally liable partners of Gebruder Heppenheimer on March 19, 1919 . *See* Reparations Request for Adolph Heppenheimer,
submitted by his daughter Hilde Cronberger and filed on behalf of herself, her
sister Trude Morgenthau and her brother Heinz (Henry) Heppenheimer, HH-
Staw 518-14874. Since Benny worked for the business during the war, it seems
logical that he was part of the decision-making processes with his brother and
cousin. Based on how Max was treated by his brothers and cousin after the war, it
may be that Max was not a part of the decision-making processes of the company
when it came to future investments.

393. Metallschmelzwerk Rheinau Aktiengesellschaft, Landesarchiv Baden-Württem-
berg- Generallandesarchiv Karlsruhe, File No. 276 Nrs. 1888, 1889, 1890.

394. As explained earlier, Joseph and Henry's older brother Maier Heppenheimer
had also structured his company in Frankenthal as an OHG, in which all of the
partners are fully liable and fully liable to third party creditors. We do not know
when Gebruder Heppenheimer was first structured as an OHG.

395. Metallschmelzwerk Rheinau Aktiengesellschaft, Landesarchiv Baden-Würt-
temberg- Generallandesarchiv Karlsruhe, File No. 276 Nrs. 1888, 1889, 1890. In
the 1920 Mannheim Address Book, the directors of the company are listed as
Adolph, Jacob and Benny Heppenheimer in Frankfurt and Max Heppenheimer
in Mannheim; this was the first year Max appeared in the Mannheim Address
Book. Max and Benny were registered in the Frankfurt Commercial Registry as
personally liable partners of Gebruder Heppenheimer on August 7, 1922. *See*
Reparations Request of Benny Heppenheimer, Hessisches Landesarchiv Hauptstaatsarchiv Wiesbaden, HHStaw_518_8241.

396. Krohn, "Ein 'Gruss aus Frankfurts schonstem Stadtteil,'" in Ostend: Blick in Ein
Judisches Viertel, 13; https://www.frankfurt.de/sixcms/detail.php?id=2855&_ff-
mpar%5b_id_inhalt%5d=9351421; https://www.frankfurt.de/sixcms/detail.
php?id=11627242&_ffmpar%5b_id_inhalt%5d=10115166.

397. *See* https://www.frankfurt.de/sixcms/detail.php?id=2855&_ffmpar%5b_id_in-
halt%5d=9351421; https://www.frankfurt.de/sixcms/detail.php?id=11627242&_
ffmpar%5b_id_inhalt%5d=10115166.

398. In 1921, Gebruder Heppenheimer had thirteen tenants in both buildings other
than Gebruder Heppenheimer. In 1935, the last year Gebruder Heppenheimer
owned both buildings, they also had thirteen tenants.

399. The building had been built in 1878 and had been a hotel. *See* https://www.
wikiwand.com/de/Liste_der_Kulturdenkm%C3%A4ler_in_Frankfurt-Bahnhofs-
viertel#/Gutleutstrasse_001. This building is now listed as a cultural monument
of Frankfurt because of its history as a hotel. *Ibid.*

400. Nordmeyer, *Gastronomie in Alt-Frankfurt,* 105

401. Ibid., 107.

402. Max was referred to as a "chemist" by Rudolph Henninger, a long-time employee of Gebruder Heppenheimer. *See* Hessisches Landesarchiv Hauptstaatsarchiv
Wiesbaden, HHStaw 518—14874.

403. Max's marriage will be discussed in more detail in the next chapter.

404. For example, Benny told his children that Max was an intellectual and not a businessman.

405. Kaufvertrag zu Werk Kuppersteg, Hessisches Landesarchiv Hauptstaatsarchiv Wiesbaden, HHStAW 2092, 4845; for the history of the facility, *see* http://www.businesschemistry.org/article/?article=74. At the time of the proposed purchase, the facility had 2,500 employees. *Ibid.*

406. *See* http://www.businesschemistry.org/article/?article=74.

407. *See* http://www.albert-gieseler.de/dampf_de/firmen1/firmadet11268.shtml.

408. Reparations request for Henny Heppenheimer, submitted by daughter Bettina Schnitzler, Bayerisches Hauptstaatsarchiv, BAYHstA LEA-49673.

409. Ibid.

410. Ibid. Jacob remained a personally-liable partner with A&B Heppenheimer until January 4, 1924, when he moved back to Strasbourg. *Ibid.*

411. "The Weimar Republic," at https://encyclopedia.ushmm.org/content/en/article/the-weimar-republic; Gay, *The Jews of Germany,* 240.

412. "Weimar Republic (1918-1933)," at https://www.yadvashem.org/odot_pdf/Microsoft%20Word%20-%207794.pdf.

413. Jonathan Steinberg, *All or Nothing: The Axis and the Holocaust 1941-1943,* (London: Routledge,1990), 235.

414. Paul Mendes-Flohr, "Jews Within German Culture," *German-Jewish History in Modern Times,* Volume 4, 182. In fact, by 1933, thirteen of the thirty-three German Nobel prize winners were of Jewish (or half-Jewish) descent. Bach, *The German Jew: A Synthesis of Judaism and Western Civilization, 1730-1930,* 245.

415. Sarah Gordon, *Hitler, Germans, and the Jewish Question,* (Princeton: Princeton University Press, 1984), 14.

416. Friedman, *The Lion and the Star,* 32.

417. Bach, *The German Jew: A Synthesis of Judaism and Western Civilization, 1730-1930,* 214.

418. Ibid., 215.

419. Levinson, *Jewish Germany: An Enduring Presence from the Fourth to the Twenty-First Century,* 122-23. The Frankfurt Jews took this self-image with them when they fled Frankfurt for New York in the 1930s, so that the neighborhood they settled in (Washington Heights, on the upper west side in Manhattan) became known as "Frankfurt on the Hudson." Ibid.

420. B.E. Kent, "Reparation and the German Financial System, 1919-1924," (Thesis submitted to Australian National University, 1962), 35, at https://core.ac.uk/download/pdf/156626529.pdf.

421. Fergusson, *When Money Dies,* 9, 16, 31.

422. Aly, *Why the Germans? Why the Jews?,* 112.

423. Ibid., 36-38.

424. Ibid., 62.

425. Feldman, *Iron and Steel in the German Inflation 1916-1923,* 280.

426. Fergusson, *When Money Dies*, 121-22. The Ruhr basin in 1923 provided nearly 85 percent of Germany's remaining coal reserves and 80 percent of its steel and pit-iron production. *Ibid.*, 128.

427. Aly, *Why the Germans? Why the Jews?*, 191.

428. The Mainkur smelter facility was located in Fechenheim, which at the time was in the district of Hanau. Fechenheim became a part of Frankfurt in 1928. https://www.frankfurt.de/sixcms/detail.php?id=2835&_ffmpar[_id_inhalt]=61756.

429. Institut für Stadtgeschichte, Frankfurt am Main, Signatur 680, 681. One of the reasons given by the tax authorities for the significant tax on inventory was because the size of the inventory increased significantly in 1922. It is possible that, like other metals companies, Gebruder Heppenheimer was hoarding its inventory as a hedge against hyperinflation. In fact, businesses were purchasing inventory as quickly as possible, since cash had no value. *See* Fergusson, *When Money Dies*, 109.

430. Fergusson, *When Money Dies*, 73-74.

431. Request for Reduction of Municipal Trade Tax, Stadtarchiv Worms, Abt. 5 Nr. 973.

432. Ibid.

433. https://history.state.gov/milestones/1921-1936/dawes.

434. Ibid.

435. Feldman, *Iron and Steel in the German Inflation 1916-1923*, 349.

436. Walter A. McDougall, *France's Rhineland Policy, 1914-1924: The Last Bid for a Balance of Power in Europe*, (Princeton: Princeton Legacy Library, 1978), 373. Still, the provisions of the Versailles Treaty reduced the size of Germany by 13.05 percent, including the loss of the Lorraine iron area, so that the German iron and steel industry was forced to rely more upon foreign sources of supply. *See* Carl T. Schmidt, "The Treaty of Versailles, Inflation and Stabilization," in German Business Cycles, 1924-1933, (1934), 5, https://www.nber.org/chapters/c4933.pdf.

437. Unlike the scrap metal businesses run by the various Heppenheimers, Jews who were on fixed incomes from savings and investments were ruined during the hyperinflation period. Friedman, *The Lion and the Star*, 38.

438. "Frankfurt am Main as the Place of the Metal Trade," Jahrbuch der Frankfurter Bürgerschaft, (1925), 177, http://sammlungen.ub.uni-frankfurt.de/periodika/periodical/pageview/8836358?query=gebruder%20heppenheimer.

439. Ibid.

440. Hessisches Landesarchiv Hauptstaatsarchiv Wiesbaden, HHStaw 518—14874.

441. Ibid. The Reichsmark ("RM") replaced the German mark in 1924. *See* Fergusson, *When Money Dies*, 209.

442. Martina Hessler, *"Do Companies Know What Women Want?: The Introduction of Electrical Domestic Appliances During the Weimar Republic,"* (Ann Arbor: University of Michigan Library, 1998-1999), https://quod.lib.umich.edu/cgi/t/text/text-idx?cc=mfsfront;c=mfs;c=mfsfront;idno=ark5583.0013.002;g=mfsg;rgn=main;view=text;xc=1.

443. Alfred Reckendrees, *"Companies, Industry, and Crafts Trades,"* Copenhagen Business School, http://www.deutschland-in-daten.de/en/companies-industry-and-crafts-and-trades/.

444. Metallschmelzwerk Rheinau Aktiengesellschaft in Frankfurt, Landesarchiv Baden-Württemberg- Generallandesarchiv Karlsruhe, File No. 276-1888. Louis Vollweiler resigned as a Prokurist for Gebruder Heppenheimer a few months after the establishment of the joint-stock company on August 7, 1922. *See* Hessisches Landesarchiv Hauptstaatsarchiv Wiesbaden, HHStaw 518—14874.

445. Ibid.

446. Ibid.

447. In the 1918 Mannheim Address Book, Gebruder Heppenheimer is identified as the owner of the Rheinau facility, with Adolf and Jacob Heppenheimer specifically identified as owners. Louis Vollweiler is identified as the Prokurist of the company. In the 1919 Mannheim Address Book, Adolf, Jacob, Benny and Max are identified as owners of the company and Louis Vollweiler is identified as the Prokurist.

448. http://www.wormserjuden.de/; Landesarchiv Baden-Württemberg- Generallandesarchiv Karlsruhe, File No. 480-8086.

449. Landesarchiv Baden-Württemberg- Generallandesarchiv Karlsruhe, File No. 480-8086.

450. http://www.wormserjuden.de/; Landesarchiv Baden-Württemberg- Generallandesarchiv Karlsruhe, File No. 480-8086.

451. Landesarchiv Baden-Württemberg- Generallandesarchiv Karlsruhe, File No. 480-8086.

452. http://www.wormserjuden.de/

453. Landesarchiv Baden-Württemberg- Generallandesarchiv Karlsruhe, File No. 480-8086.

454. Ibid.

455. Reparations Request of Walter Schwarz, Hessisches Landesarchiv Hauptstaatsarchiv Wiesbaden, 518-50789.

456. Jacques Semelin, *The Survival of the Jews in France 1940-44,* (New York: Oxford University Press, 2018), 17.

457. Ibid.

458. According to Jean Horgen's memoirs (Jean was married to Lazarus' son Jacob's granddaughter), Robert moved to Strasbourg in the 1920s. As discussed later, Robert was divorced from his wife in 1927, so he may have left Frankfort for Strasbourg that year. It does not appear that Robert ever owned his own business, but it has been described by others that he was a scrap metal dealer, so he may have worked for his brother Jacob when he moved to Strasbourg. We know from Robert's daughter that Robert was living in Frankfurt in the mid-1930s, so he must have moved back to Frankfurt at some point in the early 1930s. He may have worked for one of his brothers in Frankfurt as a scrap metal dealer when he returned.

459.   *See* https://www.genteam.at/index.php?option=com_gesamt. The marriage certificate states that the marriage ceremony was performed by Dr. Freudenthal, who was the rabbi of the Reform synagogue in Nuremberg. *Ibid.* Nuremberg's Jewish population was smaller than the Jewish population in Frankfurt, numbering 8,603 in 1915 and 9,000 by 1933. *See* https://www.jewishvirtuallibrary.org/ nuremberg.

460.   Submission of Alice Adler; Stadtarchiv Nurnberg C 22/II Nr. 118/5400 An.

461.   Submission of Alice Adler; Stadtarchiv Nurnberg C 22/II Nr. 127/4540 An; Submission of Alice Adler; Stadtarchiv Nurnberg C 22/II Nr. 147/3911 An.

462.   By 1925, the number of Jews in both the Westend and Ostend were roughly even. Friedman, *The Lion and the Star,* 201, n. 39.

463.   Hessisches Landesarchiv Hauptstaatsarchiv Wiesbaden, HHStaw 518—14874; https://lisa.gerda-henkel-stiftung.de/binaries/content/6793/steinlestrasse_adress-buchzusammenfassung_1900_-_1975_a0q_1.pdf?t=1463652333

464.   Claussen, *Theodor Adorno: One Last Genius,* 21.

465.   Friedman, *The Lion and the Star,* 232, n. 70.

466.   By the mid-1920s, Arthur was living at Zeil 62, Berthold was living at Seiler-strasse 23, and Robert was living at Fahrgasse 115—all within several blocks of each other in the Innenstadt.

467.   Richard F. Hamilton, *Who Voted for Hitler,* (Princeton: Princeton University Press, 1982), 215.

468.   Ibid.

469.   http://www.xn--jdische-gemeinden-22b.de/index.php/gemein-den/m-o/1263-mannheim-baden-wuerttemberg

470.   Hamilton, *Who Voted for Hitler,* 216.

471.   Jacob Borut, "Antisemitism in Tourist Facilities in Weimar Germany," 5-6, at https://www.yadvashem.org/odot_pdf/Microsoft%20Word%20-%203123.pdf. This was certainly the case for the Heppenheimers family members, who no longer had any relatives in Eichtersheim.

472.   Ibid, 6; Kaplan, *Jewish Daily Life in Germany, 1618-1945,* 336.

473.   Borut, "Antisemitism in Tourist Facilities in Weimar Germany," 28.

474.   The "cure" was a popular ritual for the well-to-do, who drank the waters, dieted, and walked in beautiful natural surroundings. *See* Ron Chernow, *The Warburgs: The Twentieth-Century Odyssey of a Remarkable Jewish Family,* (New York: Vintage Books, 1993), 127.

475.   "Jews on Norderney," Museum Nordseeheilbad Norderney, at https://web. archive.org/web/20100725110546/http://www.museum-norderney.de/html/ juden_auf_norderney.html. Norderney had a synagogue, a large Jewish hotel, and various shops run by local Jews. *See* "More Nazi Cities in Lower Saxony," at https://www.tracesofevil.com/2016/09/more-sites-in-lower-saxony.html. While Norderney was encouraging of Jewish vacationers, other resorts in the North Sea banned Jewish visitors during the 1920s. Norderney changed when the Nazis took control; in 1933, Nordernay was declared to be "free of Jews." *See* "More Nazi Cities in Lower Saxony," at https://www.tracesofevil.com/2016/09/more-sites-in-lower-saxony.html.

476.　"Frankfurt on the Main," at https://www.jewishvirtuallibrary.org/frankfurt-on-the-main.

477.　"Frankfurt Jews in the Weimar Republic," http://www.frankfurt1933-1945.de/. Gebruder Heppenheimer provided support for the Jewish community's nursing home, contributing 500 marks in 1921. *See* http://sammlungen.ub.uni-frankfurt. de/cm/periodical/pageview/2153723?query=heppenheimer.

478.　Pulzer, *Jews and the German States,* 111-13. Until the establishment of Frankfurt University, professorships were essentially closed to Jews. *Ibid.* Because of the donations of more than 80 donors, Frankfurt University was the best equipped university in Germany after the University of Berlin. *See* "The Frankfurt University Foundation in and After the Nazi Era: Negation of Jewish Founder Tradition," at http://www.frankfurt1933-1945.de.

479.　Avraham Barkai, "Population Decline and Economic Stagnation," *German-Jewish History in Modern Times, Volume 4,* 31-32

480.　Friedman, *The Lion and the Star,* 30.

481.　Recha was born in Darmstadt on December 22, 1895 to Hermann Lehmann and Amalie Lehmann (born Neu). Max likely met Recha through his brother Jacob, whose wife had an older brother Josef, who was married to Recha's sister Frieda Lehmann. Recha's father Hermann was in the butcher supply business with his brother Max in Darmstadt. *See* Darmstadt Address books at http://tudigit.ulb. tu-darmstadt.de/show/_md_search?md_query_cat=sammlung&md_query_ var=sammlung27&md_query_sort=sort_shelfLocator_sdocval+asc. The business also sold intestine casings and spices. Herman was likely a successful businessman, since he owned both the apartment building in which he lived (at Bismarkstrasse 56) and the office building where his business was located (Bismarkstrasse 80). Hermann died in 1935.

482.　Joseph also saw the marriage of a grandchild just after the war. Bertha's daughter Bettina, who was born on March 19, 1901, met her future husband Siegmund Hirsch while attending the Philanthropin—he was a teacher and she was his student. Siegmund had begun teaching at the Philanthropin in 1914. http://sammlungen.ub.uni-frankfurt.de/cm/periodical/pageview/3092567?query=%22siegmund%20hirsch%22.

483.　Donna-Marie Bohan, "Gender as a Destabilising Factor of Weimar Society," *History Studies, vol. 13* (2012), 2, https://ulsites.ul.ie/historystudies/sites/default/ files/historystudies_13_bohan_gender_0.pdf.

484.　Selma, who married Lippmann Lewin in 1929, would also divorce her husband, but not until 1941. This divorce is discussed in Chapter 8. In terms of Alice's move back to Frankfurt, during the 1920s, Nuremberg had become the home of the Nazi Party, and Jews began to feel unsafe in the streets. *See* https://www. jewishvirtuallibrary.org/nuremberg. A National Socialist weekly was published in Nuremberg beginning in 1923, and by the late 1920s, Nuremberg became widely known as the center of anti-Semitism in Germany. *See* Klaus Scholder, *A Requiem for Hitler: and Other New Perspectives on the German Church Struggle,* (Eugene, Oregon: Wipf & Stock, 1989), 6-7. With the rise of anti-Semitism in Nuremberg, and the fact that her family was in Frankfurt, it may have been an easy decision for Alice to move back to Frankfurt.

485.　Larissa R. Stiglich, "A Crisis of Marriage? The Debate of Marriage Reform in the Social Democratic Weimar Women's Press 1919-1933," University of North Carolina at Chapel Hill, 24, https://cdr.lib.unc.edu/indexablecontent/uuid:0ba2f75e-d7ce-4922-93e3-b13d301a70be.

486. Ibid., 20-21.

487. Eric D. Weitz, *Weimar Germany: Promise and Tragedy*, (Princeton: Princeton University Press, 2018), 305. In fact, in Berlin, 35 percent of married couples were childless in 1933. *Ibid.*

488. Friedman, *The Lion and the Star*, 30.

489. Heuberger, *100 Years Western Synagogue Frankfurt am Main 1910-2010*, 27. Those plans ended in 1933 with the Nazi takeover. *Ibid.*

490. Friedman, *The Lion and the Star*, 26.

491. Friedman, *The Lion and the Star*, 211, n. 69.

492. *Recollections of Herb Harvey.*

493. Adolph's son Heinz had his bar mitzvah in the Hauptsynagoge in 1930. *See* http://sammlungen.ub.uni-frankfurt.de/cm/periodical/pageview/3097374?query=heinz%20heppenheimer.

494. *Recollections of Herb Harvey.* As discussed earlier, many Jews kept their businesses open on Saturday after Germany mandated in 1905 that all businesses close on Sunday.

495. Niewyk, *The Jews in Weimar Germany*, 102.

496. Ibid. Since the Frankfurt Gemeinde was considering the construction of another Orthodox synagogue to address the growing Orthodox community, the low attendance must have reflected low attendance in the Reform synagogues. This contrasts to the period just after World War I, when attendance for the high holidays in the Westend synagogue was so high that the auditorium of the Philanthropin was required.

497. *See* http://www.jewishencyclopedia.com/articles/9365-klaus.

498. Karl Otto Watzinger, *Geschichte der Juden in Mannheim 1650-1945*, (Stuttgart: Verlag W. Kohlhammer, 1984), 47.

499. Walther Killy (Ed.), *Dictionary of German Biography: Thibaut-Zyncha*, (Munich: K.G. Saur, 2006), 164.

500. Ibid.

501. Watzinger, *Geschichte der Juden in Mannheim 1650-1945*, 52.

502. Inge Gross, whose parents were friends of Max and Recha Heppenheimer, observed that the Heppenheimers were her parents' only friends who kept kosher. Inge's parents were not at all religious. *Recollections of Inge Gross.*

503. Michael Brenner, *The Renaissance of Jewish Culture in Weimar Germany*, (New Haven: Yale University Press, 1996), 59-60.

504. Friedman, *The Lion and the Star*, 76; Mendes-Flohr, "Jewish Cultural and Spiritual Life," *German-Jewish History in Modern Times, Volume 4*, 136.

505. Friedman, *The Lion and the Star*, 76.

506. Ernst discussed his education in Benjamin Ortmeyer (Ed.), *Eyewitnesses Speak Out Against Denial: Testimonials of 100 Surviving Jewish Students of Their School Days in Frankfurt on Main/Germany During the Nazi Era*, (Witterschlick/Bonn:

Verlag Marg., 1995), 130. https://schulzeituntermhitlerbild.files.wordpress.com/2010/12/excerpt_eyewitnesses_speak_out_against.pdf.

507. Reparations request of Melanie Horn, Hessisches Landesarchiv Hauptstaatsarchiv Wiesbaden, HHStAW 518-17162. While Melanie likely attended the Philanthropin for her earlier education, it was not uncommon for Jewish girls to attend a city high school, particularly the Viktoriaschule, where over 30 percent of the students in 1928 were Jewish. Friedman, *The Lion and the Star*, 74-76. The Viktoriaschule emphasized a foreign language education. *See* "Oral history testimony of Simone Bernays Dessayer,: at https://collections.ushmm.org/search/catalog/irn44639.

508. The Philanthropin was in the city, so Herb had to take a trolley from Mainkur to and from school. *Recollections of Herb Harvey.*

509. *Ibid.*

510. Friedman, *The Lion and the Star,* 50.

511. Paul Mendes-Flohr, "Jewish Cultural and Spiritual Life," *German-Jewish History in Modern Times, Volume 4,* 138.

512. Ibid., 139-40.

513. Roberta Louis Goodman and Betsy Dolgin Katz, *The Adult Jewish Education Handbook: Planning, Practice, and Theory,* (Denver: A.R.E. Publishing, 2004), 21.

514. Ibid., 141.

515. Ibid. Given the size of the student body, it is reasonable to imagine some of the Heppenheimer family attended classes.

516. Ibid.

517. Ibid., 141. Martin Buber reopened the Lehrhaus during the Third Reich. *Ibid.,* 143.

518. Oded Heilbronner, "A Tale of Three German Cities," *People of the City: Jews and the Urban Challenge*, Ezra Mendelsohn (Ed.) (New York: Oxford University Press, 1999), 183.

519. *Recollections of Herb Harvey.*

520. Ambrose Evans-Pritchard, *"Metal Prices Fall Further Than During the Great Depression,"* The Telegraph, (December 2, 2008), https://www.telegraph.co.uk/finance/newsbysector/industry/mining/3543370/Metal-prices-fall-further-than-during-Great-Depression.html.

521. Helmut Waszkis, *Phillip Brothers: The History of a Trading Giant, 1901-1985,* (Metal Bulletin Books, 1987), 14. DeVries, *Of Mettle and Metal,* 130; http://www.fundinguniverse.com/company-histories/metallgesellschaft-ag-history/.

522. DeVries, *Of Mettle and Metal,* 130; Hannah Ahlheim, *Deutsche, kauft nicht bei Juden!,* (Gottingen: Wallstein Verlag, 2008), 117 n. 36.

523. Metallschmelzwerk Rheinau Aktiengesellschaft in Mannheim (HRB XXVI/53) / 1923-1932, Landesarchiv Baden-Württemberg- Generallandesarchiv Karlsruhe, File No. 276_1889. Except as otherwise noted, the information contained in the rest of this paragraph and the following paragraph is from this file.

524. The world copper industry was hit hard by the depression, with both sharp price declines and steep reductions in production, so any speculation in the copper

market would have been risky. *See* "The World Copper Industry: Its Changing Structure and Future Prospects," Kenjo Takeuchi, et. al., World Bank Staff Commodity Working Papers, p. 15 (1986), at http://documents.worldbank.org/curated/en/825891468739289854/pdf/SCP15.pdf. For example, in 1929, the price of copper on the London Metal Exchange was about 100 pounds sterling per ton, but then dropped to below 30 by 1931. *See CU 150: The History of the Copper Group, Aurubis AG, 144, n. 18.*

525. Reparations Requests for Gebruder Heppenheimer and for Benny Heppenheimer, Hessisches Landesarchiv Hauptstaatsarchiv Wiesbaden, HHStAW 518-8240 and 518-8241.

526. Hessisches Landesarchiv Hauptstaatsarchiv Wiesbaden, HHStaw 518—14874; https://lisa.gerda-henkel-stiftung.de/binaries/content/6793/steinlestrasse_adressbuchzusammenfassung_1900_-_1975_a0q_1.pdf?t=1463652333

527. Hessisches Landesarchiv Hauptstaatsarchiv Wiesbaden, HHStaw 518—14874.

528. Ibid.

529. Adolph was not unlike many of his generation following World War I. Seeing the relatively small profit margins available in the scrap metal business, and having survived the Great War, this generation of scrap metal dealers was more interested in metals speculation and other opportunities than simply warehousing metals. *See* Alfred Marcus, *Die Wirtschaftliche Krise des Deutschen Juden,* (Berlin: Verlag von Georg Stilke, 1931), 43-44.

530. Hessisches Landesarchiv Hauptstaatarchiv Wiesbaden, HHStaw-518-14874.

531. Reparations Request of Isidor Wolfsheimer, Hessisches Landesarchiv Hauptstaatsarchiv Wiesbaden, HHStAW 676-6177.

532. Ibid.

533. Ibid

534. Ibid.

535. Ibid.

536. Reparations Request of Berthold Heppenheimer, Hessisches Landesarchiv Hauptstaatsarchiv Wiesbaden, HHStAW 581-14875.

537. Ibid.

538. Bayerisches Hauptstaatsarchiv, BAYHstA LEA-49673.

539. Ibid.

540. Information in this paragraph was derived from Reparations Request of Sally Heppenheimer, Landesarchiv Baden-Württemberg- Generallandesarchiv Karlsruhe, File No. 480-8086.

541. Niewyk, *The Jews in Weimar Germany,* 52, 79.

542. Nordmeyer, *Gatronomie in Alt-Frankfurt,* 59.

543. Friedman, *The Lion and the Star,* 23. In the months after he was named German chancellor in 1933, Adolf Hitler declared that portions of the Versailles treaty were null and void. *See* Aly, *Why the Germans, Why the Jews,* 111.

544. Parket Abt, "The Nazi Fiscal Cliff: Unsustainable Financial Practices Before World War II," *The Gettysburg Historical Journal,* Volume 16, Article 5, (2017), 20.

545.   Aly, *Why the Germans, Why the Jews*, 29.

546.   Heilbronner, "A Tale of Three German Cities," *People of the City: Jews and the Urban Challenge*, 183. "1929: A Turning Point During the Weimar Period," at https://www.facinghistory.org/weimar-republic-fragility-democracy/readings/1929-turning-point. But Jews suffered, as well, with more than one-third of the approximately one hundred thousand Jewish office and factory workers out of work during the depression. Avraham Barkai, "Exclusion and Persecution: 1933-1938," *German-Jewish History in Modern Times, Volume 4,* 203. During the depression, the unemployment rate for Jewish men under the age of twenty-five in Frankfurt was higher than the rate for non-Jews—36 versus 30 percent. Friedman, *The Lion and the Star,* 38.

547.   Abraham Ascher, *Was Hitler a Riddle? Western Democracies and National Socialism,* (Stanford: Stanford University Press, 2021), 21.

548.   Barkai, "Exclusion and Persecution: 1933-1938," *German-Jewish History in Modern Times, Volume 4,* 197.

549.   "The Nazi Party: Background & Overview," https://www.jewishvirtuallibrary.org/background-and-overview-of-the-nazi-party-nsdap.

550.   Barkai, "Exclusion and Persecution: 1933-1938," *German-Jewish History in Modern Times, Volume 4,* 199.

551.   "Philanthropin—School of the Israelite Community," at http://www.frankfurt1933-1945.de. Because of these restrictions and the increasing anti-Semitism experienced by Jewish students in public schools, the number of students in the Philanthropin increased from 376 in 1933 to 701 in 1934. *Ibid.*

552.   Ibid; Barkai, "Exclusion and Persecution: 1933-1938," *German-Jewish History in Modern Times, Volume 4,* 201.

553.   "Frankfurt am Main—The City and the Holocaust," on http://www.holocaustresearchproject.org/nazioccupation/frankfurt.html.

554.   Ibid.

555.   "Memorandum from the Wirtschaftsamt (the Economic Office), February 17, 1934," at http://www.frankfurt1933-1945.de. The Memorandum noted that the Jewish population in Frankfurt was greater in terms of percentage than the Reich as a whole and that the Jewish share in the business life of the City was far greater than its share of the population—the Jewish population in Frankfurt was 6.3, and yet Jews owned 35% of Frankfurt's businesses. The Economic Office was concerned that Frankfurt could experience losses in tax revenue as a result of the closure of Jewish businesses and the transfer of assets outside of Germany. Relevant to the Heppenheimer family, the Memorandum noted that there were 77 scrap metal businesses in Frankfurt in 1934, with 32 (or 41.6%) owned by Jews.

556.   Barkai, "Exclusion and Persecution: 1933-1938," *German-Jewish History in Modern Times, Volume 4,* 210-11.

557.   *Recollections of Herbt Harvey.*

558.   *See* http://sammlungen.ub.uni-frankfurt.de/cm/periodical/pageview/3098621?query=%22walter%20hirsch%22. Walter was Bertha's daughter Bettina's son.

559.   *See* http://sammlungen.ub.uni-frankfurt.de/cm/periodical/pageview/3099519?query=joseph%20heppenheimer.

560. Heuberger (Ed.) *100 Years Western Synagogue Frankfurt am Main 1910-2010*, 14. Rabbi Salzberger was the last rabbi to leave Frankfurt, emigrating to England in April 1939. Friedman, *The Lion and the Star, p. 166.*

561. Richard J. Evans, *The Third Reich in Power*, (New York: The Penguin Press, 2005), 338-39.

562. Erin Blakemore, "Germany's World War I Debt Was So Cruchsing it Took 92 Years to Pay Off," History.Com, at https://www.history.com/news/germany-world-war-i-debt-treaty-versailles; "Chapter VIII—Economic Aspects of the Conspiracy," *Nazi Conspiracy and Aggression Volume I*, The Avalon Project, at https://avalon.law.yale.edu/imt/chap_08.asp.

563. Abt, "The Nazi Fiscal Cliff: Unsustainable Financial Practices Before World War II," *The Gettysburg Historical Journal*, 22.

564. "A Program for German Economic and Industrial Disarmament," *A Study Submitted by the Foreign Economic Administration to the Subcommittee on War Mobilization on the Committee on Military Affairs*, United States Senate, 19th Cong. 2nd Session, p.138. Germany was increasingly directing expenditures to rearmament through the 1930s, so that, by 1939, 70 percent of German government expenditures were going to rearmament. *See* Abt, "The Nazi Fiscal Cliff: Unsustainable Financial Practices Before World War II," *The Gettysburg Historical Journal*, 22. Steel production increased 330 percent between 1933 and 1938. *Ibid.*

565. Charles Will Wright, "The Iron and Steel Industries of Europe," *United States Department of the Interior Economic Paper 19*, (1930), 9. Germany did not have enough iron and steel to satisfy its rearmament needs; shortages in steel, iron ore, and non-ferrous metals required that Germany import these materials, as well as scrap. Abt, "The Nazi Fiscal Cliff: Unsustainable Financial Practices Before World War II," *The Gettysburg Historical Journal*, 29. Restrictions were placed on the export of scrap metal, so that imports of scrap dwarfed exports. For example, in 1938, 1,127,927 tons of scrap were imported by Germany, while just 17,645 tons were exported. Imperial Institute, *The Mineral Industry of the British Empire and Foreign Countries: Statistical Summary 1936-1938*, (London, 1939), 195,202.

566. "Louis Pinczower zum 100. Geburtstag," *Mitteilungen des Verbandes Ehemaliger Breslauer und Schlesie*r in Israel, No. 28, (September 1970), 12.

567. Ibid.

568. John V. H Dippel, *Bound Upon a Wheel of Fire: Why So Many German Jews Made the Tragic Decision to Remain in Nazi Germany*, (New York: Basic Books, 1996), 139.

569. This is in contrast to the Heppenheimer scrap metal dealers who were critical to the war effort in World War I, but enthusiastically supported that effort.

570. Evans, *The Third Reich in Power*, 355.

571. Nietzel, *Handeln und Uberleben: Judische Unternehmer aus Frankfurt am Main 1924-1964*, 112-13.

572. Ibid., 114-15.

573. Ibid. This is not surprising, since the push for boycotting Jewish scrap metal dealers began with the takeover of Germany by the Nazi party. For example, Fritz Schunemann, a German scrap metal dealer, sent a letter to the Mayor of Munich on March 25, 1933, urging that the city stop selling scrap metal to Jewish

companies. Bearbeitet von Wold Gruner, *The persecution and murder of Europe-an Jews by the National Socialist Germans 1933-1945: German Reich 1933-1937,* (Munchen: R. Oldenbourg Verlag Munchen, 2008), 91. Stating that 90 percent of scrap metal companies were in the hands of Jews (a great exaggeration), Schunemann argued that recycled metals were of critical importance to Germany and should be in the hands of Christian Germans. *Ibid.*

574.   Nietzel, *Handeln und Uberleben: Judische Unternehmer aus Frankfurt am Main 1924-1964,* 116.

575.   Ibid, 117-18.

576.   Roberta S. Kremer (Ed.), *Broken Thread: The Destruction of the Jewish Fashion Industry in Germany and Austria,* (Oxford: Berg Publishers, 2007), 14.

577.   Ibid., 84-85.

578.   Alice Falkenstein, "Documents Related to Jewish Business," June 14, 1941, United States Holocaust Memorial Museum, at https://www.ushmm.org.

579.   Since 1897, the German trade guilds had an examinations monopoly that was approved by the particular state, so Alice likely needed to pass an examination and comply with all other requirements in the state of Hesse before she could become a member of the guild. *See* Wolf-Dietrich Greinert, *Mass Vocational Education and Training in Europe,* Cedefop Panaorama Series, 75. Originally, Jews had been excluded from all guilds, but that began to change following Jewish emancipation in 1871. *See* Kaplan, *Jewish Daily Life in Germany,* 131, 138. The fact that she could pass the master's examination suggests that Alice had received formal dressmaker training, likely from the arts and crafts school in Nuremberg, and likely had an apprenticeship after her graduation.

580.   Evans, *The Third Reich in Power,* 436. Alice must have successfully navigated these new hurdles, since she remained a dues-paying member of the Dressmakers Guild until December 31, 1938. *See* Alice Falkenstein, "Documents Related to Jewish Business," June 14, 1941, United States Holocaust Memorial Museum, at https://www.ushmm.org.

581.   Peter Longerich, *Holocaust: The Nazi Persecution and Murder of the Jews,* (Oxford: Oxford University Press, 2010), 41.

582.   Alfred Falkenstein, a watch salesman, was born on December 9, 1896 in Frankfurt. He graduated from the Realschule der Israelitischen Religionsgesellschaf, the yeshiva established by Samson Raphael Hirsh, in 1912. *See* http://sammlungen.ub.uni-frankfurt.de/cm/periodical/pageview/2583272?query=alfred%20falkenstein. While Alfred's family may have been members of the separatist Orthodox Jewish synagogue, he likely did not remain Orthodox. Alfred served as a soldier for Germany in World War I. After the war, Alfred moved to Nuremberg and married there on January 10, 1921. See https://www.genteam.at/index.php?option=com_gesamt. It is certainly possible that Alice knew Alfred in Nuremberg and it may be that both Alice and Alfred decided to marry after they divorced their spouses.

583.   Kremer, *Broken Thread: The Destruction of the Jewish Fashion Industry in Germany and Austria,* 86.

584.   Irene Guenther, *Nazi Chic? Fashioning Women in the Third Reich,* (Oxford: Berg Publishing, 2004), 157.

585. Robert B. Kahn, "Reflections by Jewish Survivors from Mannheim," (New York: Mannheim Reunion Committee, 1990), 76, at https://www.jewishgen.org/yizkor/Mannheim/images/Mannheim%20Survivors%20Reflections%20June1990.pdf

586. Before the Nazis took power, Jewish children excelled in the Mannheim public schools. During the Weimar Period, the proportion of Jewish students in the high school was three to four times higher than the Jewish population as a whole, and, in the 1932-33 school year, the Gymnasium Kurt had attended had 43 Jewish students out of a total of 475 students. Watzinger, *Geschichte der Juden in Mannheim 1650-1945, 50.*

587. Rudolph Henninger, the long-time employee of Gebruder Heppenheimer, stated that it was the business difficulties that caused Max's suicide. *See* reparations request of Benny Heppenheimer, Hessisches Landesarchiv Hauptstaatsarchiv Wiesbaden, HHStAW 518-8241.

588. Armin Nolzen, "The Nazi Party and its Violence Against the Jews, 1933-1939," 6. https://www.yadvashem.org/articles/academic/nazi-party-and-violence-against-jews.html.

589. Armin Nolzen, "Violence as a Historiographical Concept," (2003), 11. http://www.yadvashem.org/odot_pdf/Microsoft%20Word%20-%207001.pdf.

590. City Archive Mannheim, 6/1967_00224 Jews in Court/Rassenchande II (1937), Hakenkreuzbanner, June 4, 1936.

591. Ibid., Neue Mannheimer Zeitung, Nr. 249, June 4, 1937.

592. Ibid.

593. Ibid., Neue Mannheimer Zeitung, 263, June 12, 1937.

594. Ibid., Hakenkreuzbanner, Nr. 250, June 3, 1937.

595. Ibid.

596. Abraham J. Peck (Ed.), *The German-Jewish Legacy in America, 1938-1988: From Buldung to the Bill of Rights*, (Detroit: Wayne State University Press, 1989), 81.

597. Dippel, *Bound Upon a Wheel of Fire: Why So Many German Jews Made the Tragic Decision to Remain in Nazi Germany*, 99.

598. Friedman, *The Lion and the Star*, 140.

599. After Erna emigrated to the United States, she married Arthur Wertheimer (later changed to Worth), and they had a daughter Sue.

600. Reparations request of Melanie Horn, Hessisches Landesarchiv Hauptstaatsarchiv Wiesbaden, HHStAW 518-17162. The remainder of the information in this paragraph is from this reparations request.

601. Melanie and Paul arrived in Palestine with only a tourist visa. Until 1938, many German Jews reached Palestine on tourist visas. *See* Hagit Lavsky, *Before Catastrophe: The Distinctive Path of German Zionism,* (Detroit: Wayne State University Press, 1996), 252. While Melanie's immigration on a tourist visa was illegal, legal immigration to Palestine by German Jews did occur. This legal emigration to Palestine was facilitated by the Haavara Transfer Agreement, which was signed by representatives of the Zionist movement in Germany and Palestine and the Nazi government on August 27, 1933, and allowed for the transfer of a significant portion of the emigrants' assets in exchange for the export to Germany of much-needed goods such as citrus fruit. *See* Evans, *The Third Reich in Power,*

557. Melanie and Paul had three children after their emigration: Yael, Ada, and Immanuel. In 1970, Melanie and Paul were passengers on Swissair Flight 330 en route to Israel and were killed when a bomb planted by terrorists exploded upon takeoff in Switzerland.

602.   Ortmeyer, *Eyewitnesses Speak Out Against Denial: Testimonials of 100 Surviving Jewish Students of Their School Days in Frankfurt on Main/Germany During the Nazi Era,* 130.

603.   Ibid.

604.   The Taunus is a mountain range in Hesse and Grosser Feldberg is one of its most striking mountain peaks. See https://www.frankfurt-rhein-main.de/en/Region/Hochtaunus-District2/Grosser-Feldberg.

605.   Ortmeyer, *Eyewitnesses Speak Out Against Denial: Testimonials of 100 Surviving Jewish Students of Their School Days in Frankfurt on Main/Germany During the Nazi Era,* 130.

606.   Ibid.

607.   Ibid.

608.   Ibid. On the ship's manifest, Ernst noted that he paid for the passage himself and that he was arriving with $800. At this point, German Jews still had financial resources and could emigrate with some of those resources. That would change as German Jews tried to emigrate later in the decade.

609.   Barkai, "Exclusion and Persecution: 1933-1938," *German-Jewish History in Modern Times, Volume 4,* 205.

610.   Ibid.

611.   Dippel, *Bound Upon a Wheel of Fire: Why So Many German Jews Made the Tragic Decision to Remain in Nazi Germany,* 139.

612.   Friedman, *The Lion and the Star,* 140.

613.   Gay, *The Jews of Germany,* 257.

614.   Kurt Heppenheimer Application for a U.S. Visa, Visa No. 10227.

615.   Max's son Kurt had been told that Max's brothers provided financial support to Recha after Max's suicide. Such support may have been enough for the family to pay for the smaller apartment, and was likely more important after Kurt emigrated to America. While the Gebruder Heppenheimer OHG company was no longer in the business of trading metals, it still owned all the business properties and was likely the entity receiving the rents from the various tenants. Since Max was one of the owners of the OHG company at the time of his death, Recha may have been receiving Max's share of the rental income after his death, which may have been enough to survive. If that was the case, this may have been the "financial support" that Recha was receiving from Max's brothers.

616.   Kurt Heppenheimer Application for a U.S. Visa, Visa No. 10227.

617.   Ibid.

618.   Martin Münzel, "Expulsion—Plunder—Flight: Businessmen and Emigration from Nazi Germany," in *Immigrant Entrepreneurship: German-American Business Biographies, 1720 to the Present,* vol. 4, edited by Jeffrey Fear. German Historical

Institute. Last modified March 24, 2014. http://www.immigrantentrepreneurship.org/entry.php?rec=174

619. Ibid.

620. Eggerz, *The German-Jewish Epoch of 1743-1933: Tragedy or Success Story.*

621. Münzel, "Expulsion—Plunder—Flight: Businessmen and Emigration from Nazi Germany."

622. Dippel, *Bound Upon a Wheel of Fire: Why So Many German Jews Made the Tragic Decision to Remain in Nazi Germany*, 208.

623. Ibid.

624. Ibid., 230.

625. Ibid., 231-32.

626. https://www.ushmm.org/wlc/en/article.php?ModuleId=10005201

627. "Gestapo" is an acronym derived from the German Geheimstaatspolizei, or Secret State Police. *See* https://encyclopedia.ushmm.org/content/en/article/gestapo.

628. Evans, *The Third Reich in Power*, 582-83.

629. Ibid.

630. Ortmeyer, "Eyewitnesses Speak Out Against Denial: Testimonials of 100 Surviving Jewish Students of Their School Days in Frankfurt on Main/Germany During the Nazi Era," 106-07.

631. Rabbi Salzberger, the last remaining Reform rabbi, emigrated to England after Kristallnacht. But the chief cantor of the reform synagogues, Nathan Saretzki, continued to hold services for the Jewish community, using the Philanthropin's auditorium for the services, since all the synagogues were either damaged or destroyed. On August 18, 1942, the cantor and his wife were deported to Theresienstadt and were murdered at Auschwitz. *See* "Nathan Saretzki, Last Chief Cantor of the Main Synagogue," at http://www.frankfurt1933-1945.de.

632. Peter Loewenberg, "The Kristallnacht as a Public Degradation Ritual," *Year Book XXXII of the Leo Baeck Institute*, (London: Secker & Warburg, 1987), 314.

633. Ibid., 313.

634. "Deportations to Buchenwald," at http://www.frankfurt1933-1945.de; https://www.ushmm.org/learn/timeline-of-events/1933-1938/buchenwald-concentration-camp-opens.

635. *See Recollections of Herb Harvey.*

636. Evans, *The Third Reich in Power*, 591.

637. https://www.ushmm.org/wlc/en/article.php?ModuleId=10005198.

638. http://www.holocaustresearchproject.org/othercamps/buchenwald.html.

639. Ibid.

640. Ibid.

641. Tax records of Heinrich Bauernfreund, Hessisches Landesarchiv Hauptstaatsarchiv Wiesbaden, HHStAW 676-5689. In a letter to the German tax office on March 31, 1939, Heinrich stated that his wife's scrap metal company was being

liquidated because of his arrest and committed to shutting down the company. *Ibid.*

642. Evans, *The Third Reich in Power*, 360.

643. Ibid, 389.

644. Ibid., 593.

645. Ibid., 595.

646. Ibid.

647. Ibid.

648. Ibid.

649. Ibid., 222.

650. Martin Munzel, "Expulsion—Plunder—Flight: Businessmen and Emigration from Nazi Germany (1933-1945)," at https://www.immigrantentrepreneurship. org/entries/expulsion-plunder-flight-businessmen-and-emigration-from-nazi-germany. In April 1938, the Jews were required to register their property, which later enabled the Reich to obtain precise data on Jewish property, which was essential for the Nazis to implement their policy of Aryanizing the German economy.

651. Evans, *The Third Reich in Power*, 596.

652. Ibid.

653. Manfred Kohler, "Boycotted, Harassed, Forced to Sell," *Frankfurter Allgemeine*, (August 11, 2013).

654. Ibid.

655. The relatively high number of takeovers and liquidations between 1939 and 1942 reflects the fact that the process of settlement of the business and its deletion from the commercial register took time to complete. *See* Nietzel, *Handeln und Uberleben: Judische Unternehmer aus Frankfurt am Main 1924-1964*, 161.

656. Ibid., 158 and 163.

657. Ibid.

658. Reparations Request of Benny Heppenheimer, Hessisches Landesarchiv Hauptstaatsarchiv Wiesbaden, HHSttaw 518-8241. Reparations Request for Jacob Heppenheimer, Hessisches Landesarchiv Hauptstaatsarchiv Wiesbaden, HHSttaw 518-8242. The Aryanization of Jewish businesses represented one of the biggest transfers of ownership in German history, and the transfer of the businesses into non-Jewish hands was generally for much less than its real value. *See* Munzel, "Expulsion—Plunder—Flight: Businessmen and Emigration from Nazi Germany (1933-1945)." Rudolph Henninger, the long-standing Gebruder Heppenheimer employee, joined Birkenbach as a silent partner during the war, and then joined Birkenbach as a full partner in 1948 when the company was renamed Heinrich Birkenbach & Co. Because Henninger was one-quarter Jewish, he was not classified as a Jew under the Nuremberg Laws, but he still may have faced some anti-Semitism and thus chose to remain "silent."

659. Diskus-Werke had been located adjacent to the smelter facility.

660. Liquidation of Gebruder Heppenheimer, Institut fur Stadtgeschichte, Frankfurt am Main, Signatur 1.1240, 1.1241.

661. Hessisches Landesarchiv Hauptstaatsarchiv Wiesbaden, HHSttaw 518-8241.

662. Ibid.

663. Ibid.

664. For Jews emigrating after September 1939, the fee deducted from blocked accounts was 96 percent. *See* "The Beneficiaries of Aryanization: Hamburg as a Case Study," Frank Bajohr, p. 5, at https://www.yadvashem.org/download/about_holocaust/studies/bajohr_full.pdf.

665. Hessisches Landesarchiv Hauptstaatsarchiv Wiesbaden, HHStaw 518-8241.

666. The buildings on Untermain Anlange survived the allied bombings and remain standing and in use to this day. The buildings on Dominikanergasse and Kloster-gasse, however, were destroyed during the allied bombings of March 1944, which destroyed much of the old city. *See* "The March Attacks in 1944," at http://www.frankfurt1933-1945.de. Following the war, the old Borneplatz became a whole-sale flower market and then a parking lot. C.H. Beck, *The Judengasse in Frankfurt,* (Frankfurt am Main: Museum Judengasse Frankfurt, 2016), 47-49. In the 1980s, a public utility building was erected over the Borneplatz and the old Judengasse, including the portion of Dominikanergasse on which Gebruder Heppenheimer had been located. *Ibid.,* 49-50. After much controversy over the location of this public utility building over the old Judengasse, the builders agreed to locate a new Frankfurt Jewish Museum in the basement of the building. *Ibid.,* 51.

667. Landesarchiv Baden-Württemberg- Generallandesarchiv Karlsruhe, File No. 480-8086.

668. Ibid.

669. Business records of Sally Heppenheimer, Stadtarchiv Worms Abt. 13 Nr. 1519; Abt. 27 Nr. 32; Landesarchiv Baden-Württemberg- Generallandesarchiv Karl-sruhe, File No. 480-8086.

670. Ludwig Heppenheimer business records, Landesarchiv Speyer J 10 Nr. 2968.

671. "Confiscation of Jewish Property in Europe," Symposium Proceedings of the United States Holocaust Memorial Museum, 94, at https://www.ushmm.org/m/pdfs/Publication_OP_2003-01.pdf.

672. Ibid., 12.

673. Ibid., 96.

674. Ibid; Geraldine Schwarz, *Those Who Forget—My Family's Story in Nazi Germany,* (New York: Scribner, 2017), 44.

675. "Confiscation of Jewish Property in Europe," Symposium Proceedings of the United States Holocaust Memorial Museum, 97.

676. Munzel, "Expulsion—Plunder—Flight: Businessmen and Emigration from Nazi Germany (1933-1945)." The intent of these taxes was, in part, to impoverish Jewish refugees so that they would become a burden on the host country and provoke anti-Semitism. *Ibid.* But the intent of these taxes was also to raise capital for the German war effort. *Ibid.* In fact, a recent study commissioned by the German ministry found that the money stolen from all European Jews during the war financed at least 30 percent of the German war effort. *See https://www.*

telegraph.co.uk/news/worldnews/europe/germany/8119805/Confiscated-Jewish-wealth-helped-fund-the-German-war-effort.html.

677.   Munzel, "Expulsion—Plunder—Flight: Businessmen and Emigration from Nazi Germany (1933-1945)." The process for obtaining a U.S. visa was particularly onerous. An applicant would first place his or her name on a waiting list and then work to obtain the following: (1) five copies of the visa application; (2) two copies of the applicant's birth certificate; (3) two sponsors (U.S. citizens or legal permanent residents), who each completed six copies of an Affidavit of Support and Sponsorship; (4) certified copy of the most recent tax return; (5) affidavit from a bank regarding the applicant's accounts; (6) affidavit from any other responsible person regarding other assets; (7) certificate of Good Conduct from German police authorities, including two copies of any police dossier, prison record, military record and other government records; (8) affidavits of good conduct from several responsible disinterested persons (which was imposed after September 1940); (9) physical examination at U.S. consulate; (10) proof of permission to leave Germany (which was imposed beginning September 30, 1939); and (11) proof that passage had been booked to the Western hemisphere (which was imposed beginning in September 1939). *See* "Documents Required to Obtain a Visa, at https://www.ushmm.org/wlc/en/article.php?ModuleId=10007456.

678.   Herbert A. Strauss, "The Immigration and Acculturation of the German Jew in the United States of America," *The Leo Baeck Institute Year Book, Volume 16, Issue 1*, January 1971, 65.

679.   Ibid., 68.

680.   Ibid., 66. Instead, many of the German Jews choosing to emigrate in the early years of the Nazi regime chose to emigrate to Palestine. *See* "History of Jewish Immigration to Israel (Aliyah)," at https://reformjudaism.org/history-jewish-immigration-israel-aliyah.

681.   "Refugees," at https://encyclopedia.ushmm.org/content/en/article/refugees.

682.   Ibid.

683.   https://www.ushmm.org/wlc/en/article.php?ModuleId=10005139; https://kehila-links.jewishgen.org/berlin/Jews_in_Germany.html.

684.   Ibid.

685.   Recha's sister Frieda was deported from Darmstadt on March 24, 1942, along with 1000 other Jews, and died in the Piaski Ghetto in Poland. *See* http://www.statistik-des-holocaust.de/list_ger_hhn_420324.html.

686.   "The Outbreak of World War II and Anti-Jewish Policy," at https://www.yadvashem.org/holocaust/about/outbreak-of-ww2-anti-jewish-policy.html.

687.   Avraham Barkai, "In a Ghetto Without Walls." *German-Jewish History in Modern Times, Volume 4*, 335. For example, a Jewish ration card could not be used to purchase meat, fish, regular milk, butter, eggs, fruit, better baked goods, coffee, or tea.

688.   Gay, *The Jews of Germany*, 281.

689.   Avraham Barkai, "In a Ghetto Without Walls." *German-Jewish History in Modern Times, Volume 4*, 339.

690.   Ibid.

691. Lucy S. Dawidowicz, *The War Against the Jews, 1933-1945*, (New York: Bantam Books, 1975), 82.

692. Munzel, "Expulsion—Plunder—Flight: Businessmen and Emigration from Nazi Germany (1933-1945);" Dalia Ofer, *Escaping the Holocaust: Illegal Immigration to the Land of Israel, 1939-1944*, (Oxford: Oxford University Press, 1990), 98

693. Beate Meyer, *A Fatal Balancing Act: The Dilemma of the Reich Association of Jews in Germany, 1939-1945*, (New York: Berghahn Books, 2013), 81.

694. Ibid. at 20-21. The name of the association and its mission were changed to reflect the fact that there were no longer any "German Jews" in Germany following the Nuremberg Laws, only Jews in Germany. *See* https://www.jewishvirtualli-brary.org/reichsvereinigung.

695. Meyer, *A Fatal Balancing Act: The Dilemma of the Reich Association of Jews in Germany, 1939-1945*, 24-25.

696. Ibid, 30, 252.

697. *See* https://www.yadvashem.org/holocaust/about/final-solution-beginning/mass-murder-in-ussr.html#narrative_info. More than 1.5 million Jews were murdered this way.

698. *See* the International Institute for Holocaust Research at http://db.yadvashem. org/deportation/transportDetails.html?language=en&itemId=5091969. At the same time that Himmler was preparing for the deportation of Jews in Western Europe, he began organizing for the mass murder of Jews in Eastern Europe. This operation, later know as Operation Reinhard, involved the construction of three death camps—Belzec, Sobibor, and Treblinka —for the purpose of killing Jews. *See* "Sobibor: Key Dates," at https://encyclopedia.ushmm.org/content/en/article/ sobibor-key-dates.

699. Meyer, *A Fatal Balancing Act: The Dilemma of the Reich Association of Jews in Germany, 1939-1945*, 116.

700. Ibid., 128, 152.

701. Ibid., 154.

702. "The Wannsee Conference," https://www.yadvashem.org/holocaust/about/fi-nal-solution-beginning/wannsee-conference.html.

703. *See* German Jews During the Holocaust, 1939-1945, https://www.ushmm.org/ wlc/en/article.php?ModuleId=10005469.

704. Ibid.

705. Ibid.

706. Bertha's daughter Bettina and her husband Siegmund were still in Frankfurt at the start of the war, and Bettina remained in Frankfurt until 1941. Their only child, Walter, had emigrated to America in 1938 at the age of 17, but died in December 1939 in New York. Siegmund obtained his visa on January 8, 1940, and left for America on April 30, 1940. Siegmund, however, emigrated alone, with his passage paid by Erna's husband. Bettina was not able to emigrate with her husband "due to unfortunate circumstance," although we do not know what those circumstances were. *See* Hessisches Landesarchiv Hauptstaatsarchiv Wiesbaden, HHStAW 519-3_25959. After her husband emigrated, Bettina was able to survive only through assistance from the Jewish community, since she had no assets.

See Hessisches Landesarchiv Hauptstaatsarchiv Wiesbaden, HHStAW 519-3-707. Bettina received her tax clearance certificate in March 1941. *See* Hessisches Landesarchiv Hauptstaatsarchiv Wiesbaden, HHStAW 519-3_25959. Bettina obtained her visa to enter the United States on March 7, 1941 and departed for America on April 19, 1941 from Bilbao, Spain, nearly a year after her husband emigrated.

707.   Except as otherwise noted, the information in this section about Johanna and Isidor Wolfsheimer is derived from the reparations request and tax records of Isidor Wolfsheimer, Hessisches Landesarchiv Hauptstaatsarchiv Wiesbaden, HHStAW 676-6177; HHStAW 518-80394. Except as otherwise noted, the information about Franz and Martha Neumeier is derived from their reparations request and tax records, Hessisches Landesarchiv Hauptstaatsarchiv Wiesbaden, HHStAW 518-8646; HHStAW 676-6204.

708.   Wolfgang Benz, "Emigration as Rescue and Trauma: The Historical Context of the Kindertransport," *SHOFAR*, Fall, 2004, Vol. 23, No. 1, 4.

709.   Salome Lienert, "Swiss Immigration Policies 1933-1939," *Bystanders, Rescuers or Perpetrators? The Neutral Countries and the Shoah,* eds. Corry Buttstadt, et al. (Berlin: Metropol Verlag & IHRA, 2016), 43.

710.   Simon Erlanger, "The Politics of 'Transmigration': Why Jewish Refugees had to Leave Switzerland from 1944 to 1954," Jewish Political Studies Review 18:1-2 (Spring 2006). http://www.jcpa.org/phas/phas-erlanger-s06.htm

711.   Peter Hayes (Ed.), *How Was it Possible? A Holocaust Reader,* (Lincoln: University of Nebraska Press, 215), 219.

712.   Lienert, "Swiss Immigration Policies 1933-1939," 47.

713.   Franz makes no mention of any Swiss bank account in his reparations request, and in fact suggested that he had to borrow money from friends while living in Switzerland. But any mention of financial resources in Switzerland would likely not have helped his request for reparations from the German government.

714.   The Neumeiers fought to have their money released from Deutsche Bank while living in Switzerland, but the entire amount was ultimately seized by the Nazi authorities in April 1941.

715.   Lisbon became the only neutral transatlantic harbor in Western Europe following the occupation of France by Germany in June 1940. *See* https://portal.ehri-project.eu/countries/pt. There were a few ships leaving from Spain during this period, but the voyages were irregular and were frequently canceled, and hence were unreliable. *See* Kaplan, *Hitler's Jewish Refuges,"* 252 n. 43.

716.   Irene Flunser Pinmental, "Portugal and the Holocaust," in *Portuguese Jews, New Christians, and "New Jews,"* eds. Claude B. Stuczynski and Bruno Feitler, (Leiden: Brill, 2018), 441.

717.   Ibid., 444.

718.   Ibid.

719.   About 80,000 to 100,000 Jews and other refugees were able to flee Nazi-controlled Europe through Lisbon. *See* https://portal.ehri-project.eu/countries/pt. This included nearly 40,000 Jews between June of 1940 and early 1942. *See* https://www.holocaustrescue.org/introduction-to-rescue-in-portugal.

720.   Marion Kaplan, *Hitler's Jewish Refugees: Hope and Anxiety in Portugal,* (New Haven: Yale University Press, 2020), 43. The Joint Distribution Committee was founded during World War I as an international Jewish relief organization, and provided critical aid in helping Jews escape from Germany. The JDC had established the Transmigration Bureau, which helped refugees from countries like Germany emigrate to the U.S. Its primary role was to accept deposits from friends or family overseas towards the travel costs of Jews emigrating from Europe. *See* http://www.jdc.org/about/.

721.   Kaplan, *Hitler's Jewish Refugees: Hope and Anxiety in Portugal*, 43.

722.   Ibid.

723.   "German Refugees Transported to Lisbon in Sealed Trains," Jewish Telegraph Agency (Jan. 23, 1941), at https://www.jta.org/1941/01/23/archive/german-refu-gees-transported-to-lisbon-in-sealed-trains.

724.   Stephen Halbrook, *Swiss and the Nazis: How the Alpine Republic Survived in the Shadow of the Third Reich,* (Haverton, PA: Casemate, 2006), 102.

725.   Marion Kaplan, "Lisbon is Sold Out! The Daily Lives of Jewish Refugees in Portugal During World War II," Tikvah Working Paper 01/13, The Tikvah Center for Law & Jewish Civilization, (2013), 16.

726.   "Introduction to Refuge in Portugal," at https://www.holocaustrescue.org/intro-duction-to-rescue-in-portugal. There were also no ships going directly to Haiti. In order to get to Haiti, the Wolfsheimers would have had to first sail to Cuba, which would have required that they obtain a Cuban transit visa, if one was available. Marion Kaplan, *Hitler's Jewish Refugees: Hope and Anxiety in Portugal,* (New Haven: Yale University Press, 2020), 162.

727.   Kaplan, "Lisbon is Sold Out! The Daily Lives of Jewish Refugees in Portugal During World War II," 16-17, 20. By 1941, passage to America was a challenge. While sixty-one ships carrying Jewish refugees arrived in New York harbor from all over Europe in the month of June 1939, in the month of June 1941, only 14 ships arrived, almost all from Lisbon. *See* https://medium.com/@HolocaustMu-seum/german-bombs-and-us-bureaucrats-how-escape-lines-from-europe-were-cut-off-1b3e14137cc4.

728.   Kaplan, *Hitler's Jewish Refugees: Hope and Anxiety in Portugal,* 160.

729.   Kaplan, "Lisbon is Sold Out! The Daily Lives of Jewish Refugees in Portugal During World War II," 19.

730.   While the Wolfsheimers were not able to take advantage of the JDC's train passage to Lisbon, they were able to take advantage of the JDC's Transmigration Bureau while in Lisbon. Because emigrants could not purchase steamship tickets in local currency, the Transmigration Bureau enabled American family or friends to place money in an account, to be used to pay for the steamship ticket once the reservation was secured and all the necessary travel documentation was in order. *See* explanation at https://www.ancestry.com/search/collections/ajjdctransmigra-tion/. An account had been established on behalf of the Wolfsheimers (although there is no record of an account for the Neumeiers).

731.   Unless otherwise noted, all information regarding Benny and Margot was obtained from the *Recollections of Herb* Harvey, as well as the reparations requests of Benny Heppenheimer on behalf of himself and his wife, Hessisches Landesar-chiv Hauptstaatsarchiv Wiesbaden, HHStAW 518-8241; HHStAW 518-14877.

732.   Evans, *The Third Reich in Power,* 597.

733.   Wolf Gruner, *Jewish Forced Labor Under the Nazis: Economic Needs and Racial Aims, 1938-1944,* (Cambridge: Cambridge University Press, 2006), xvii. By May 1939, around 15,000 German Jews were already employed as forced laborers, and by the summer of 1939, about 20,000 German Jews were employed doing heavy construction work. Evans, *The Third Reich in Power,* 597. In terms of Frankfurt, by April 1940, 11,500 Jews still lived in the city, but only about 1,000 were deemed capable of full-time manual work. Gruner, *Jewish Forced Labor Under the Nazis: Economic Needs and Racial Aims, 1938-1944,* 10. Of these, 546 performed manual labor—331 in brick or excavation work and 215 carrying coal or similar jobs. *Ibid.* By the following April, the number of Jewish forced laborers increased—a total of 1,628 Jews (1,104 men and 524 women) were working as forced laborers in Frankfurt. *Ibid,* 15. Private companies took advantage of these forced laborers. In Frankfurt, over 220 companies used forced laborers, including 80 companies involved in war operations. *Ibid.,* 278.

734.   Herb's brother Bill may have continued his schooling in the Philanthropin, although this Jewish school was also under siege. Following Kristallnacht in November 1938, male teachers from the school were deported to Buchenwald and returned to Frankfurt in January 1939. In the spring of 1939, only 160 students remained in the high school. In April 1939, Frankfurt seized the property and forced the school to rent the building from the city. The Reich finally shut down all Jewish schools in April 1941, including the Philanthropin. *See* "Philanthropin—School of the Israelite Community," at http://www.frankfurt1933-1945.de/.

735.   Barkai, "In a Ghetto Without Walls," *German-Jewish History in Modern Times, Volume 4*, 344. The policy of moving Jews out of their existing homes and apartments and concentrating them in Jewish neighborhoods in the homes or apartments owned by other Jews began in 1939, and was intended to create a Jewish ghetto without the need for physical barriers. *See* Hans Riebsamen, "Before Deportation to the "Ghetto House"," *Frankfurter Allgemeine, November 9, 2010.* https://www.faz.net/aktuell/rhein-main/frankfurt/ns-zeit-in-frankfurt-vor-der-deportation-ins-gettohaus-11068046.html. There may have been as many as 300 Jewish Houses in Frankfurt. When the Nazis began the deportations, they began with the Jews that were living in the best neighborhoods in Frankfurt. *See* "Ghettoization of the Jews in Frankfurt (1938-1942)," at http://www.frankfurt1933-1945.de/.

736.   To avoid becoming a "public charge," Jewish immigrants were required to have a certain amount of money in an account before they could emigrate to America. Susanne Heim, "The Attitude of the US and Europe to the Jewish Refugees From Nazi Germany," *Refugee Policies from 1933 until Today: Challenges and Responsibilities,* (Berlin: Metropol Verlag, 2018), 58, at https://www.holocaustremembrance.com/sites/default/files/inline-files/Refugee%20Policies%20Publication.pdf. The amount of money was left up to the consuls, most of whom were aware of the anti-immigration climate in the U.S. *Ibid,* 58-59. As discussed below, the family believed that the American consulate officials in Stuttgart, where they would need to obtain their visas, were particularly anti-Semitic, so we can assume that they imposed a relatively high funding requirement for the family. Of course, because all monies were deposited in a blocked account, the family would have no access to the money once they emigrated to America.

737. The German government closed all the American consulates in July 1941. Christoph Strupp, "Observing a Dictatorship: American Consular Reporting on Germany, 1933-1941," GHI Bulletin No. 39, (Fall 2006), 80.

738. Herb suspected that the Vice Consul in the Stuttgart office, Julius C. Jensen, purposely lied about Margot's x-ray results, thinking that the family would not leave without her. *See Recollection of Herb Harvey.*

739. Because German Jews who finally received visas were limited in what they could take and anticipating that any registered wealth would ultimately be confiscated, Benny had already begun to move certain valuables out of Germany ahead of emigration, beginning in 1938. Benny's wife Margot had sent her jewelry and the jewelry of her mother, as well as the jewelry of her sisters-in-law Bertha Marx and Johanna Wolfsheimer (Benny's sisters) to a family member in Switzerland, who then carried that jewelry with him when he emigrated to America. *See Recollection of Herb Harvey.*

740. By this point, the U.S. State Department was no longer issuing visas to people in Germany or German-occupied countries, so Cuba was Margot's only hope. Rebecca Boehling and Uta Larkey, *Life and Loss in the Shadow of the Holocaust: A Jewish Family's Untold Story,* (Cambridge: Cambridge University Press, 2011), 199. After the U.S. consulates closed, there was a run on Cuban visas, with 35,000 visas issued between September and November 1941. *Ibid.,* 301 n. 139.

741. *See* the International Institute for Holocaust Research at http://db.yadvashem.org/deportation/transportDetails.html?language=en&itemId=5091969

742. "Jewish Deportation from October 1941 to June 1942," in http://www.frankfurt1933-1945.de/.

743. https://deportation.yadvashem.org/index.html?language=en&itemId=9437819&ind=-1.

744. The SA, also known as Storm Troopers or Brown Shirts, was the Nazi Party militia that helped Hitler rise to power in Germany. By 1941, the SA was no longer a dominant organization within the Reich, but its members continued to terrorize so-called enemies of the Nazi regime. *See* https://www.yadvashem.org/odot_pdf/Microsoft%20Word%20-%205986.pdf.

745. Meyer, *A Fatal Balancing Act: The Dilemma of the Reich Association of Jews in Germany, 1939-1945,* 255.

746. "Jewish Deportation from October 1941 to June 1942," in http://www.frankfurt1933-1945.de/.

747. Ibid.

748. Ibid.

749. https://deportation.yadvashem.org/index.html?language=en&itemId=9437819&ind=-1.

750. "Jewish Deportation from October 1941 to June 1942," at http://www.frankfurt1933-1945.de/. Heppenheimer family members, including Joseph, had lived in the Ostend earlier in the century.

751. Memorial at the Frankfurt Grossmarkt—Two phase competition, p. 30, at https://www.competitionline.com/upload/downloads/12xx/1209_3016174_Auslobung-competition%20brief_.pdf.

752. https://deportation.yadvashem.org/index.html?language=en&itemId=9437819&ind=-1.

753. Memorial at the Frankfurt Grossmarkt—Two phase competition, p. 33.

754. Ibid.

755. Ibid., 30.

756. Gay, *The Jews of Germany,* 281.

757. https://deportation.yadvashem.org/index.html?language=en&itemId=9437819&ind=-1.

758. *See* information from the Judisches Museum Frankfurt; https://www.pz-ffm.de/stichwortdesmonats.html?&tx_ttnews[tt_news]=159&cHash=4a68da7fff66d52b-11d3a4348b437007. The site http://www.statistik-des-holocaust.de/list_ger_hhn_420818.html contains the transport list for Lodz. This was the only transport to leave Frankfurt for Lodz. Later transports from Frankfurt went to other ghettos, including Theresienstadt, as well as concentration and death camps.

759. Benny continued to work through the war to secure a visa for Margot. As late as August 11, 1944, Benny was seeking information regarding Margot's last location to obtain an immigration visa. *See* Request to Hebrew Sheltering and Immigrant Society, U.S. Immigration and Naturalization Service, File #56,213-685.

760. https://www.holocaust.cz/en/history/concentration-camps-and-ghettos/the-lodz-ghetto/

761. *See* the International Institute for Holocaust Research at http://db.yadvashem.org/deportation/transportDetails.html?language=en&itemId=5091969

762. Ibid.; *see also* https://www.holocaust.cz/en/history/concentration-camps-and-ghettos/the-lodz-ghetto/

763. *See* the International Institute for Holocaust Research at http://db.yadvashem.org/deportation/transportDetails.html?language=en&itemId=5091969. Living conditions were brutal, so that more than 20 percent of the ghetto's population ultimately died as a direct result of the harsh living conditions. *Ibid.*

764. https://www.jewishgen.org/databases/Holocaust/0194_Lodz_letters.html#P2.

765. Lucjan Dobroskzycki (Ed.), *The Chronicle of the Lodz Ghetto 1941-1944,* (New Haven: Yale University Press, 1984), 165.

766. Karel Margry (Ed.), "After the Battle: The Lodz Ghetto," Battle of Britain International Ltd., (2018), 17. https://www.prchiz.pl/pliki/The_Lodz_Ghetto.pdf.

767. Dobroskzycki, *The Chronicle of the Lodz Gehtto 1941-1944,* 166.

768. Isaiah Trunk, *Lodz Ghetto: A History,* (Bloomington: Indiana University Press, 2006), xxxii-xxxxv.

769. https://www.jewishgen.org/databases/Holocaust/0194_Lodz_letters.html#P2. Of the 20,000 Western Jews that arrived in Lodz, nearly 4,000 had died at this point because of hunger or disease. Dobroskzycki, *The Chronicle of the Lodz Gehtto 1941-1944,* 166; 180.

770. Trunk, *Lodz Ghetto: A History,* 234.

771. Dobroskzycki, *The Chronicle of the Lodz Gehtto 1941-1944,* 154.

772. Ibid.

773. https://www.jewishgen.org/databases/Holocaust/0194_Lodz_letters.html#P2.

774. Trunk, *Lodz Ghetto: A History*, 235.

775. Dobroskzycki, *The Chronicle of the Lodz Gehtto 1941-1944*, 160.

776. Ration Sheet for Inhabitants of Lodz Ghetto, National Archives in Lodz, April/May 1942.

777. *See* https://www.jewishgen.org/databases/Poland/LodzGhetto.html.

778. To add to the evidence that both Margot and her mother were deported to Chelmno in May 1941, in May of 1945, Margot's son Herb was member of the U.S. Armed Forces stationed in Germany and visited a family in Frankfurt that had been friends of Margot. This family had sent money to Margot immediately after her deportation to Lodz. They continued to send money, but the last letter was returned to them in the summer of 1942 with the stamp "Moved to Unknown Destination." *See Recollections of Herb Harvey.* This supports the conclusion that Margot and her mother received the "eviction" notice (which is why she was no longer at the housing she had been assigned) and they were on one of the transports to Chelmno that left Lodz in May.

779. https://www.yadvashem.org/odot_pdf/Microsoft%20Word%20-%205915.pdf.

780. Ibid.

781. https://www.jewishgen.org/ForgottenCamps/Camps/ChelmnoEng.html.

782. https://www.theholocaustexplained.org/the-final-solution/the-death-camps/chelmno/.
In all, 320,000 people were murdered at Chelmno. *See* https://www.yadvashem.org/odot_pdf/Microsoft%20Word%20-%205915.pdf.

783. Dobroskzycki, *The Chronicle of the Lodz Gehtto 1941-1944*, 164.

784. Ibid., 159.

785. Ibid., 164.

786. Ibid., 161.

787. Ibid., 172.

788. Ibid., 164-65.

789. Ibid., 161.

790. https://www.jewishgen.org/databases/Holocaust/0194_Lodz_letters.html#P2.

791. https://www.jewishgen.org/databases/Holocaust/0194_Lodz_letters.html#P2.

792. Dobroskzycki, *The Chronicle of the Lodz Gehtto 1941-1944*, 188.

793. http://www.yadvashem.org/odot_pdf/Microsoft%20Word%20-%205915.pdf.

794. Ibid.

795. Ibid.

796. Ibid.

797. Ibid.

798. https://www.jewishgen.org/ForgottenCamps/Camps/ChelmnoEng.html

799. Ibid.

800.   Ibid. http://www.yadvashem.org/odot_pdf/Microsoft%20Word%20-%205915. pdf.

801.   Ibid.

802.   Unless otherwise noted, the information regarding Alice and Alfred Falkenstein is derived from their tax records, Hessisches Landesarchiv Hauptstaatsarchiv Wiesbaden, HHStAW 676-8335 and Alfred's arrest records, Hessisches Landesarchiv Hauptstaatsarchiv Wiesbaden, HHStAW 409-3_12344 and 474-3_220.

803.   "Britta Bopf, "Economic Discrimination and Confiscation: The Case of Jewish Real Estate," *Confiscation of Jewish Property in Europe, 1933-1945,* (Washington, D.C., United States Holocaust Memorial Museum, 2003), 112.

804.   It is not clear when Alice and Alfred decided to try to leave Germany. It may be that, like Benny and Margot, they decided to leave after Kristallnacht.

805.   Oto Luthar, *Margins of Memory: Anti-Semitism and the Destruction of the Jewish Community in Prekmurje,* (ZRC Publishing House, 2012), 146.

806.   For example, a lawyer in Hamburg was accused of having a relationship with a non-Jewish woman, even though there was no evidence of a relationship and the real reason for the prosecution was a dispute about rent. *See* "Discrimination by Rescission of Emancipation: The Nuremberg Laws 1935," The International Association of Jewish Lawyers and Jurists, No. 22 Winter 1999, 12. http://www. intjewishlawyers.org/main/files/Justice%20No.22%20Winter1999.pdf.

807.   Jüdisches Museum Frankfurt, Datenbank Gedenkstätte Neuer Börneplatz.

808.   Alice and Alfred were still living there when the 1939 German Minority census was taken in May 1939. The 1939 German Minority Census was conducted by the German government and required that the head of each household fill out a card marking the Jewish background of each of the resident's four grandparents. *See* https://www.mappingthelives.org/.

809.   Alice Falkenstein, "Documents Related to Jewish Business," Jan. 27, 1941, United States Holocaust Memorial Museum, at https://www.ushmm.org.

810.   Alice Falkenstein, "Documents Related to Jewish Business," Jan. 20, 1941, United States Holocaust Memorial Museum, at https://www.ushmm.org. In the letter, she explained that she had owned a women's tailoring shop from 1933 through 1938, and had 2-3 employees.

811.   Gruner, *Jewish Forced Labor Under the Nazis: Economic Needs and Racial Aims, 1938-1944,* 15.

812.   Alice Falkenstein, "Documents Related to Jewish Business," Mar. 4, 1941, United States Holocaust Memorial Museum, at https://www.ushmm.org.

813.   Alice Falkenstein, "Documents Related to Jewish Business," June 14, 1941, United States Holocaust Memorial Museum, at https://www.ushmm.org.

814.   Ibid. In general, the craft guilds supported the Nazi government and the changes the government made to the guilds. Evans, *The Third Reich in Power,* 436. The fact that the Guild went out of its way to offer support to a Jew at a time when Jews were banned from owning businesses in Germany suggests that Alice may have been a valued member of the guild.

815.   Alice Falkenstein, "Documents Related to Jewish Business," Sept. 5, 1941, United States Holocaust Memorial Museum, at https://www.ushmm.org. By the time

Alice received her work assignment, the number of Jews employed as forced laborers in Frankfurt had risen to 2,020—1,265 men and 755 women. *See* Gruner, *Jewish Forced Labor Under the Nazis: Economic Needs and Racial Aims, 1938-1944*, 18.

816. "Jewish Deportation from October 1941 to June 1942," in http://www.frankfurt1933-1945.de/; Meyer, *A Fatal Balancing Act: The Dilemma of the Reich Association of Jews in Germany, 1939-1945*, 255.

817. Meyer, *A Fatal Balancing Act: The Dilemma of the Reich Association of Jews in Germany, 1939-1945*, 255.

818. "Document: Deportation Notification Form," in http://www.frankfurt1933-1945.de/. The notification instructed the person to do the following: (1) list all assets on the asset declaration form (which would then become property of the German government); (2) leave behind all valuables other than a wedding ring; (3) take no more than 50 Reichmarks, which was to be used to pay for the transport (the money was taken from Jewish community funds if the person did not have the resources); (4) pack a small suitcase with warm clothes; and (5) pack a handbag with food for three days. *Ibid.*

819. "Document: State Police Order on Deportation," in http://www.frankfurt1933-1945.de/.

820. Friedman, *The Lion and the Star*, 171.

821. Ibid.

822. "Jewish Deportation from October 1941 to June 1942," in http://www.frankfurt1933-1945.de/. To make room for the incoming transports of German Jews into Lithuania, 27,000 Jews from the ghettos in Riga were executed in the woods outside the city limits. Friedman, *The Lion and the Star*, 170-71.

823. Dokumente zur Geschichte der Frankfurter Juden, prepared by Kommission zur Erforschung der Geschichte der Frankfurter Juden, Verlag Waldemar Kramer, p. 525 (1963).

824. Ibid.

825. Ibid.

826. Ibid., 525, 527.

827. Ibid., 526.

828. Ibid.

829. *See* https://www.jewishgen.org/yizkor/pinkas_lita/lit_00542.html

830. Ibid.

831. Ibid.

832. David Downing, *Sealing Their Fate: The Twenty-Two Days That Decided World War II*, (London: Da Capo Press, 2009), 145.

833. Ibid.

834. Ibid.

835. Unless otherwise noted, the information regarding Lippmann Lewin is derived from his prison records, Hessisches Landesarchiv Hauptstaatsarchiv Wiesbaden, HHStAW 409/3-13594, 409/3-13593, and 409/4-4127. Unless otherwise noted,

the information regarding Selma Lewin is derived from a lawsuit she filed and from her divorce proceeding against Lippmann, Hessisches Landesarchiv Hauptstaatsarchiv Wiesbaden, HHStAW 474/4-251 and 474/3-861.

836. Rogow was, at the time of Lippmann's birth, part of Germany, but following Germany's defeat in World War I, was returned to Poland. *See* http://www.polishroots.org/Research/GenPoland/ProvinzPosen/tabid/461/Default.aspx. When Lippmann was in his teens, Lippmann was sent to Rotterdam, the Netherlands, for an apprenticeship. Between June 18, 1917 and November 1918, Lippmann served in the German army. After the war, Lippmann became a salesman for a wholesale coffee company.

837. Before moving in with Selma and Lippmann, Emma had been living in the same apartment she had lived in with Joseph, on Roderberg Weg in the Ostend. While some of Joseph's children had moved to fancier neighborhoods in Frankfurt during the 1920s, Emma had remained in the Ostend. Emma's step-daughter Bertha continued to live with Emma on Roderberg Weg until Emma moved in with her daughter Selma.

838. Hessisches Landesarchiv Hauptstaatsarchiv Wiesbaden, HHStaw 518—8241.

839. Selma was represented by Siegfried Popper, a "Jewish consultant." As a result of the 5th Ordinance on the Reich Citizenship Act of September 27, 1938, all Jewish lawyers lost their law licenses as of November 30, 1938. 84 lawyers were affected by this edict in Frankfurt. Recognizing that Jews seeking to emigrate still required representation, and such representation could not be performed by "Aryan" lawyers, a small number of the excluded former lawyers were granted permission to be "Jewish consultants." Siegfried Popper was among the initial nine former lawyers who were granted permission to practice as Jewish consultants, with the permission being granted for a short period of time and requiring subsequent requests for extension. *See "The Jewish Consultants," at https://www.frankfurt1933-1945.de/nc/beitraege/show/1/thematik/boykott-und-arisierung/artikel/die-juedischen-konsulenten/.* Popper remained Selma's consultant until her divorce was granted. Popper, his wife, and two children were deported to Theresienstadt on March 17, 1943 and all perished in Auschwitz in 1944.

840. Marion A. Kaplan, *Beyond Dignity and Despair: Jewish Life in Nazi Germany,* (New York: Oxford University Press, 1998), 88.

841. Ibid.

842. Lippmann was planning to emigrate to Palestine through Trieste. Attempting to emigrate to Palestine at the end of the 1939 seems like an odd choice. By 1936, the British government had begun to cut back on the number of immigration permits it would issue, particularly after the Arab revolt that began in April 1936. Hagit Lavsky, *Before Catastrophe: The Distinctive Path of German Zionism,* (Detroit: Wayne State University Press, 1996), 253. Over 60,000 German Jews had immigrated to Palestine during the 1930s, but the British White Paper in May 1939 contained measures that severely limited Jewish entry into Palestine. *See* https://www.ushmm.org/wlc/en/article.php?ModuleId=10005139. But through the efforts of the German Foreign Office, which was still working at the time to encourage emigration, in September 1939, Britain stated that it would be willing to honor permission that had been granted to 1,450 German Jews to enter Palestine, if they could pick up their permits in Trieste. *See* Christopher R. Browning, *The Origins of the Final Solution—The Evolution of Jewish Policy, September 1939-March 1942,* (Lincoln: University of Nebraska Press, 2004), 195-95.

Lippmann and one or more of his siblings were likely among the 1,450 German Jews who had received permission to enter Palestine, since, at that time, there was no other legal way to emigrate to Palestine through Trieste.

843. By the 1939 German Minority Census, four of Lippmann's siblings (Robert, Julius, Rosa and Gertrud) were living together in an apartment in Frankfurt, and his sister Johanna was living in a separate apartment in Frankfurt. *See* https://www.mappingthelives.org/.

844. The regulations provided that, at least three weeks prior to emigration, a customs official from the Foreign Exchange Office was to be notified, and then the customs official would conduct an audit in the dwelling of the emigrant. As a general rule, only goods purchased before 1933 and a very limited number of valuables could be shipped abroad. The customs official would check the information contained in the removal lists to make sure that they matched the items to be packed and that no valuables were being shipped. The emigrant would then receive a customs seal. The regulations were clear that false statements or inclusion in the shipment of valuables would be subject to severe penalties under the Foreign Exchange Act. "Document: Leaflet of the Exchange Office S Frankfurt for the Transport of Goods by Jewish Emigrants in 1939," at http://www.frankfurt1933-1945.de.

845. Browning, *The Origins of the Final Solution—The Evolution of Jewish Policy, September 1939-March 1942,* (Lincoln: University of Nebraska Press, 2004), 196.

846. Ofer, *Escaping the Holocaust: Illegal Immigration to the Land of Israel, 1939-1944,* 102. Given the value of the items, it is highly unlikely that Lippmann would have ever received permission to ship the items to Trieste, which is probably why he needed to find a customs official to bribe.

847. This house had been owned by Alfred and Irmgard Marx, and the house had been used by Dr. Alfred Marx for his medical practice. *See* Initiative Stolperstein Frankfurt am Main, Dokumentation 2016, 66, at http://www.stolpersteine-frankfurt.de/downloads/doku2016_web.pdf. By the late 1930s, Dr. Marx was forced to stopped practicing medicine and to make his home a Judenhaus. *Ibid.* A biography of another resident of Eschersheimer Landstrasse 39 referred to it as a Jewish Home. *See* http://www.erinnerung.org/gg/haeuser/wr18.html. Alfred and Irmgard Marx were deported to Theresienstadt on September 15, 1942 and both were murdered in Auschwitz. *Initiative Stolperstein Frankfurt am Main, Dokumentation 2016, p. 66.*

848. Marion Kaplan, *Between Dignity and Despair: Jewish Life in Nazi Germany,* (New York: Oxford University Press, 1998), 154-55.

849. Ibid.

850. Italy declared war on Britain and France in June 1940, entering World War II as Germany's ally. *See* https://www.ushmm.org/wlc/en/article.php?ModuleId=10005455.

851. The customers official Wagner, who had no authority to conduct the inspection or issue the seal of approval, was convicted on November 15, 1940 and sentenced to one year in prison. The court stated that Lippmann, through his actions, had "plunged a previously immaculate official into misery."

852. "Diez Prison," Frank Falla Archive, at https://www.frankfallaarchive.org/prisons/diez-prison/.

853. Selma had a foreign exchange account in Frankfurt bank. *See* https://collections. arolsen-archives.org/en/archive/70357579/?p=1&s=Heppenheimer&doc_ id=70357579. Before the middle of 1938, a foreign exchange account was required before a German Jew could emigrate (so that the Nazis could deplete the assets in the account following emigration). *See* Albrecht Ritschl, "Fiscal Destruction Confiscatory Taxation of Jewish Property and Income in Nazi Germany," 3, at http://eh.net/eha/wp-content/uploads/2019/06/RItschl.pdf. But on April 26, 1938, all German Jews were ordered to register their domestic and foreign assets and at the end of 1938, all German Jews were required to establish a blocked account. *See* Harold James, *The Deutsche Bank and the Nazi Economic War Against the Jews: The expropriation of Jewish-Owned Property,* (Cambridge: Cambridge University Press, 2004), 197. We do not know whether Selma established her account because she intended, at some point, to emigrate, or whether she did this because she was directed to do so at the end of 1938.

854. *See* https://www.frankfurt.de/sixcms/detail.php?id=1907322&_ffmpar[_id_inhalt]=29627381.

855. http://www.juedische-pflegegeschichte.de/das-krankenhaus-der-israelitischen-gemeinde-in-der-gagernstrasse-36/.

856. *See* http://www.juedische-pflegegeschichte.de/historical-institutions-of-jewish-elderly-care-and-aged-care-work-in-frankfurt-am-main/.

857. https://www.ushmm.org/wlc/en/article.php?ModuleId=10007258.

858. "The Wannsee Conference," https://www.yadvashem.org/holocaust/about/final-solution-beginning/wannsee-conference.html.

859. Ibid. As previously discussed, plans had already been made for the construction of three death camps.

860. Friedman, *The Lion and the Star,* 172.

861. Ibid., 173.

862. "Jewish Deportation from October 1941 to June 1942," in http://www.frankfurt1933-1945.de/

863. Aufbau, July 24, 1942, p. 9, at https://archive.org/stream/aufbau81942germ#page/n472/mode/1up/search/Frankfurt

864. Ibid.

865. *See* http://www.statistik-des-holocaust.de/list_ger_hhn.html. There are total numbers of passengers for each transport: the May 8th transport carried 938 Jews, the May 24th transport carried 959 Jews, and the June 11th transport carried 1254 Jews. *Ibid.*

866. Monica Kingreen, "Gewaltsam verschleppt aus Frankfurt Die Deportation der Juden in den Jahren 1941-1945," in *Nach der Kristallnacht: Judisches Leben und Antijudische Politik in Frankfurt am Main 1938-1945,* ed. Monica Kingreen (Frankfurt: Campus Verlag, 1999), 369.

867. "Ghettoization of the Jews of Frankfurt (1938-1942), at http://www.frankfurt1933-1945.de.

868. See *Glossary of Terms and Abbreviations,* Holocaust Survivors and Victims Resource Center, 80, at https://secure.ushmm.org/individual-research/Glossary. pdf. The information on the foreign exchange accounts was not always accurate.

For example, Lippmann's account information stated that he had emigrated to Palestine.

869. After the Wannsee Conference, Izbica, a Polish town which already had a Jewish ghetto, was chosen as the main transitory ghetto for Czech, German and Austrian Jews because of its proximity to Belzec, Sobibor, and Treblinka. https://www. holocausthistoricalsociety.org.uk/contents/ghettosa-i/izbica.html. Belzec became operational in March 1942. *Ibid*. The first deportations to Sobibor began in May 1942. *See* https://www.ushmm.org/wlc/en/article.php?ModuleId=10007258. Treblinka began operations in July 1942. *See* https://www.ushmm.org/wlc/en/article. php?ModuleId=10005193.

870. https://deportation.yadvashem.org/index.html?language=en&itemId=5604908&ind=-1.

871. Ibid.; http://db.yadvashem.org/deportation/transportDetails.html?language=en&itemId=9439240.

872. Ibid. Another resident in the Jewish House in which Selma was living on Eschersheimer Landstrasse 39, Fritz Wulf, died in Majdanek on July 7, 1942. *See* https://yvng.yadvashem.org/nameDetails.html?language=en&itemId=11659167&ind=1. To have been deported to Majdanek meant that he had been on one of the transports from Frankfurt to Izbica. It is possible that Fritz Wulf and Selma were placed on the same deportation list since they were living in the same Jewish House (and, as previously explained, the Gestapo ordered the Reichsvereinigung to gather the names of all those in the area of the persons to be "evacuated," and then the Gestapo created a deportation list from this pool of names), with Fritz leaving the train with the other men in Majdanek and Selma remaining on the train until Izbica.

873. https://deportation.yadvashem.org/index.html?language=en&itemId=5604908&ind=-1.

874. Ibid.

875. Ibid.

876. https://www.holocausthistoricalsociety.org.uk/contents/ghettosa-i/izbica.html.

877. https://ipfs.io/ipfs/QmXoypizjW3WknFiJnKLwHCnL72vedxjQkDDP1mX-Wo6uco/wiki/Izbica_Ghetto.html.

878. Ibid.

879. https://www.holocausthistoricalsociety.org.uk/contents/ghettosa-i/izbica.html.

880. https://deportation.yadvashem.org/index.html?language=en&itemId=5604907&ind=-1.

881. https://www.jewishvirtuallibrary.org/the-deportation-of-austrian-and-german-jews.

882. https://www.ushmm.org/wlc/en/article.php?ModuleId=10005192.

883. Ibid.

884. On October 14, 1943, likely emboldened by news of the Warsaw ghetto uprising and determined to defy the Nazis, the Jews of Sobibor killed the camp's Nazi SS officers and led an escape from the camp. Of the 600 prisoners, 300 were killed in the attempt, but the remaining prisoners made it successfully into the woods and evaded capture. Of those prisoners who escaped, SS and police personnel from

the Lublin district recaptured and shot some 100. Upon hearing of the escape, Heinrich Himmler, head of the Nazi SS, closed the camp within days, killed all remaining prisoners, destroyed all evidence of the camp, and planted the area over with trees. By the war's end, only 47 Sobibor prisoners had survived and only those survivors knew about Sobibor. They told the world about the horrors of Sobibor. *See* http://jcfgp.org/thomas-toivi-blatt/; https://www.ushmm.org/wlc/en/article.php?ModuleId=10007258.

885. *See* https://www.lagis-hessen.de/de/subjects/xsrec/current/101/pageSize/50/mode/abstract/setmode/abstract/sn/edb?q=YToxOntzOjc6ImJlcmVpY2giO3M-6MTY6IkrDvGRpc2NoZXMgTGViZW4i4iO30=.

886. *See* http://www.statistik-des-holocaust.de/list_ger_hhn_420818.html, which has the transport lists for transports to Theresienstadt.

887. Ibid.

888. https://www.jewishvirtuallibrary.org/theresienstadt-the-ldquo-model-rd-quo-ghetto.

889. Avraham Barkai, "The Final Chapter", in *German-Jewish History in Modern Times, Volume 4*, 371.

890. Ibid., 375.

891. https://www.jewishvirtuallibrary.org/theresienstadt-the-ldquo-model-rd-quo-ghetto.

892. Ibid.

893. Ibid.

894. http://www.yadvashem.org/holocaust/about/ghettos/theresienstadt.html#narrative_info.

895. Of the 33,000 Jews who perished in the Theresienstadt Ghetto, more than 20,000 death certificates were issued. https://blog.ehri-project.eu/2016/02/18/death-certificate-of-gabriel-frankl-from-the-terezin-ghetto/. There is no death certificate for Emma.

896. http://www.thehistoryreader.com/military-history/theresienstadt/.

897. https://deportation.yadvashem.org/index.html?language=en&itemId=5091987&ind=-1.

898. Ibid.

899. Ibid.

900. Ibid. The Treblinka operations were very similar to those at Sobibor. The transport trains ended their journey at the station in the village of Treblinka, 4 km from the camp. From there, the deportees were sent to the camp 20 trucks at a time. The deportees were taken out of the trucks, the men were separated from the women and children, and all were forced to strip naked. Then they were driven down to the "bath house," where they were gassed. *See* https://www.holocaust.cz/en/history/concentration-camps-and-ghettos/treblinka-3/.

901. http://www.thehistoryreader.com/military-history/theresienstadt/. Responding to pressure from the Red Cross, the Nazis created a façade suggesting a model life for Jews, which was toured by the Red Cross on June 23, 1944, but it was just a façade. *See* http://www.yadvashem.org/holocaust/about/ghettos/theresienstadt.

html#narrative_info. Of the more than 154,000 Jews deported to Theresienstadt during the war, 88,000 were deported to death camps and 33,000 died of hunger, disease, and brutal treatment in Theresienstadt. *Ibid.*

902.   Lippmann's siblings Robert, Julius, Rosa and Gertrud were deported to Minsk on November 12, 1941. *See* http://www.statistik-des-holocaust.de/list_ger_hhn_411112.html. All perished. Lippmann's sister Johanna was deported to the Theresienstadt Ghetto on August 18, 1942, and she died in the Theresienstadt Ghetto on August 22, 1943 of heart failure. *See* https://www.holocaust.cz/data-baze-dokumentu/dokument/98117-lewin-johanna-oznameni-o-umrti-ghet-to-terezin/.

903.   Ibid.

904.   http://db.yadvashem.org/deportation/transportDetails.html?language=en&itemId=5092432. Jews living in so-called "privileged" mixed marriages were exempted from the deportations. Beate Meyer, "The Mixed Marriage: A Guarantee of Survival or a Reflection of German Society During the Nazi Regime," in *Probing the Depths of German Antisemitism: German Society and the Persecution of the Jews, 1933-1941,* David Bankier (Ed.) (New York: Berghahn, 2000), 62. Unfortunately, that would change in the later years of the war.

905.   *http://db.yadvashem.org/deportation/transportDetails.html?language=en&itemId=5092432.*

906.   https://deportation.yadvashem.org/index.html?language=en&itemId=5092734&ind=-1. Lippmann was not on the list of deportees, but the list contains only Berlin residents and an historian has noted that there were persons "from various cities in Germany" on the train. *Ibid.*

907.   Ibid.

908.   One sixth of all Jews murdered by the Nazis were gassed at Auschwitz. https://www.myjewishlearning.com/article/auschwitz-birkenau/, citing The Yad Vashem Encyclopedia of the Ghettos during the Holocaust.

909.   http://auschwitz.org/en/history/life-in-the-camp/the-order-of-the-day.

910.   Ibid. Twenty brick buildings were adapted, and 8 new blocks were added by the first half of 1942. The blocks were designed to hold about 700 prisoners, but in practice they housed up to 1,200. *Ibid.* The first Polish political prisoners arrived in Auschwitz in June 1940, and by March 1941, there were 10,900 prisoners, the majority of whom were Polish. https://www.myjewishlearning.com/article/auschwitz-birkenau/, citing *The Yad Vashem Encyclopedia of the Ghettos during the Holocaust.* The Polish prisoners were also subjected to inhumane conditions.

911.   Ibid.; https://www.myjewishlearning.com/article/auschwitz-birkenau/, citing *The Yad Vashem Encyclopedia of the Ghettos during the Holocaust.*

912.   Ibid. The gas chambers in the Auschwitz complex constituted the largest and most efficient extermination method employed by the Nazis. Four chambers were in use at Birkenau, each with the potential to kill 6,000 people daily. They were built to look like shower rooms in order to confuse the victims. New arrivals at Birkenau were told that they were being sent to work, but first needed to shower and be disinfected. They would be led into the shower-like chambers, where they were quickly gassed to death with the highly poisonous Zyklon B gas. *See* https://www.myjewishlearning.com/article/auschwitz-birkenau/, citing *The Yad Vashem Encyclopedia of the Ghettos during the Holocaust.*

913. Beginning in March 1942, trains carrying Jews arrived daily. In many instances, several trains would arrive on the same day, each carrying one thousand or more victims coming from the ghettos of Eastern Europe, as well as from Western and Southern European countries. Throughout 1942, transports arrived from Poland, Slovakia, the Netherlands, Belgium, Yugoslavia, and Theresienstadt. Jews, as well as Gypsies, continued to arrive throughout 1943. Hungarian Jews were brought to Auschwitz in 1944, alongside Jews from the remaining Polish ghettos. *See* https://www.myjewishlearning.com/article/auschwitz-birkenau/, citing *The Yad Vashem Encyclopedia of the Ghettos during the Holocaust.*

914. Construction of brick barracks began in the fall of 1941, and those barracks would each hold 700 prisoners. http://auschwitz.org/en/history/life-in-the-camp/. Wooden barracks, built later, had no windows and would hold more than 400 prisoners per barracks. *Ibid.*

915. Ibid; http://www.wollheim-memorial.de/en/kz_bunamonowitz_en. Given the availability of slave labor, the German chemical industry conglomerate I. G. Farben Industrie placed one of its synthetic rubber plants near Auschwitz, and built Monowitz immediately adjacent to the factory site to house the workers for its facility. Ewa K. Bacon, "The Prisoner Hospital at Buna-Monowitz," in *History 1933-1948: What We Chose to Remember,* eds. Margarte Monahan Hogan and James M. Lies, (Portland: University of Portland, 2011), 161-62.

916. https://www.jewishvirtuallibrary.org/history-and-overview-of-auschwitz-birkenau.

917. Another ramp for selection was built inside the Birkenau camp, in connection with the anticipated arrival of Hungarian Jews, but that did not go into operation until after Lippmann had arrived at Auschwitz. *See* http://auschwitz.org/en/history/auschwitz-and-shoah/the-unloading-ramps-and-selections.

918. Ibid.

919. Ibid.

920. Ibid.

921. Ibid.

922. http://www.yadvashem.org/yv/en/exhibitions/album_auschwitz/auschwitz-birkenau.asp.

923. Ibid; Jüdisches Museum Frankfurt, Datenbank Gedenkstätte Neuer Börneplatz.

924. https://phdn.org/archives/www.ess.uwe.ac.uk/genocide/gcpol10.htm.

925. Ibid.

926. Ibid.

927. Ibid.

928. "The Order of the Day," at http://auschwitz.org/en/history/life-in-the-camp/the-order-of-the-day.

929. Ibid.

930. Ibid.

931. "Nutrition," at http://auschwitz.org/en/history/life-in-the-camp/nutrition.

932. "The Order of the Day," at http://auschwitz.org/en/history/life-in-the-camp/the-order-of-the-day.

933. Ibid; "Nutrition," at http://auschwitz.org/en/history/life-in-the-camp/nutrition.

934. https://www.theholocaustexplained.org/the-final-solution/auschwitz-birkenau/transport-and-arrival/

935. The Death Books of Auschwitz Concentration Camp prisoners had been "lost" until 1989, when the then Soviet Union released some of the German documentation, death certificates, roll-calls, cremation lists, etc, that had been found at Auschwitz in January 1945. The Soviets turned over 46 volumes, recording the deaths of 69,000 Auschwitz prisoners, covering the years 1941, 1942 and 1943. But there are volumes still missing for 1944 and 1945, and it is not known whether Russia still has the missing volumes. *See* http://www.dobra.org/documents/auschwitz.html.

936. *See* https://www.hdot.org/debunking-denial/ab2-death-books/.

937. From the archives of the State Museum Auschwitz-Birkenau in Oświęcim.

938. Alan M. Kraut, "The State Department, the Labor Department, and German Jewish Immigration, 1930-1940," et. al., *Journal of American Ethnic History*, Vol. 3, No. 2, (Spring 1984), 25.

939. Immigration Records of Leopold Heppenheimer, U.S. Citizenship and Immigration Services, A-File A003839569.

940. Ibid

941. Leopold died in Pittsburgh, Pennsylvania on January 1, 1958.

942. Unless otherwise noted, the information in this section about Sally Heppenheimer is derived from the Reparations Request submitted by his wife, Landesarchiv Baden-Württemberg- Generallandesarchiv Karlsruhe, File No. 480-8086.

943. https://www.thegreyfolder.com/deported-to-gurs.

944. Ibid.

945. Ibid.

946. The deportations also included Jewish citizens from the Palatinate and Saarland, and came after the occupation of parts of France (including Alsace and Lorraine) by Nazi Germany in May 1940. Determining that this region (which now included Alsace and Lorraine) should be "purely German," the Administrators of Baden and the Palatinate were ordered to deport the Jews in their states, as had already been done in Alsace and Lorraine. *See* "The 'Wagner-Burckel Action,'" at https://gurs.saarland/lager/wagner-buerckel-aktion. The deportation of Jews from Alsace and Lorraine is discussed later in this chapter with respect to Jacob Heppenheimer, Lazarus' son.

947. Jette Heppenheimer, who is on this list, was not a relative of Curtis Heppen, although she perished in the Holocaust on September 9, 1941 at the age of 90. *See* https://yvng.yadvashem.org/nameDetails.html?language=en&itemId=11519296&ind=1.

948. https://www.thegreyfolder.com/deported-to-gurs.

949. Ibid. Gurs was under the authority of the collaborationist Vichy government of France. *Ibid.*

950. Ibid.

951. Ibid.

952. Of the 7,500 Jews deported to Gurs, 1,940 were ultimately able to emigrate. *See* https://www.ushmm.org/wlc/en/article.php?ModuleId=10005298. As emigration became impossible for Jews living in Milles and Gurs, these camps became centers for deportation to a concentration or death camp. *Ibid.*

953. Charmian Brinson, William Kaczynski, *Fleeing from the Fuhrer: A Postal History of Refugees from Nazism*, (Gloucestershire : The History Press, 2011), 20.

954. Bertha was in a different camp, since Camp de Milles was just for men.

955. Eric T. Jennings, *Escape from Vichy: The Refugees Exodus to the French Caribbean,* (Cambridge: Harvard University Press, 2018), 47.

956. We know that Sally and Bertha were on the Wyoming because this ship left Marseille when Sally and Bertha left Marseilles, there were no subsequent ships that left Marseille for the Western Hemisphere, and the passengers on this ship were sent to the same camp in Morocco, as discussed later. The Wyoming was carrying approximately four hundred passengers. *Ibid.*

957. *See* Interview of Ralph Hockley, at https://collections.ushmm.org/oh_findingaids/RG-50.030.0873_trs_en.pdf.

958. Michael Dobbs, *The Unwanted: America, Auschwitz, and a Village Caught Between,* (New York: Alfred A. Knopf, 2019), 194.

959. Ibid., 193.

960. Ibid.

961. Ibid.; Lisa Moses Leff, *The Archive Thief: The Man who Salvaged French Jewish History in the Wake of the Holocaust,* (Oxford: Oxford University Press, 2015), 71; Guide to Papers of Werner and Gisella Cahnman, http://digifindingaids.cjh.org/?pID=192287#b3f46.

962. http://corrieberghuis.blogspot.com/2011/03/een-meisje-van-18-in-het-kamp-van-oued.html; "Oral History Interview with Hans Cahnmann," May 28, 1989, https://collections.ushmm.org/search/catalog/irn511473.

963. *See* Guide to Papers of Werner and Gisella Cahnman, http://digifindingaids.cjh.org/?pID=192287#b3f46.

964. Georffrey P. Megargee (Ed.), *The United States Holocaust Memorial Museaum Encyclopedia of Camps and Gehttos 1933-1945, (Bloomington: Indiana University Press, 2018),* 289.

965. "Oral History Interview with Hans Cahnmann," May 28, 1989, https://collections.ushmm.org/search/catalog/irn511473.

966. http://corrieberghuis.blogspot.com/2011/03/een-meisje-van-18-in-het-kamp-van-oued.html.

967. Ibid.

968. "More Refugees to Arrive Here; 12,000 Entered," *The Jewish Floridian*, Volume 14, No. 33, (August 15, 1941), 1.

969. "600 More Refugees Saved by JDC Reach New York," *Jewish Telegraphic Agency*, (August 11, 1941).

970. Sally died on June 2, 1950 at the age of 70 and Bertha died in November 1978 at the age of 95.

971. Unless otherwise noted, the information in this section is derived from the reparations request of Walter Schwarz, Hessisches Landesarchiv Hauptstaatsarchiv Wiesbaden, HHStAW 518-50789 and the tax records of the Bauernfreunds, Hessisches Landesarchiv Hauptstaatsarchiv Wiesbaden, HHStAW 676-5689.

972. Heinrich had owned a metal trading business, Bauernfreund and Co., which was established around 1922. Around 1933, Heinrich filed for bankruptcy, perhaps experiencing the same challenges that other metals dealers experienced during the depression. Unfortunately for Heinrich, he was convicted of bankruptcy offenses, and he spent several months in prison. *See* Hessisches Landesarchiv Hauptstaatsarchiv Wiesbaden, HHStAW 409/3-6219. It is not clear whether this conviction was truly an offense relating to the bankruptcy or related to the fact that Heinrich was Jewish. When he was released from prison, Heinrich was unable to re-open his business. Instead, his wife Johanna started J. Bauernfreund & Co., likely in 1935.

973. In their effort to force Jews to sell or liquidate their businesses, revenue offices often came up with dubious back taxes against the Jewish business owner, which certainly may have been the case for the Bauernfreunds. *See* Christof Kreutzmuller, *Final Sale in Berlin: The Destruction of Jewish Commercial Activity 1930-1945,* (New York: Berghahn Books, 2015), 164.

974. https://www.frankfurt.de/sixcms/detail.php?id=1907322&_ffmpar[_id_inhalt]=2004636. This apartment was about a block from the now-damaged Westend Synagogue, but still in the fashionable Westend.

975. The foreign exchange accounts of both Heinrich and his mother-in-law Berta noted that they had emigrated to Cuba. While this is clearly not correct, it was likely based on the fact that both had Cuban visas. *See* Ancestry.com. *Europe, Registration of Foreigners and German Victims, 1939-1947* [database online]. Lehi, UT, USA: Ancestry.com Operations, Inc., 2019.

976. Martha Jelenko, "Germany," *The American Jewish Year Book,* Vol. 44, (Sept. 12, 1942-Sept. 29, 1943), 186.

977. Marion A. Kaplan, "When the Ordinary Became Extraordinary: German Jews Reacting to Nazi Persecution, 1933-1939, in *Social Outsiders in Nazi Germany,* eds. Robert Gellately and Nathan Stoltzfus, (Princeton: Princeton University Press, 2001), 86.

978. In fact, just nineteen Jews were able to leave Germany in October 1941—three on October 14 and sixteen on October 17. *See* Yehuda Bauer, *American Jewry and the Holocaust: The American Jewish Joint Distribution Committee, 1939-1945,* (Detroit: Wayne State University, 1981), p. 64.

979. Boehling, *Life and Loss in the Shadow of the Holocaust: A Jewish Family's Untold Story,* 301 n. 139.

980. Because the Bauernfreunds had moved to a new apartment within the Westend, their apartment remained in a desirable location for the Nazis and they were thus early targets for deportation.

981. *See* List of Jewish victims from the Memorial book "Victims of the Persecution of Jews under the National Socialist Tyranny in Germany 1933—1945" prepared by the German Federal Archives, https://www.bundesarchiv.de/gedenkbuch/index.

html.en. There does not appear to be a death certificate for Johanna, so we do not know what the basis is for the conclusion in the German records that Johanna died in Lodz.

982. Ibid.

983. Ibid; *See* the International Institute for Holocaust Research at http://db.yad-vashem.org/deportation/transportDetails.html?language=en&itemId=5091969. There was a second deportation in September 1942, but that deportation targeted the sick, the elderly, and the very young. This transport is discussed later in this chapter regarding the fate of Robert Heppenheimer, Berta Schwarz's cousin. Work Identification Cards were required for the approximately 75,000 workers in the Lodz ghetto, but the Lodz archives contain only 13,000 ID cards. *See* https://www.jewishgen.org/databases/Holocaust/0147_Lodz_work_cards.html. Johanna and her sons are not among those who are listed as having received the ID cards, so we have no way of knowing whether they remained in Lodz after the 1942 deportations.

984. http://db.yadvashem.org/deportation/transportDetails.html?language=en&itemId=5091969

985. Ibid.

986. Ibid. Lodz was supposed to be a temporary ghetto, but by 1944, Jews had been working there as slave laborers for four years. While this ghetto was profitable for the Germans and was particularly important for the German war effort, ideology won out in 1944 and the decision was made to liquidate the ghetto. "The Final Days of the Lodz Ghetto," Sheryl Silver Ochayon, http://www.yadvashem.org/articles/general/the-final-days-of-the-lodz-ghetto.html.

987. *See* the International Institute for Holocaust Research at http://db.yadvashem.org/deportation/transportDetails.html?language=en&itemId=5091969. While crematoria had been added to Chelmo in 1944, the use of Zyklon B gas at Auschwitz was determined to be more efficient, thus allowing for a faster liquidation process, which explains the shift of deportations from Chelmno to Auschwitz. "Shoah Resource Center: Chelmo," http://www.yadvashem.org/odot_pdf/Microsoft%20Word%20-%205915.pdf. Chelmno was destroyed by the Nazis in September 1944 and they tried to erase all evidence of mass murder at that site. *See* https://www.theholocaustexplained.org/the-final-solution/the-death-camps/chelmno/

988. Except as otherwise noted, information on Jacob Heppenheimer was obtained from Jean Horgen, the husband of Jacob's granddaughter Eliane.

989. https://www.yadvashem.org/odot_pdf/Microsoft%20Word%20-%205729.pdf

990. Ibid.

991. The family could not take everything, and so a Matisse painting was left behind. The family never recovered the painting.

992. Ibid.; Dreyfus, "Alsace-Lorraine," in *The Greater German Reich and the Jews: Nazi Persecution Policies in the Annexed Territories 1935-1945,* Wolf Gruner & Jorg Osterloh (Eds.) New York: Berghahn, 2017), 325.

993. Semelin, *The Survival of the Jews in France 1940-44,* 68. On the eve of World War II, Lyon had a Jewish population of 5,000. See https://www.jewishvirtuallibrary.org/lyons.

994. https://www.yadvashem.org/articles/general/historical-review.html.

995. Ibid.

996. Semelin, *The Survival of the Jews in France 1940-44*, 60.

997. https://www.yadvashem.org/articles/general/historical-review.html.

998. Michael R. Marrus and Robert O. Paxton, *Vichy France and the Jews,* (Stanford: Stanford University Press, 1981), 334; http://jewishtraces.org/histoire/lyon-1942-1944/. While the local French population often refused to collaborate with the Germans, deportations of Jews continued until France was liberated by the Allies. *Ibid.*

999. Semelin, *The Survival of the Jews in France 1940-44*, 76.

1000. https://www.jewishgen.org/databases/jgdetail_2.php. Getrude's daughter, Eliane, was born on October 5, 1944 in Lausanne, Switzerland. *See Ibid.*; https://www.myheritage.com/research/record-40000-43933088/eliane-myriam-horgen-born-reich-in-geni-world-family-tree?s=573925011; http://schoenberg.com/WebTree/ps72/ps72_431.htm

1001. "Invasion of Southern France", https://ww2db.com/battle_spec.php?battle_id=110.

1002. Dreyfus, "Alsace-Lorraine," in *The Greater German Reich and the Jews: Nazi Persecution Policies in the Annexed Territories 1935-1945*, 331.

1003. Semelin, *The Survival of the Jews in France 1940-44*, 11.

1004. Jüdisches Museum Frankfurt, Datenbank Gedenkstätte Neuer Börneplatz.

1005. Stadtarchiv Munchen, Auszug aus der Datenbank Biografischen Gedenkbuch der Münchner Juden.

1006. Jüdisches Museum Frankfurt, Datenbank Gedenkstätte Neuer Börneplatz. In the 1939 Jewish Minority Census, Bettina's maiden names is listed as "Guggenheimer," which was an error. *See* https://www.mappingthelives.org/bio/da0add8c-a7e1-4c6f-946c-fdaac282bf41.

1007. Reparations Request of Bettina Schnitzler on behalf of Henny Heppenheimer, Bayerisches Hauptstaatsarchiv, BAYHStA LEA-49673.

1008. Meyer, *A Fatal Balancing Act: The Dilemma of the Reich Association of Jews in Germany, 1939-1945*, 257. While Munich may have been hostile to Jews, at the time Henny and Bettina moved to Munich, there was still a sizeable Jewish community. In 1933, 9,005 Jews lived in Munich, and the size of the Jewish community had been reduced only slightly by the time Henny and her family had moved to Munich, but only because the thousands of Jews who had left Munich had been replaced by Jews from the smaller surrounding towns, who hoped that life under the Nazis would be more bearable in a larger Jewish community. *See* Susanna Schrafstetter, "Submergence into Illegality: Hidden Jews in Munich, 1941-45," in *The Germans and the Holocaust: Popular Response to the Persecution and Murder of the Jews*, eds. Susanna Schrafstetter & Alan E. Steinweis, (New York: Berghahn Press, 2016), 111 (2016). But Kristallnacht, as well other actions against the Jews in Munich, took its toll on the Jewish community—by November 1941, there were just 3,200 Jews still living in Munich. *Ibid*, 112.

1009. Jüdisches Museum Frankfurt, Datenbank Gedenkstätte Neuer Börneplatz; "Biography of Ilse Liselotte Nussbaum," at https://www.gedenken9nov38.de/archiv/

biografien-2016/ilse-liselotte-nussbaum/ (which identified the house as a Jewish House).

1010. Meyer, *A Fatal Balancing Act: The Dilemma of the Reich Association of Jews in Germany, 1939-1945,* 263.

1011. Ibid., 264.

1012. Ibid.; http://www.statistik-des-holocaust.de/OT411120-33.jpg.

1013. Meyer, *A Fatal Balancing Act: The Dilemma of the Reich Association of Jews in Germany, 1939-1945,* 264.

1014. http://holocaustcontroversies.blogspot.com/2012/10/the-jager-report-6_17.html, relying on information from the German historian Wolfram Wette's biography of Karl Jager, an SS officer who maintained a report of the killings in Nazi-occupied Lithuania.

1015. Ibid.

1016. Ibid.

1017. Meyer, *A Fatal Balancing Act: The Dilemma of the Reich Association of Jews in Germany, 1939-1945,* 323.

1018. Unless otherwise noted, the information in this section about Bettina was derived from her CM/1 files, at https://collections.arolsen-archives.org/en/search/people/79711985/?p=1&s_lastName=asc.

1019. Beate Meyer, "The Mixed Marriage: A Guarantee of Survival or a Reflection of German Society During the Nazi Regime," in *Probing the Depths of German Antisemitism: German Society and the Persecution of the Jews, 1933-1941,* ed. David Bankier (New York: Berghahn, 2000), 62. The Nazi government granted such privileged status in order to placate the "German-blood" relatives. *Ibid.,* 60.

1020. During the war, many Jewish forced laborers in Munich were not working in military-related factories, but instead in private companies, such as Firma Brettschneider. Susanna Schrafstetter, *Flucht und Versteck: Untergetauchte Juden in Munchen—Verfolgungserfahrung und Nachkriegsalltag,* (Gottingen: Wallstein Verlag, 2015), 48.

1021. The Nazis had built more than 400 forced labor camps in Munich. "Ein Lebendiger Erinnerungsort," Von Helmut Reister, Judische Allgemeine Nr. 44/18, (November 2018), 15. Because Bettina was allowed to live at home, she managed to avoid the horrible working conditions and violence faced by those living in the forced labor camps. *See* Cord Pagenstecher, "'We Were Treated Like Slaves.' Remembering Forced Labor for Nazi Germany," in *Human Bondage in the Cultural Contact Zone,* eds. Raphael Hormann and Gesa Mackenthun, (Munster: Waxmann, 2010), 278.

1022. Bayerisches Hauptstaatsarchiv, BAYHStA LEA-49673.

1023. "To Field an Army: A Short History of the Draft," at https://warfarehistorynetwork.com/2016/01/23/to-field-an-army-a-short-history-of-the-draft/.

1024. "Chapter I: The German Military System," at https://www.ibiblio.org/hyperwar/Germany/HB/HB-1.html.

1025. *See* https://themunicheye.com/wwii-relics-still-threaten-bavaria-1971.

1026.   Schrafstetter, "Submergence into Illegality: Hidden Jews in Munich, 1941-45," in *The Germans and the Holocaust: Popular Response to the Persecution and Murder of the Jews,* 113.

1027.   "Maximilian Strnad Discusses Fates of Intermarried Jews in Nazi Germany," USC Shoah Foundation Institute News, (November 23, 2015), at https://sfi.usc.edu/news/2015/11/10434-maximilian-strnad-discusses-fates-intermarried-jews-nazi-germany.

1028.   Ibid.

1029.   Ibid.

1030.   "Maximilian Strnad Discusses Fates of Intermarried Jews in Nazi Germany," USC Shoah Foundation Institute News, (November 23, 2015), at https://sfi.usc.edu/news/2015/11/10434-maximilian-strnad-discusses-fates-intermarried-jews-nazi-germany.

1031.   Meyer, *A Fatal Balancing Act: The Dilemma of the Reich Association of Jews in Germany, 1939-1945,* 269.

1032.   Files of the Joint Distribution Committee, at http://search.archives.jdc.org/multimedia%2FDocuments%2FVMB_cardindex%2F31157_176226%2F31157_176226-00215.jpg. *See* "Juden in München," AUFBAU, p. 21 (24 Aug 1945), at https://archive.org/stream/aufbau111945germ#page/n558/mode/1up

1033.   https://www.jewishvirtuallibrary.org/munich. Approximately 17,000 Jews were in Thereisenstadt when it was liberated in 1945. *See* https://www.jewishvirtuallibrary.org/theresienstadt-the-ldquo-model-rdquo-ghetto.

1034.   Ibid. About half the Jewish displaced persons in Germany, Austria, and Italy—about 120,000 —emigrated to Palestine/Israel, while about 80,000-90,000 emigrated to the United States. *See https://www.myjewishlearning.com/article/displaced-persons-after-the-holocaust/*

1035.   https://www.familysearch.org/ark:/61903/3:1:3QS7-L942-CPCX-?i=1012&cc=1923888

1036.   Bettina Schnitzler Application for Immigration Visa and Alien Registration, No. 1-1062571. Bettina died in Richmond, Virginia on February 23, 2006. Bettina was not the only Heppenheimer family member to survive in Germany because she was married to a non-Jew. Henry Heppenheimer's only child living in Germany during the 1930s—Adolph —emigrated to America in the 1938. Adolph's daughter Trude emigrated in 1933 and his son Heinz emigrated in 1936. But Adolph's daughter Hilde and her Protestant husband Lothar Cronberger lived in Dresden, Germany throughout the war. Hilde was one of 213 Jews married to non-Jews still living in Dresden as of January 1945. *See* "Dresden Jewish Records," at https://www.jewishgen.org/databases/jgdetail_2.php. In February 1945, Dresden was heavily bombed, which essentially destroyed the city. *See* "Bombing of Dresden," at https://www.history.com/topics/world-war-ii/battle-of-dresden. Following Germany's surrendered, Hilde and her husband moved to a Displaced Persons camp, and emigrated to America on August 22, 1946. *See* https://collections.arolsen-archives.org/en/archive/81650012/?p=1&s=cronberger&doc_id=81650012.

1037.   The Socialist Workers Party was working against the Nazis before the war. Robert had written letters in 1934 and 1935 that are in the Socialist Workers Party database. *See* http://www.argus.bstu.bundesarchiv.de/ry13/rightframe.htm?high-

light=true&search=heinrich&KontextFb=KontextFb&searchVolumes=selected
&vid=ry13&kid=388e2478-1631-40fc-92e4-8352be8c4c0e&uid=313e23cb-0e05-
-465e-931e-0265fec5e92b&searchPos=1041.

1038.   Robert explained in his request that he had to leave Germany for political reasons. *See* https://www.holocaust.cz/en/database-of-victims/victim/141720-rob-
ert-heppenheimer/. Unless otherwise noted, the information about Robert is
derived from the reparations request of his daughter Gerturd, Hessisches Landesarchiv Hauptstaatsarchiv Wiesbaden, HHStAW 518-14878.

1039.   *See* "Prague" in the YIVO Encyclopedia of Jews in Eastern Europe, at http://
www.yivoencyclopedia.org/article.aspx/Prague; "Anti-Jewish Policy After the
Establishment of the Protectorate of Bohemia and Moravia," at https://www.holo-
caust.cz/en/history/final-solution/the-final-solution-of-the-jewish-question-in-
the-bohemian-lands/anti-jewish-policy-after-the-establishment-of-the-protec-
torate-of-bohemia-and-moravia/. In November 1938, Czechoslovakia registered
12,392 Jewish refugees, and that number grew to 15,186 by December 1938. *See*
Wolf Gruner, "Protectorate of Bohemia and Moravia," in *The Greater German
Reich and the Jews: Nazi Persecution Policies in the Annexed Territories 1935-1945,*
103.

1040.   "Jewish Life in Prague," at http://www.holocaustresearchproject.org/ghettos/
prague.html.

1041.   Between October 1938 and the end of July 1939, 20,000 Jews left the country,
including the refugees who had been directed to leave. *See* Gruner, "Protectorate
of Bohemia and Moravia," in *The Greater German Reich and the Jews: Nazi Persecution Policies in the Annexed Territories 1935-1945,* 110.

1042.   https://www.ushmm.org/wlc/en/article.php?ModuleId=10005688

1043.   Jüdisches Museum Frankfurt, Datenbank Gedenkstätte Neuer Börneplatz.

1044.   https://www.holocaust.cz/en/database-of-digitised-documents/docu-
ment/421078-heppenheimer-robert-nezpracovano/. Robert's friend Adolf Simon
was among those who were arrested. Adolf never saw Robert again.

1045.   "Anti-Jewish Policy After the Establishment of the Protectorate of Bohemia
and Moravia," at https://www.holocaust.cz/en/history/final-solution/the-final-
solution-of-the-jewish-question-in-the-bohemian-lands/anti-jewish-policy-af-
ter-the-establishment-of-the-protectorate-of-bohemia-and-moravia/.

1046.   "Jewish Life in Prague," at http://www.holocaustresearchproject.org/ghettos/
prague.html.

1047.   Ibid.

1048.   "Ghetto Without Walls," at https://www.holocaust.cz/en/history/final-solution/
the-final-solution-of-the-jewish-question-in-the-bohemian-lands/ghetto-with-
out-walls/

1049.   "Jewish Life in Prague," at http://www.holocaustresearchproject.org/ghettos/
prague.html.

1050.   Ibid.

1051.   In July of 1939, the Centre for Jewish Emigration was established and represented the only path to legal emigration. *See* Anti-Jewish Policy After the Establishment of the Protectorate of Bohemia and Moravia," at https://www.holocaust.
cz/en/history/final-solution/the-final-solution-of-the-jewish-question-in-the-

bohemian-lands/anti-jewish-policy-after-the-establishment-of-the-protecto-rate-of-bohemia-and-moravia/. Between 1939 and 1941, 26,093 Jews out of a total of 118,000 were able to leave the Protectorate legally, but it became more difficult to emigrate as time went on. *See Ibid.* For example, in order to receive an exit visa, Robert would have been required to pay an exorbitant fee. *See* http://www.holocaustresearchproject.org/nazioccupation/sudetenland.html.

1052. https://www.holocaust.cz/en/database-of-digitised-documents/document/421077-heppenheimer-robert-nezpracovano/

1053. *See* the International Institute for Holocaust Research at http://db.yadvashem.org/deportation/transportDetails.html?language=en&itemId=5091969.

1054. Ibid.

1055. Robert's train arrived in Lodz on October 19. Of the nearly 5,000 Jews that were deported in that 17-day period, just 276 survived the Holocaust. *See* https://kehilalinks.jewishgen.org/lodz/statistics.htm.

1056. https://www.holocaust.cz/en/database-of-victims/victim/141720-robert-heppenheimer/.

1057. https://www.jewishgen.org/databases/jgdetail_2.php

1058. https://www.jewishgen.org/databases/Holocaust/0194_Lodz_letters.html.

1059. Ibid.

1060. http://www.lodz-ghetto.com/litzmannstadt_ghetto_-_the_calendar.html,2-42.

1061. http://www.yadvashem.org/holocaust/this-month/august/1944-3.html.

1062. For example, death certificates were issued upon the deaths of Berta Schwarz and Heinrich Bauernfreund.

1063. Many Jews died in the ghetto of a variety of diseases. For example, in 1942, 103,034 Jews lived in the Lodz ghetto, and 18,046 died during that year in the ghetto. *See* https://kehilalinks.jewishgen.org/lodz/statistics.htm.

1064. Ibid.

1065. Ibid.

1066. http://www.holocaustresearchproject.org/holoprelude/mischlinge.html.

1067. At the time, a passport was required only for persons traveling to foreign countries. Robert M. W. Kempner, *The German National Registration System As Means of Police Control of Population,* 36 J. Crim. L. & Criminology, p. 385 (1945-1946).

1068. We know that the name on her passport was Gertrud Adeleid Auelmann, based on an event that will be discussed later in this section.

1069. Following the enactment of the Nuremberg Laws, the "Law for the Protection of the Hereditary Health of the German People" was enacted, which required that all prospective marriage partners obtain a "certificate of fitness to marry" from the public health authorities. *See* Michael Burleigh and Wolfgang Wippermann, *The Racial State Germany 1933-1945,* (Cambridge: Cambridge University Press, 1991), 49. Gertrud would have been required to prove that she was an Aryan by submitting to the local health authority a copy of her own birth certificate, as well as the birth certificates of both of her parents. *See* William Lee Baruah-Young, *From Hobby to Necessity: The Practice of Genealogy in the Third Reich,* Doctoral Thesis for the University of Glasgow, (2014), 45. http://theses.gla.ac.uk/5306/.

According to Gertrud's marriage record that she submitted with her reparations request (the record was not an original copy, but simply a statement that the marriage occurred), when Gertrude married, she married a Protestant and identified her religion as Protestant. The record also indicates that Gertrud's maiden name was "Heppenheimer." Had she used her actual maiden name and original birth certificate, her Jewish ancestry would have been discovered. Therefore, I believe that the marriage record was "corrected" in 1957, and that Gertrud used her mother's maiden name instead at the time of her marriage, based on what occurred in 1941.

1070.   Gertrud did have a second child, a daughter who was born in 1942. This child was identified in her reparations request and was sixteen years old when Gertrud's reparations request was submitted. *See https://www.myheritage.com/ research/record-1-236975081-1-500030/gertrud-fokuhl-geb-heppenheimer-in-my-heritage-family-trees?s=573925011*

1071.   This record is how we know that Gertrud's passport is based on a lie, since she used her mother's maiden name as her birth name. Since Gertrud's passport contained the last name "Auelmann," it seems likely that she used that name for her marriage certificate, as well. The death record was corrected in 1957 (the correction is actually recorded on the original death record in ink) to reflect that Gertrud's maiden name was actually Heppenheimer. *See* https://www.ancestry.de/imageviewer/collections/61119/ images/47106_b307014-00020?treeid=&personid=&hintid=&useP-UB=true&usePUBJs=true&_ga=2.150658227.405973345.1617805134-1506133108.1612887506&pId=601053681. Since Gertrud submitted her reparations request for her father around the time the death record was corrected, it seems likely that the correction was made as a result of the reparations request.

1072.   As with her marriage license, in order to avoid having a "J" (meaning Jew) stamped on the front of the passport, Gertrud would have been required to prove her Aryan descent to and including her grandparents without interruption. Bernhard Kuschey, *Die Wodaks. Exil und Rückkehr.* (Vienna: *New Academic Press, 2008), 166.*

1073.   "Conversion to Christianity and Conversion to Judiasm During the Era of Nazi Rule," a presentation by Professor Dan Michman at Bar-Ilan University (June 5, 1997), at https://www.biu.ac.il/JH/Parasha/eng/kedoshim/michman.htm.

1074.   Bernard Edinger, "Living Submerged: Jews Hiding as Non-Jews in Nazi Germany," *The Jerusalem Post* (March 11, 2017).

1075.   "The 'Invisibles' Reveals How Some Jews Survived Nazi Germany by Hiding in Plain Sight," National Public Radio (January 29, 2019), at https://www.npr.org/2019/01/29/689272533/the-invisibles-reveals-how-some-jews-survived-nazi-germany-by-hiding-in-plain-si.

1076.   *See* Diana Tovar, Summary of Peter Wyden's *Stella* University of California, Santa Barbara (Fall 2005), at http://marcuse.faculty.history.ucsb.edu/classes/33d/projects/jewishlife/JewishStellaDiana.htm. One of the most notorious catchers was Stella Kubler (born Goldschlag), a Berlin Jew who turned in between 600 and 3,000 Jews posing as non-Jews. Orit Arfa, "The Poisonous Blonde of Berlin: The Controversial Stella Goldschlag Story," in *The Jerusalem Post (Sept. 24, 2017).*

1077.   Barkai, "The Final Chapter," *German-Jewish History in Modern Times: Volume 4,* 381.

1078.   By marrying a Protestant, Gertrud was violating the Nuremberg Laws, and running the risk of imprisonment. The punishment for violating the "Blood Law" would have been lengthy prison sentences for both Gertrud and her husband. *See Kritsen Rundle,* "The Impossibility of an Exterminatory Legality: Law and the Holocaust," in *The University of Toronto Law Journal,* Vol. 59, No. 1, (Winter 2009), 71.

1079.   Eva Noach-Mosse, *Last Days of Theresienstadt,* (Madison: University of Wisconsin Press, 2018), xi.

1080.   "The Food Situation in Frankfurt During the Second World War," Frankfurt am Main 1933-1945, at http://www.frankfurt1933-1945.de.

1081.   "The March Attacks 1944," Frankfurt am Main 1933-1945, at http://www.frankfurt1933-1945.de.

1082.   "The Food Situation in Frankfurt During the Second World War," Frankfurt am Main 1933-1945, at http://www.frankfurt1933-1945.de.

1083.   Ibid.

1084.   The Aufbau published the list of names in its April 27, 1945 edition. *See* https://archive.org/stream/aufbau111945germ#page/n265/mode/1up

1085.   Lynn Rapaport, *Jews in Germany After the Holocaust: Memory, Identity, and Jewish-German Relations,* (Cambridge: Cambridge University Press, 1997), 28.

1086.   Ibid.

1087.   Tom Tugend, "New Generation Shifts Holocaust Conversation in 'Germans & Jews,'" in *Jewish Journal* (Sept. 7, 2016, https://jewishjournal.com/current_edition/189595/.

1088.   Gertrud died in 2004 in Frankfurt at the age of 84. *See* https://www.myheritage.com/research/record-1-236975081-1-500030/gertrud-fokuhl-geb-heppenheimer-in-myheritage-family-trees.

1089.   Advertisement in the Gemeindeblatt October 1935, found at http://sammlungen.ub.uni-frankfurt.de/cm/periodical/pageview/3099704?query=%22david%20seidel%20u.%20frau%22.

1090.   "The 1939 German Minority Census" at https://www.mappingthelives.org/bio/45f68684-4585-462e-860f-e2876ebceede.

1091.   Unless otherwise noted, the information in this section is derived from the Reparations Request of David Zejdel, Hessisches Landesarchiv Hauptstaatsarchiv Wiesbaden, 518-518-58184; Reparations Request of David Zejdel for Gustav Heppenheimer, Hessisches Landesarchiv Hauptstaatsarchiv Wiesbaden, 518-14876; the tax records of David Seidel (Zejdel), Hessisches Landesarchiv Hauptstaatsarchiv Wiesbaden, HHStAW 676-6463; and the Reparations Request of Alfred Zejdel for his Mother Pessa, Hessisches Landesarchiv Hauptstaatsarchiv Wiesbaden, HHStAW 518-59175.

1092.   Pessa had purchased this small office building at Klostergasse 4, just down the street from the Gebruder Heppenheimer Dominikanergasse facility, in 1921. After she married David Seidel, ownership of the building was transferred to David. They continued to rent out offices in the building until forced to sell the building.

1093. In 1938, there were approximately 50,000 Jews with Polish citizenship living in Germany. *See* https://www.holocaust.cz/en/history/events/the-expulsion-of-pol-ish-jews-from-germany/.

1094. Uta Larkey, "Fear and Terror: The Expulsion of Polish Jews from Saxony/Germany in October 1938," *Dapim: Studies on the Holocaust,* Vol. 31, Issue 3 (2017), 6.

1095. The mandatory residency registration with the local police for all Jews in Germany had made it easy for authorities to produce lists of names and addresses of Polish Jews in a relatively short time. *See Ibid.,* 7-8.

1096. https://www.holocaust.cz/en/history/events/the-expulsion-of-polish-jews-from-germany/.

1097. "The Friedel Mayer Collection," at https://www.juedischesmuseum.de/en/ex-plore/documents-and-photos/detail/polenaktion-1938/.

1098. Even after the war began in 1939, the German government continued to issue passports to Jews in Germany, including the "stateless" Jews mostly of Polish origin. *See* https://www.jewishgen.org/databases/Holocaust/0044_TempPassports-ForGermanJews1938to1941.html. The passports were usually of limited duration (Pessa's passport expired on August 1, 1942), and were intended to facilitate the departure of the recipient from Germany. *See* J.A.S. Grenville, *The Jews and Germans of Hamburg: The Destruction of a Civilization 1790-1945,* (Abington: Routledge, 2012), 192.

1099. We know that Gustav never received a German passport because he stated at a later time that he had not been issued a passport and only had the identity card. Germany required that identity cards be issued to all Jews in Germany beginning in January 1939. *See* Grenville, *The Jews and Germans of Hamburg: The Destruction of a Civilization 1790-1945,*192.

1100. "Great Britain," at https://www.yadvashem.org/odot_pdf/Microsoft%20 Word%20-%206312.pdf.

1101. Jüdisches Museum Frankfurt, Datenbank Gedenkstätte Neuer Börneplatz.

1102. Pessa and her family were not the only Jews who ignored the deportation orders. Approximately 6,500 German Jews ignored deportation orders and went into hiding. Of this number, approximately 1,700 survived. Sebastian Huebel, "Disguise and Defiance: German Jewish Men and Their Underground Experiences in Nazi Germany, 1941-45," *Shofar,* Vol. 36, No. 3, (Winter 2018, 110).

1103. Pessa likely saw Jacob and his family when Jacob lived in Frankfurt from 1919 to 1924. And since Pessa did not remarry until 1923, Jacob may have served as a father figure to young Gustav.

1104. When Germany invaded and conquered northern France in 1940, Metz (which had been the second largest Jewish community in Alsace-Lorraine after Strasbourg) was immediately annexed to the Third Reich. *See* https://www.yadvashem. org/odot_pdf/Microsoft%20Word%20-%205729.pdf. As discussed earlier, by July 1940, all Jews had been expelled from Alsace-Lorraine. Thus, when the Zejdel family arrived in Metz, the city was already "Jew-free." *Ibid.*

1105. Because crossing the border was illegal, Jewish families crossing at that time relied upon human smugglers for assistance. *See* Frank Caestecker, "Review of Insa Meinen, Ahlrich Meyer: Verfolgt von Land Zu Land: Judische Fluchtlinge in Westeuropa 1938-1944," *H-Migration,* H-Net Reviews, (Feb. 2014), https:// networks.h-net.org/node/8382/reviews/11468/caestecker-insa-meinen-verfolgt-von-land-zu-land-j%C3%BCdische-fl%C3%BCchtlinge. One Jewish family that crossed the German border into Belgium in 1939 told of taking a train to the border and then paying a smuggler to walk them through fields and forests so as not to be detected by the German border guards. *See* Recollection of Survivor David Katz, http://jewishva.org/node/748. By the time Pessa, Gustav, and Alfred crossed the German border, it was even harder for Jews to cross undetected.

1106.   Diemut Majer, "Non-Germans" Under the Third Reich: The Nazi Judicial and Administrative System in Germany and Occupied Eastern Europe, with Special Regard to Occupied Poland, 1939-1945, (Baltimore: The Johns Hopkins University Press, 1993), 171.

1107.   Alfred Zejdel's family was told that a sympathetic German police officer assisted the family. That assistance may have occurred while the family was in hiding in Frankfurt or when Gustav was trying to find help to get the family across the Belgium/German border. Alfred's family was also told that Gustav and his brother were being sought by the Gestapo for selling medical supplies on the black market. While Alfred's reparation request does not mention this as the reason they were being sought by the Gestapo, it may be that Gustav and Alfred were selling medical supplies on the black market to supplement the family's meager earnings. Jewish doctors had lost their medical licenses in 1938, and very few were allowed to treat Jewish patients. Kaplan, *The Jewish Daily Life in Germany*, 312. These doctors could no longer be called "Doctor," but were instead referred to as "Practitioner for the sick." *Ibid.* By 1941, the Germans had cut off medical supplies to the Jewish hospital. Martin Gilbert, *Final Journey: The Fate of the Jews of Nazi Europe*, (Rosetta Books, 1979), p. 82. It would thus make sense that there were opportunities to both help the Jewish community and to make money by selling medical supplies.

1108.   Caestecker, "Review of Insa Meinen, Ahlrich Meyer: Verfolgt von Land Zu Land: Judische Fluchtlinge in Westeuropa 1938-1944."

1109.   Ibid.

1110.   Frank Caestecker and Denis Scuto, "The Benelux and the Flight of Refugees from Nazi Germany: The Luxembourg Specificity," Histoire Generale, The Government of the Grand Duchy of Luxembourg, 407. http://orbilu.uni.lu/handle/10993/29290

1111.   Schram Laurence "The Transit Camp for Jews in Mechelen: The Antechamber of Death," February 6, 2008, at http://www.sciencespo.fr/mass-violence-war-massacre-resistance/en/document/transit-camp-jews-mechelen-antechamber-death.

1112.   "Belgium and its Jews During the War," The Journal of Historical Review, Mark Weber (March/April 1999), at http://www.ihr.org/jhr/v18/v18n2p-2_Weber.html; Corry Guttstadt, *Turkey, the Jews, and the Holocaust*, (Cambridge: Cambridge University Press, 2009), 251.

1113.   David Fraser, "*A Passive Collaboration: Bureaucracy, Legality, and the Jews of Brussels 1940-1944*," in Brooklyn Journal of International Law, Vol. 30 Issue 2, p. 383 n. 66.

1114.   Before the war, over 1,000 German Jews had found shelter in Luxembourg, out of a total Jewish population in Luxembourg of 3,500. https://www.ushmm.org/wlc/en/article.php?ModuleId=10005363. By mid-August of 1938, the Luxembourg government essentially shut down the border to German Jewish emigrants, and in February of 1939 received the assistance of the German customs officials to end the illegal immigration of Jews to Luxembourg. "The Benelux and the Flight of Refugees from Nazi Germany: The Luxembourg Specificity," Histoire Generale, Frank Caestecker and Denis Scuto, The Government of the Grand Duchy of Luxembourg, p. 390. From August 8, 1940 until the Germans forbade emigration on October 15, 1941, 2,500 Jews left Luxembourg. *See* https://www.ushmm.org/wlc/en/article.php?ModuleId=10005363. Germans interned the remaining 800 Jews. Ibid.

1115. From the State Archives in Belgium, A404165; A404096. The registration does not identify "Mr. Rohr," but Lina and Fredrich Rohr were living in Brussels at the time and were from Frankfurt. Moreover, Lina was born in Kalisz, Poland, which was the same town Pessa was born in, and so it is entirely possible that Pessa knew this family (or was related to Lina). Both Lina and Fredrich Rohr perished in the Holocaust. *See* https://yvng.yadvashem.org/index.html?language=en&s_lastName=rohr&s_firstName=&s_place=brussels&s_dateOfBirth=&s_inTransport=.

1116. By the time Pessa had entered Belgium, all German Jews had lost their citizenship, so Belgium allowed Jews to register as stateless persons. *See* David Fraser, "*A Passive Collaboration: Bureaucracy, Legality, and the Jews of Brussels 1940-1944,*" Brooklyn Journal of International Law, Vol. 30 Issue 2, (2005), 409.

1117. From the State Archives in Belgium, A404165; A404096.

1118. Ibid. This is how we know that Gustav did not have a passport and only had a German identity card.

1119. Following their registration with the Brussels authorities, the Brussels police sent requests for information to the Luxembourg police regarding Pessa and Gustav and to the Frankfurt police regarding Gustav, presumably to verify the information contained in their respective registrations. The Luxembourg police responded that they had no information on either person. The Frankfurt police stated that the information regarding Gustav's birthdate is correct and that nothing is known about his moral or political character. From the State Archives in Belgium, A404165; A404096.

1120. *See* https://portal.ehri-project.eu/units/be-002157-8.

1121. In Germany, the Nazis had mandated that, by January 1, 1939, all Jewish men and women bearing first names of non-Jewish origin add "Israel" and "Sara," respectively, to their given names. https://www.ushmm.org/learn/timeline-of-events/1933-1938/law-on-alteration-of-family-and-personal-names.

1122. From the State Archives in Belgium, A404165; A404096.

1123. *See* http://www.yadvashem.org/odot_pdf/microsoft%20word%20-%20122. pdf. As it turned out, moving to Brussels rather that Antwerp gave Gustav and his family a better chance of survival. Before the war, the majority of Jews in Belgium lived in Antwerp. During the German occupation, 42 percent of Jews in all of Belgium who were registered were deported. Of the Jews registered in Brussels, 37 percent were deported, while in Antwerp, 65 percent were deported. The difference stems from the fact that the authorities in Antwerp were more cooperative and collaborative with the Germans than were the Brussels authorities. *See* Lieven Saerens, "Why Did So Many of the Jews in Antwerp Perish in the Holocaust," http://www.yadvashem.org/odot_pdf/microsoft%20word%20-%205430.pdf.

1124. "Brussels," at http://www.yadvashem.org/odot_pdf/microsoft%20word%20-%20 122.pdf. Pessa's son Alfred had been a talented musician in Frankfurt, and hoped to be a professional musician. When they fled Germany, Alfred took with him his violin. At some point, the family was forced to sell the violin for food, suggesting that any work they were able to secure was not enough to support the family.

1125. Ibid.

1126. Ibid.

1127. Ibid.

1128. Mark Weber "Belgium and its Jews During the War," *The Journal of Historical Review,* (March/April 1999), http://www.ihr.org/jhr/v18/v18n2p-2_Weber.html. The Dossin Barracks had been a military barracks, and the Germans had converted the Barracks into a detention and deportation camp. *See* https://www.ushmm. org/wlc/en/article.php?ModuleId=10005430.

1129. https://www.facinghistory.org/resource-library/text/anti-jewish-measures-netherlands-and-belgium-between-1940-and-1944.

1130. Ibid.

1131. Ibid.

1132. Caestecker, "Review of Insa Meinen, Ahlrich Meyer: Verfolgt von Land Zu Land: Judische Fluchtlinge in Westeuropa 1938-1944."

1133. Ibid. https://www.facinghistory.org/resource-library/text/anti-jewish-measures-netherlands-and-belgium-between-1940-and-1944.

1134. Alfred was arrested twice, but managed to avoid deportation to the Dossin Barracks. After Gustav was arrested, Alfred found work at a hotel, and he lived in the hotel until liberation. The hotel's owner took advantage of Alfred's illegal immigration status by overworking him. After liberation, Alfred worked as an interpreter for the British Army, and then was reunited with his father David. Feeling restless and without his father's permission, Alfred volunteered to fight in the Israel War of Independence, and later received a medal for his service. He remained in Israel until 1951, and then returned to England and worked as a tailor. Both Alfred and his father became British citizens.

1135. Suzanne Vromen, "Unique Aspects of Jewish Armed Resistance and Rescue in Belgium," in *Jewish Resistance Against the Nazis,* ed. Patrick Henry, (Washington, D.C.: The Catholic University of America Press, 2014), 137.

1136. Escapes from the transports leaving the Dossin barracks were not uncommon. Of the 28 transports that left the Dossin barracks, 538 people escaped by jumping from the trains. *See* "The Deportation of the Jews from the Nazi Transit Camps Drancy (France) and Malines (Belgium), at https://training.ehri-project.eu/ deportation-jews-nazi-transit-camps-drancy-france-and-malines-belgium.

1137. http://auschwitz.org/en/museum/auschwitz-prisoners/.

1138. http://www.auschwitz.org/en/museum/auschwitz-prisoners/; http://auschwitz. org/en/history/auschwitz-iii/ig-farben.

1139. http://ftp.auschwitz.org/en/history/auschwitz-iii/general-numbers.

1140. http://auschwitz.org/en/history/auschwitz-iii/living-conditions-and-number-of-victims.

1141. http://auschwitz.org/en/history/auschwitz-iii/living-conditions-and-number-of-victims.

1142. Ibid.

1143. Florain Schmaltz, "The Death Toll at the Buna/Monowitz Concentration Camp," *Norbert Wollheim Memorial*, 7, at http://www.wollheim-memorial.de/files/1058/original/pdf_Florian_Schmaltz_The_Death_Toll_at_the_BunaMonowitz_Concentration_Camp.pdf.

1144. From the archives of the State Museum Auschwitz-Birkenau in Oświęcim. All the information regarding Gustav in the rest of this section of the chapter was obtained from the archives. The prisoner infirmary in Monowitz (*Häftlingskrankenbau or HKB*) had been established in 1942. http://www.wollheim-memorial.de/en/krankenbau_aufnahme_und_behandlung_en. Anyone seeking treatment in the infirmary would come to the outpatient clinic after evening roll call and join the long line of those waiting to be admitted. *Ibid.* The prisoners stood outdoors in any weather, and anyone who was declared an *Arztvormelder* (a patient presenting a medical concern) by the clinic's male nurses in the evening had to show up again the next morning to be definitively accepted or rejected after superficial examination by a doctor. *Ibid.* Admission to the HKB meant a shower, a shave, and assignment to the appropriate ward of the infirmary. *Ibid.* Intake was done with the prisoner barefoot and naked, and his bowl and spoon, like all other possessions, had to be handed over. *Ibid.* After admission, the patients received a shirt and trousers from the HKB's stocks. Infirmary admission was a mixed blessing for a camp inmate: while he was granted a few days of rest, he was also subject to selections by the SS. *Ibid.* Conditions in the infirmary were less than hygienic: beds often had to be shared by prisoners and only a portion of the HKB had running water, so that pails were used for toilets. *See* http://www.wollheim-memorial.de/en/der_haeftlingskrankenbau_im_kz_bunamonowitz_geschichte_und_aufbau.

1145. Bacon, "The Prisoner Hospital at Buna-Monowitz," in *History 1933-1948: What We Chose to Remember,* 173.

1146. http://www.wollheim-memorial.de/en/krankenbau_aufnahme_und_behandlung_en.

1147. Bacon, "The Prisoner Hospital at Buna-Monowitz," in *History 1933-1948: What We Chose to Remember,* 170.

1148. Ibid., 166.

1149. Ibid., 165.

1150. Ibid., 171.

1151. http://www.yadvashem.org/yv/en/exhibitions/album_auschwitz/auschwitz-birkenau.asp.

1152. Florain Schmaltz, "The Death Toll at the Buna/Monowitz Concentration Camp," *Norbert Wollheim Memorial*, 6.

1153. Ibid. For example, a selection took place in Monowitz on September 25 or 26, 1944, at which time around 600 prisoners, including 214 from the prisoner infirmary, were selected for the gas chambers. *Ibid.*

1154. http://www.wollheim-memorial.de/en/kz_bunamonowitz_en.

1155. https://www.jewishvirtuallibrary.org/number-of-prisoners-in-auschwitz-camps-january-1945.

1156. Ibid.

1157. https://www.ushmm.org/wlc/en/article.php?ModuleId=10007961; https://www.ushmm.org/learn/timeline-of-events/1942-1945/death-march-from-auschwitz.

1158. https://www.ushmm.org/wlc/en/article.php?ModuleId=10007961.

1159. https://www.theholocaustexplained.org/the-final-solution/auschwitz-birkenau/resistance/.

1160. Florain Schmaltz, "The Death Toll at the Buna/Monowitz Concentration Camp," Norbert Wollheim Memorial, 1.

1161. https://yvng.yadvashem.org/nameDetails.html?language=en&itemId=11519294&ind=0.

1162. The total number of Jews killed in Monowitz is unclear. Estimates range from a minimum of 23,000 to a maximum of 40,000. *See* Florain Schmaltz, "The Death Toll at the Buna/Monowitz Concentration Camp," Norbert Wollheim Memorial, 2. The surviving transfer lists of Monowitz only include those transferred to the Auschwitz main camp, and do not include the camp selections or those who died or were killed directly on the plant grounds. *Ibid.* at 3-4. Of the 238 persons kept for slave labor on Gustav's transport, 98 ultimately survived and of the 24,908 Jews deported from the Dossin Barracks to Auschwitz, just 1123 survived. *See* https://eurojewcong.org/communities/belgium/.

1163. Even friends tried to locate Heppenheimer family members after the war. For example, Serevina Diemer, presumably a family friend, had a paid notice placed in the September 27, 1946 edition of the Aufbau, a German newspaper published in America, seeking information on Gustav Heppenheimer, his half-brother and his mother. *See* https://archive.org/stream/aufbau1219461946germ#page/n806/mode/1up/search/heppenheimer, p. 807. Interestingly, the notice states that the family had lived in Frankfurt and was now living in the United States, so Ms. Diemer must have assumed that the family successfully emigrated to America after escaping Germany in 1941.

1164. "German Jews During the Holocaust," at https://encyclopedia.ushmm.org/content/en/article/german-jews-during-the-holocaust.

1165. Bruno Blau, "The Jewish Population of Germany 1939-1945, *Jewish Social Studies*, Vol. 12, No. 2, (Apr. 1950), 171; "German Jews During the Holocaust," at https://encyclopedia.ushmm.org/content/en/article/german-jews-during-the-holocaust. In terms of the Jews living in Frankfurt (where most of the Heppenheimers lived), approximately 26,000 Jews lived in Frankfurt in 1933, and almost 15,000 were able to emigrate. "Frankfurt am Main: The City and the Holocaust," at http://www.holocaustresearchproject.org/nazioccupation/frankfurt.html; "Emigration von Frankfurter Juden ins Ausland (Überblick)," at http://www.frankfurt1933-1945.de.

1166. Jacob's son Ernest stated that he had to borrow large sums of money to get his parents out of Germany and went into debt caring for his parents until their deaths. *See* Reparations Request for Jacob Heppenheimer, Hessisches Landesarchiv Hauptstaatsarchiv Wiesbaden, HHSttaw 518-8242.

1167.   *Recollections of Herb Harvey.*

1168.   Compensation for National Socialist Justice: Indemnification Provisions, Federal Ministry of Finance, (2018), 6. https://australien.diplo.de/blob/2151044/1ef8ff-64677da1048de4f21067a7eaa9/entschaedigung-von-ns-unrecht-2018-englisch-data.pdf.

1169.   Menachem Z. Rosensaft and Joana D. Rosensaft, "The Early History of German-Jewish Reparations," *Fordham International Law Journal,* Volume 25, Issue 6, p. S-2 (2001); Compensation for National Socialist Justice: Indemnification Provisions, Federal Ministry of Finance, p. 6.

1170.   Ibid. at 7-8. After making a modest one-time payment, Curtis Heppen was able to obtain a German pension and he collected that pension until the day he died. His widow, Millie, collected survivor benefits until her own death in February 2019.

1171.   Landesarchiv Speyer J 10 Nr. 2968.

1172.   Ibid.

1173.   Niewyk, *The Jews in Weimar Germany,* 196.

1174.   Ibid., citing the Sociologist Franz Oppenheimer.

1175.   Bach, *The German Jew: A Synthesis of Judaism and Western Civilization, 1730-1930,* 245.

1176.   David H. Jones, *Moral Responsibility in the Holocaust: A Study in the Ethics of Character,* (Oxford: Rowman & Littlefield Publishers, Inc., 1999), 79.

1177.   Ibid

1178.   "Reparations and Restitutions," at https://www.yadvashem.org/odot_pdf/Micro-soft%20Word%20-%205817.pdf.

1179.   "Germany accepts sole responsibility for Holocaust: German FM," Radio Poland, May 2, 2018, at http://archiwum.thenews.pl/1/10/Artykul/347641,Germany-accepts-sole-responsibility-for-Holocaust-German-FM.

1180.   "Merkel at Auschwitz: Remembering Nazi Crimes Inseparable From German Identity," The Times of Israel, June 28, 2020, at https://www.timesofisrael.com/merkel-at-auschwitz-remembering-nazi-crimes-inseparable-from-german-identity/.

1181.   "Never Forget—Germany's Culture of Remembrance," https://www.deutschland.de/en/germany-year-usa-20182019-germanys-culture-of-remembrance.

1182.   "Ibid. A German artist, Gunter Demnig, began this commemoration project to remember the victims of the Holocaust by placing a concrete cube bearing a brass plate at the last place of residency, which was the place the family lived in before being forced to move into a "Jewish house," being deported, or being forced to emigrate. *See* http://www.stolpersteine.eu/en/faq/. Over 70,000 stumbling stones have been laid across Europe, including more than 1,000 in Frankfurt. *See* https://www.dpa-international.com/topic/man-behind-holocaust-memorial-cobblestones-sees-end-work-urn%3Anewsml%3Adpa.com%3A20090101%3A190124-99-707427; http://www.stolpersteine-frankfurt.de/frankfurt_en.html.

1183.   http://www.stolpersteine-frankfurt.de/downloads/doku2014_WEB.pdf.

1184.   Ibid.

1185.   There are two other sets of stumbling stones for Heppenheimer family members. In 2005, stumbling stones were laid at Mittelweg 8 in Frankfurt to remember Maier Heppenheimer's granddaughter Johanna Bauernfreund and her family (Heinrich, Hans and Fred). *See* http://www.stolpersteine-frankfurt.de/down-loads/Doku2005.pdf. While Johanna's mother Berta Schwarz (Maier's daughter) does not have a stumbling stone, her son Walter, who successfully emigrated to America, does have a stumbling stone in Stuttgart. Walter's mother-in-law Berta Kahn died in the Holocaust, but Walter was able to escape with his wife Senta. Walter's mother-in-law, Walter and Senta all have stumbling stones. *See* http://www.stolpersteine-stuttgart.de/index.php?docid=931&mid=0. The stumbling stones thus recognize that even those who were able to escape from Germany were also victims of the Nazis.

1186.   *See* https://www.marchivum.de/de/archiv/bestaende/behoerdenbestaende.